EXCAVATIONS

ON THE

FRANCISCAN

FRONTIER

✝

D1452836

Ripley P. Bullen Series
Florida Museum of Natural History

EXCAVATIONS

ON THE

Archaeology

at the

FRANCISCAN

Fig Springs

FRONTIER

Mission

Brent Richards Weisman

University Press of Florida / Florida Museum of Natural History

Gainesville Tallahassee Tampa Boca Raton Pensacola Orlando Miami Jacksonville

The University Press of Florida is the scholarly publishing agency of the State University System of Florida, comprised of Florida A & M University, Florida Atlantic University, Florida International University, Florida State University, University of Central Florida, University of Florida, University of North Florida, University of South Florida, and University of West Florida.

University Press of Florida, 15 Northwest 15th Street, Gainesville, FL 32611

Columbus Quincentenary Series

Library of Congress Cataloguing in Publication Data can be found on the last printed page of the book.

To my parents

CONTENTS

LIST OF FIGURES

LIST OF TABLES

PREFACE

✢   FIG SPRINGS HAS UNIQUE VALUE
in that many of the colonial period Spanish and aboriginal artifacts known
and perhaps better described from other sites in the Florida mission
provinces are found here in or around the remains of the buildings where
they once had been used. This book is a descriptive introduction to Fig
Springs archaeology. Many aspects of the study deserve fuller treatment
in their own right, so I hope that the overall archaeological context of the
site as presented here will provide the background and stimulus for
additional research.

That it took forty years to discover Goggin's mission makes a good
story in itself, and is a good lesson for beginning students in archaeology
as to the fortuitous nature of their chosen discipline. One can only hope
that the recent burst of public and scholarly interest in the contact and
colonial periods of Florida history proves genuine. Let us hope that it will
not be another forty years before this story is told. Already the many
successes of the 1988–1989 excavations at Fig Springs have inspired
others to return to the site. Excavations by the Florida Museum of Natural
History in the summers of 1990 and 1991 have yielded a series of
radiocarbon dates for the premission aboriginal occupation of the site
extending back to the tenth century A.D. and, in the process of excavating
burials in the cemetery for the purpose of detailed skeletal analysis, have
uncovered what may be the remains of another mission structure. Clearly
what is offered in the pages that follow is not the final story of Fig Springs
archaeology but merely a point of departure for future investigations and
discussions.

The Fig Springs project gathered a number of enthusiastic supporters
during the 1988–1989 seasons, without whom work at the site would not
have been possible. Field crew members Keith Terry, Kristen Smith,
Gwenyth Thompson, Steve Stathakis, Brack Barker, and Roan McNab
deserve first mention, as the excavation of the site is really their
accomplishment. Keith Terry and his family receive special credit for

their service and loyalty well above the duties of employment. We were ably assisted in the 1989 season by University of Florida anthropology students John Worth, Gardner Gordon (who returned to the site in summer 1989 as a paid excavator), and Pia Davis, and Matthew Tank from Kalamazoo College in Michigan. Ann Kirking Post of the Smithsonian Institution brought Frank Powers, Sam Hodge, Antoinette "Toni" Johnson, and Anne Davis to dig at the site that February, and I only regret that it was colder here than in Washington, D.C. Volunteers Mary Mitchell, Judi White, and Andy Smith contributed their labor during vacation time, and their efforts are appreciated. Fieldwork at Ichetucknee Springs State Park was a great pleasure, as might be imagined, and was made even more pleasurable by the gracious assistance of Park Manager Azell Nail and his staff.

Behind the scenes, Jim Miller of the Florida Bureau of Archaeological Research, Jerald Milanich of the Florida Museum of Natural History, and Michael Gannon of the University of Florida's Center for Early Contact Period Studies worked hard to provide the funding and logistical support necessary to keep us in the field for 16 months virtually without interruption. Lew Scruggs of the Department of Natural Resources also took an interest in the financial welfare of the project, and helped see to it that funding was available for the extended excavation season in 1989. Roy Lett of the Bureau of Archaeological Research took the artifact photographs and offered valuable advice on photography during the course of the field work.

Figures here and in the two previous technical reports were variously drafted by Ian Breheny, Merald Clark, Charles Poe of the Bureau of Archaeological Research, and by John Wolenka of the Office of Instructional Resources at the University of Florida. Todd Kurtzer is responsible for the oblique rendering of the church excavation that appears as figure 27.

John Worth wishes to acknowledge the support of the field crew comprised of Terry, Smith, Thompson, Stathakis, and Gordon (mentioned above), and appreciates the earlier review of his pottery typology by Jerald Milanich, Kenneth Johnson, Claudine Payne, and John Scarry. His revised chronology has benefited from the related work of Kenneth Johnson.

To all those who have taken part in the project, I hope they enjoy what they read here and feel that I have done their efforts justice.

A note is needed on the various spellings of Ichetucknee that appear in the text. The spelling "Ichtucknee" is maintained in referring to majolica types and blue glass beads, in keeping with Deagan (1987) following Goggin's original nomenclature. The spelling "Ichetucknee" is used according to modern usage in referring both to the name of the river and state park and to the projectile point type defined by Bullen (1975). Varieties of aboriginal pottery types first defined in this book (see Appendix D) are spelled "Ichetucknee" in keeping with modern spelling and to avoid confusion with the Ichtucknee majolica types.

1

Introduction

✝   AT A SITE BELIEVED TO HAVE
been the Franciscan mission of San Martín de Timucua—the Fig Springs
site (8 Co1) in Ichetucknee Springs State Park, Florida—excavations
were carried out in 1988 and 1989 to unearth remains of the church and
other buildings (fig. 1). Near the beginning of the project, funded by the
Florida Department of Natural Resources, no one was really sure that the
goals of reconstructing the buildings and opening them to the public
could be met. The plan was both ambitious and optimistic and, if
successful, would be the first of its kind in the southeastern United States.

Now, after the excavation units have been backfilled and those remains
have been covered and protected, the project, from an archaeological
perspective, must be considered a success. Three mission-era buildings
were indeed discovered and partially excavated, one interpreted as the
church, another as the quarters of the priest or the convento, and the third
a large structure of aboriginal construction in the associated mission
village. The mission cemetery was also located and was found to contain
the remains of Christian Indians buried in grave pits aligned with the
presumed church. Rich midden deposits were found in the mission
village, containing Spanish artifacts like glass beads, sherds of imported
majolica, or tin-enameled earthenware, fragments of olive jar and glass
bottles, and even an intact brass finger ring with its stone setting still
in place, mixed in the soil with plentiful Indian-made pottery and
stone tools.

Although much about the Fig Springs site is interesting in its own
right, it is best to begin by briefly presenting the historical and
archaeological settings out of which the project developed—that is, by
reviewing what was previously known about the Florida missions.

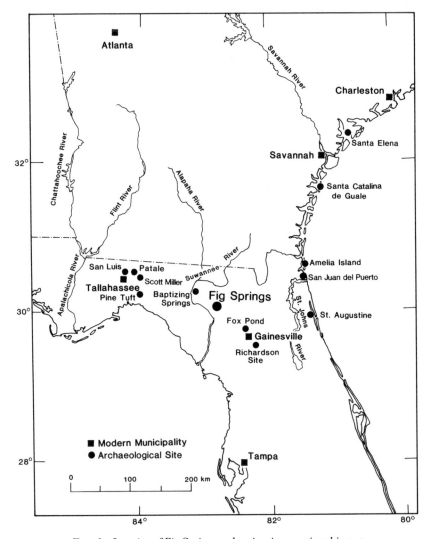

FIG. 1. *Location of Fig Springs and major sites mentioned in text.*

Florida Missions and the Development of Mission Archaeology

Outside interest in the Florida missions, sporadic during their existence, became, ironically, more acute shortly after their demise. In 1716 Diego de Peña, sent west into Creek country from St. Augustine by the Spanish colonial government to entice the Indians to resettle a Florida peninsula made vacant by years of disease and slaving raids, came upon the *ycapacha*, or old fields, of Mission Santa Fé two leagues (about 5.2 miles using the accepted modern reckoning of 2.6 miles to the league) east of the river which now bears that name (Boyd 1949). After spending the night in this place, Peña crossed the Santa Fe River, passed through a location he called *Afecta palino*, and then, four leagues from the river, ambled through the *ycapacha* of Mission San Martín. The four-league, or 10.6-mile, distance from the Santa Fe River to San Martín is close to the 11 miles that now separate the river from the archaeological site of Fig Springs, located on the uplands above the Ichetucknee River in what is now Ichetucknee Springs State Park.

The mission Indians of San Martín and the Indians of the Afuyca (sometimes spelled Ahoica or Ajoica) and Santa Catalina settlements, founded after the destruction of San Martín in the Indian rebellion of 1656, by the time of Peña's trek had long been driven from the area by British-backed slave raiding. As was the case with all the mission places visited by him, no physical remains of the mission town itself were in evidence. Leaving the San Martín old fields, Peña continued northwest five leagues to a place called by him Aquilachua, passing on the way the springs of Usichua, Usiperachua, and Afanochua. The next day Peña moved on to the first old fields of Mission San Juan Guacara, seemingly referred to by him as Calacala, on the banks of the Guacara or Suwannee River and said to have "good springs."

In 1765 the Philadelphia naturalist John Bartram visited what were probably the ruins of the mission San Juan del Puerto, on Fort George Island, just north of the St. Johns River and east of the present city of Jacksonville, and recorded his impression: "Tis very demonstrable that the Spanish had a fine settlement here, as there still remain their cedar posts on each side their fine straight avenues, pieces of hewn live-oaks, and great trees girdled round to kill them; which are now very sound, though about 60 years since they were cut" (J. Bartram 1942:48).

In 1774 John's son William, himself an accomplished botanist, encountered traces of the Spanish presence in his famous travels through the central Florida region of the great Alachua savanna. Between the Seminole town of Cuscowilla near the savanna and the Talahasochte town on the east bank of the Suwannee River was the "charming savanna and fields of Capola" (W. Bartram 1955:191), possibly the old fields of an otherwise unrecorded mission. Bartram believed, on the basis of Indian testimony, that the Spaniards had manned a fortified post at Capola (198). After spending the night with the Seminoles at Talahasochte, Bartram crossed the Suwannee and soon "passed four or five miles through old Spanish fields" (197). Like his father, Bartram observed the "plain marks" of the former Spanish presence, including fence posts, wooden pillars of buildings, ditches, corn ridges, and hills made for the cultivation of batata, or sweet potato. And although he did not venture further west into the land of the Apalachee old fields, Bartram told of the church bells, mortars, cannons, and the "vast works" of fortifications and temples that could still be seen there (198).

In 1778, just four years after Bartram, the surveyor Joseph Purcell produced a detailed map (Purcell 1778) (fig. 2) of the old Spanish road from Pensacola to St. Augustine. This was at the request of John Stuart,

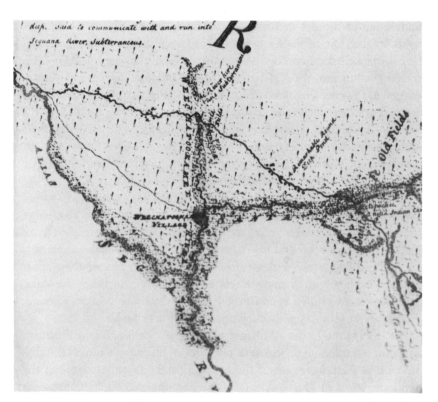

FIG. 2. *Portion of the 1778 Joseph Purcell map showing the "Weechatookamee" River (P. K. Yonge Library of Florida History).*

the British superintendent of the Indians of the southern colonies, and depicted much of the same terrain covered earlier in the century by Diego Peña. It again recorded the location of numerous old fields through which the road passed.

In the country east of the Suwannee River (called the Seguana by Purcell), Purcell passed on a well-trod path through pine woods, dotted with numerous deep springs. Just west of the Weechatookamee Old Fields, the trail skirted around the Weechatookamee River (the Creek Indian name from which "Ichetucknee" is derived) "at a place where it runs subterraneous" (Purcell 1778; Boyd 1939:19).

Clearly, early travelers across the peninsula were captivated by the ghosts of the Florida missions, signifying as they did the fragile, tenuous grasp of the white man on this still wild country. However, things Spanish, and things Indian for that matter, held no such fascination for the Americans who came to control the Florida territory after 1821, and in the absence of the monumental architecture that characterized the missions of South America, Mexico, and the American Southwest, the Florida missions were truly lost to new generations of Floridians and indeed have remained so until recent years.

Spanish Missions in Florida

After the expulsion of the fledgling French colony at Fort Caroline and the founding of St. Augustine in 1565 by Pedro Menéndez de Avilés, Philip II of Spain overcame his reluctance to colonize *La Florida* brought on by the disastrous expeditions of Narváez in 1528 and de Soto in 1539. The problem with Florida was that it had not become clear how such a colony could support itself much less contribute to the Spanish colonial empire. Mineral wealth such as had been found in the High Andes had not been found in Florida, nor did the Florida Indians seem to possess the quantities of gold, silver, and other precious objects of plunder that had so attracted the conquistadores to the Aztecs and Incas. Nor were the Florida Indians concentrated into urban areas and organized into highly stratified societies presided over by priest-kings—societies which, for all their pomp and ritual, were actually very politically unstable and relatively easily toppled.

One solution, hit upon early by Menéndez, was to establish missions among the Florida Indians. These settlements would bring together the sometimes far-flung populace of a given area into one permanent location, where the previously free Indians could easily be transformed into agricultural peasants producing foodstuffs for the colony and for export, and providing a stable labor pool which could be drawn on for various tasks.

Although priests had accompanied the conquistadores, Menéndez was the first to establish missions systematically among the Florida Indians, first at St. Augustine, then at Tequesta on the southeast coast, at Calos in the vicinity of Charlotte Harbor, and at Tocobaga on the west shore of Tampa Bay. These fortified missions, manned by soldiers as well as Jesuit priests, did not last long once the full intent of the priests was discovered. Besides being very reluctant to abandon their own deeply felt religious beliefs, the Indians became disenchanted with the priests when the latter could not supply them with the quantities and kinds of goods they desired. By 1572 the Jesuits had given up.

Just one year later the Franciscan Order was preparing to reestablish the Florida missions and by 1578 had placed priests among the Saturiwa Indians in the St. Augustine area (Deagan 1978:105). The century and a half that followed has been called the "golden age" of the Florida missions and, with some justification, the "Franciscan conquest" of the colony (Geiger 1936:2). In the words of one of the better-known priests of that era, Fray Francisco Pareja, it was the Franciscans who were "bearing the burden and the heat" and who were "conquering and subduing the land" (Oré 1936). Despite the sometimes strained relationship between the Franciscans and the colonial government in St. Augustine, it could not be denied by the authorities that the chain of missions east to west across the top of the peninsula would act as a first line of defense should either British or Indian forces decide to move against the Spanish colony from the interior.

With the exception of the Santa Catalina de Guale mission on St. Catherines Island, Georgia (Thomas 1987), the mission at San Juan del Puerto (said to have an impressive bell tower; Milanich and Sturtevant 1972), the missions of St. Augustine, and the San Luis mission at the administrative capital of the Apalachee Province, the Florida missions were humble affairs (Gannon 1965:39–40). Town plan of the mission settlements was regulated by royal ordinance and consisted of a church, convento, and kitchen or *cocina* arranged around a central plaza. Around or opposite the plaza was the Indian village, the most impressive feature of which was the main council house, or *buhiyo principal*, usually a circular thatched structure that could accommodate the entire population of the village for public meetings or other gatherings (Hann 1987; Shapiro 1987a). Many of the coastal missions and the Apalachee missions were built of wattle and daub, wet clay plastered over a framework of interwoven branches, with roofs of palmetto thatching. However, the interior mission churches of Timucua typically were constructed of vertical planking boards nailed to a post and beam frame (Hann 1988a, 1989).

Of course, as is almost always the case with plans developed from afar out of imperfect knowledge of local conditions, there was room for considerable variation from the norm, especially since the express purpose of the missions was to resettle the Indians to new locations and to alter their traditional way of life fundamentally. And despite the pedagogical training undergone by the priests in Spain and Havana, actual preparation in the survival skills needed for life in the provinces seems to have been less emphasized. How was one supposed to induce the Indians to provision the new mission community—in a territory where supplies were already scarce and could be moved only by canoe or on the human back?

Documentary sources and archaeology together suggest that perhaps the Franciscans had learned from the failed Jesuit experience. The Franciscans possessed an ample supply of European items to be given generously to the Indians as gifts. The military presence was kept to a minimum and even discouraged by the priests, who were well aware of the frictions that were likely to develop between soldier and Indian and of the disruptive influences the soldier could have on the pacification effort. Times had changed since the brief stint of the Jesuits, and the Indians themselves had developed more accommodating attitudes toward the Spanish presence. By 1597 Indians from the interior were traveling to St. Augustine to be baptized and were even requesting priests to come live with them. In April 1606, Fray Martín Prieto traveled from St. Augustine west to the region of Potano and here built a mission church which he named San Francisco (Oré 1936:110). The following year he went many times to the land he called Timucua, where the great cacique had "more than twenty places under his command" (Oré 1936:111). In 1608, the year after the English had settled at Jamestown, Fray Martín was invited by the cacique of Timucua to settle in his principal town and begin conversion, in a place soon referred to as San Martín.

The interior missions of Potano and Timucua were truly frontier settlements. Members of frontier societies, like Jamestown or the sixteenth-century urban populations of St. Augustine, find themselves having to adapt to difficult circumstances just to survive, often with survival skills suited to another place and time. The interaction between frontier societies and new environmental and social circumstances results in a unique culture, different from the parent culture of the colonists and distinct from the adaptations of the indigenous peoples. Florida mission culture was a blend of the Mediterranean ideal of the Spaniards and the woodland cultures of the Indians and differed from the better known Anglo-American frontier societies of history and folklore in that virtually all of the members of mission society were Indians native to Florida or the lower Southeast. In the interior missions of Potano and Timucua, it is probable that at any given time only one or two priests were in residence at each of the *doctrinas,* meaning in most cases that they were outnumbered by the Indians on the order of 200 to 1.

Despite the fact that Spain looked to the efforts of Christian missionaries to pacify the Indians almost from the beginning of the conquest, it would have been very difficult for either the government or the Franciscan Order to make an accurate prediction of the outcome of missionization in seventeenth century *La Florida.* In the words of a recent Franciscan historian, in Florida "Swamp land abounded . . . there was little or no agriculture or cattle-raising. No mines were located in this vast region. The land is poor and off the beaten track of commerce" (Geiger 1936:3). For the Indians as well, nothing of their prior experience was completely adequate to prepare them for mission life. At least some of the Indians of the Potano area remembered the atrocities committed by the de Soto entrada and justifiably carried an intense anger toward Christians. In the year 1606, a deafening thunderclap brought about a change of attitude toward Christianity on the part of one of these men, the aged cacique of Santa Ana, a small town near the San Francisco mission (Oré 1936:110).

Besides having to accept the Christian faith, there were other requirements of mission life that caused the Indians some difficulty. The requirement that all able-bodied men including chiefs carry loads of corn on their backs from the missions to the capital at St. Augustine was a major source of consternation to the village headmen, exempted in aboriginal society from such exertion, and was said to be one of their major grievances in provoking the Timucuan Rebellion in 1656 (Milanich

1978:65). At least after the rebellion, if not before, caciques who worked the fields for the benefit of the mission were given hoes as compensation (Hann 1987). Above the village chiefs was the "great cacique" of the province. How the great cacique was able to wield power over the village chiefs and give at least the appearance of political unity is not known, but it is clear that the Franciscans recognized that first converting the cacique would ease their attempts to bring Christianity to the provinces. It is also clear that neither commoner nor chief appreciated having the natural order of the world upset by Spanish intervention in the ordained succession of chiefly status from one person to another. In 1597, such activities on the part of the Spanish provoked the Guale Indians of the southeast Georgia coast to rise in rebellion. An unfortunate sign of things to come, this conflict pitted Christian Indians against those that rejected the Spaniards and their religion (Geiger 1940:79–81).

It would seem obvious that life in the missions meant fundamental changes in the day-to-day lives of the natives. These changes have been extremely difficult to define and measure, however, partly because the meager historical record often fails to note those mundane things that so fascinate scholars and partly because archaeologists have had trouble finding and excavating Indian villages that date to the time period just before the coming of the missionaries. A major source on the Florida Indians of the premission era is the set of engravings made by Theodore de Bry based on the watercolors of cartographer Jacques Le Moyne, a member of the French colony at Fort Caroline attacked by Pedro Menéndez in 1565.

Despite the fact that Le Moyne created the paintings and accompanying narrative in the years after his safe return to France and all but one of the originals are now lost, the pieces are used often and often uncritically to flesh out the details of native Florida culture on the eve of colonization. From Le Moyne we learn that the Outina Indians, living in circular palisaded villages on the western shore of the northern St. Johns River, tended to their fields and crops of corn and beans during the spring and summer months and by December of the year had dispersed into the woods (Lorant 1946:77). (The Outina Indians are not to be confused with the Utina Indians, a term used misleadingly by archaeologists since the studies of anthropologist John Swanton in the 1930s in referring to the historic period Indians north of the Potano tribe.) Other times during the year were set aside for gathering berries and fruits and for feasting.

Surplus crops and wild plant foods were stored in a communal granary, as were provisions of deer meat, fish, and "crocodiles" (Lorant 1946:81, 83). The chief and his wife were treated with great deference, but other than leading "councils of state" and accompanying warriors into battle (protected by a phalanx of warriors) (Lorant 1946:63) the chief's duties and responsibilities are left vague. The chief does not seem, for instance, to have been in charge of redistribution of foods from the public storehouse. Rather, the Indians would go to the storehouse individually when in need, without fear of sanction by their fellows (Lorant 1946:79). Nor did the chiefs seem to have controlled trade with other Indian tribes, as the Indians were said to have produced little for this purpose.

How the grand palisaded villages of Outina as depicted by Le Moyne have managed to elude the archaeologist's trowel is a mystery, especially since Indian villages similarly dating to the last half of the sixteenth century in other southeastern states have been partially or completely excavated (Knight 1985; Hally 1988). In Florida, however, there are at present no archaeological checks against the documentary record left by Le Moyne. Not only are village patterns archaeologically unknown, but with the possible exception of a circular or semicircular house partially exposed at the Richardson site near Orange Lake (Milanich 1972) house plans are conjectural. Oddly, it is not until the mission period of the seventeenth century that the Florida Indians again come into archaeological view, odd because it is generally assumed that by this time Indian numbers had become greatly thinned by European diseases introduced by the conquistadores. But at the San Luis mission in Tallahassee (Shapiro 1987b; Vernon and McEwan 1990) and the Baptizing Springs site near the Suwannee River in the mission province of Timucua (Loucks 1979), there are archaeological indications of populous and not especially impoverished aboriginal societies.

How long the individual missions stayed in one place depended on local conditions such as fluctuations in community size and the need to move to new agricultural plots, plus external circumstances such as the proximity to other missions and destruction by attack. In 1685, for example, the mission of Santa Catalina de Afuyca, probably located northwest of Ichetucknee Springs, was destroyed by British-backed Yamassee Indian warriors in a dawn raid. Testimony gathered by inquiry after the attack, translated by historian Amy Bushnell (1988), sets the scene quite well: "At four in the morning the enemy entered in two

groups, one by the road to Tari and the other by the road to Santa Fe, and
. . . at the appointed hour one of the groups fired a shot and the other
answered with another one and they advanced from both directions at
once, firing and yelling. Hearing the noise everyone came outside unable
to defend himself, people fleeing in every direction only to run into more
enemies, for there were a great many of them." Eighteen people were
killed and 21 carried off to the Indian town of Tari. The British governor
of Santa Elena provided the raiders with 16 shotguns and 11 cutlasses to
accomplish their aims.

The 1685 strike was but the first in a series of attacks on the Florida
missions by Yamassee and Creek Indians, supported and protected by the
British settlements on the lower Atlantic coast. In January 1704 the
boldest blow was struck when Colonel James Moore and a small army of
Creeks and Carolinian colonists moved on Apalachee Province, attacking
and taking a number of the mission towns. Assaults continued through the
summer, and by August the San Luis fort and mission were abandoned by
their inhabitants and burned to the ground. Timucua was not heavily
inhabited after 1685, and by 1704 the remaining North Florida Indians
had resettled within sight of the Spanish fort at St. Augustine (Milanich
1978:82).

The Development of Mission Archaeology

Modern archaeological interest in the Florida missions has developed in
large part from the studies of historian Mark F. Boyd, who, in a number
of publications beginning in the 1930s, made it seem possible if not
probable that many of the historically documented missions could actually
be located (Boyd 1939). Boyd was keenly interested in the collections
being made by J. Clarence Simpson of the Florida Geological Survey,
particularly in finds of Spanish olive jars, hand-wrought nails, and other
artifacts in scattered locations along the old Spanish road from St.
Augustine to Pensacola. Boyd himself discovered and partly excavated the
important Pine Tuft and Scott Miller sites.

The first systematic effort to investigate Florida's archaeological sites
representative of all periods of prehistory and the historic era began in
1946 with the establishment of the archaeological arm of the Florida Park
Service, directed by John W. Griffin and staffed at first by Hale Smith and

then by Ripley Bullen. The emphasis of the Park Service program was on building basic chronologies for different areas of Florida and on identifying artifacts that could be used as temporal markers to cross-date archaeological sites. In 1948 John Griffin conducted the first archaeological excavations at Fort San Luis by testing the moat area. Architectural hardware was found as was a fragment of a cannon and a pistol barrel. Thirty-nine rosary beads and various other glass beads were also found. Faunal remains included pig and cow bones. Also by 1948 Hale Smith was ready to define the mission period in Florida archaeologically, naming it the Leon-Jefferson period after the two counties in which the Apalachee mission sites were concentrated (Smith 1948).

The first archaeological remains of a mission church and convento were uncovered by Hale Smith at the Scott Miller site (8Je2) in 1947, although Mark Boyd had begun investigations there in 1940. The larger structure, interpreted by Smith to have been the church, actually consisted of two buildings contained within an enclosing wall. The measurements of the enclosure were 17.8 m north-south by 12.0 m east-west. The second building was located about 35 m north of the church and had dimensions of 6 m by 4.9 m. Both structures had clay floors and walls made of wattle and daub. Large numbers of both Spanish and Indian artifacts were obtained from excavations of the structures and from a clay-filled borrow pit nearby. Majolica, olive jar, and Chinese porcelain were collected, as well as architectural hardware such as an iron hinge and keyhole plate (Smith 1956:57). The borrow pit contained a particularly rich mix of materials, yielding stone pounders and grinders, an iron hoe, an anvil, spring locks, a musket and a pistol barrel, and a lead finger ring (Smith 1956:58). A charred corncob and burnt peach pits were found on the floor of the presumed church building.

Smith also explored the mission site at Pine Tuft (8Je1), thought by Mark Boyd to be Mission San Juan de Aspalaga (Boyd 1939:273), and here found Spanish majolica, aboriginal pottery, wrought-iron hardware, and, in a 1-foot-square test on top of the presumed floor of the church, the remarkably well preserved charred remains of beans, peas, corn, and possibly garlic cloves (Smith 1956:62). In 1955, John W. Griffin, by now working for the St. Augustine Historical Society after the disbanding of Florida Park Service archaeology in 1953, excavated a series of test squares at the San Juan del Puerto site (8Du53) on Fort George Island, obtaining glass beads and other Spanish artifacts in good archaeological context. The immediate result of these efforts was to demonstrate beyond doubt the archaeological potential of mission sites and that the physical remains of the buildings themselves could be found and interpreted.

During this period John M. Goggin of the University of Florida also became greatly interested in the Florida missions and, like Griffin and Smith, at first concentrated on developing an archaeological signature by which mission sites could be identified. While the work of Smith and Griffin primarily had been focused on the Apalachee missions, Goggin's attentions were on the missions of Potano and Timucua. His was the initial archaeological work at such important sites as Richardson, Fox Pond (8Al272), and Zetrouer (8Al67), not to mention his collecting forays to the Wright's Landing (8SJ3) and Shell Bluff Landing (8SJ32) sites in the St. Augustine area and to San Juan del Puerto (8Du53) further up the coast. Goggin's discovery of Fig Springs and his early collecting there are central to our story and will be discussed in more detail in chapter 2. Goggin put a great many archaeological sites on the map, but even more important was his recognition that Spanish artifacts found in Florida sites could be used as rather precise time markers for archaeological deposits that were otherwise very difficult to date. His detailed monographs on Spanish olive jar (Goggin 1960a) and majolica (Goggin 1968) are among his strongest contributions to archaeology.

In 1968, following up on the work of Boyd and Smith, the State of Florida began a project to locate previously unidentified Apalachee mission sites (Jones and Shapiro 1987). Systematic use of historical maps in combination with predicted site locations based on topographical elevation and distance to water led to the discovery and partial excavation of nine additional Apalachee missions. An important contribution of this work, much of it done almost single-handedly by state archaeologist B. Calvin Jones, was the excavation of a mission cemetery and the first recognition that the cemetery was a regular feature of the overall site plan. Jones and L. Ross Morrell returned to Smith's Pine Tuft site and almost completely exposed the architectural remains of two structures, one interpreted as the church and the smaller one the convento. The presumed church had a clay floor and several rooms defined by vertical plank partition boards (Morrell and Jones 1970:34). Like the structure at Scott Miller excavated by Smith, the Pine Tuft church was enclosed by a wattle-and-daub wall. The conjectural reconstruction of this building (Morrell and Jones 1970:42) is perhaps the most often reproduced depiction of a "typical" Florida mission.

Meanwhile, first at Florida State University and then at the University of Florida, Charles Fairbanks was working on following up Goggin's leads and continued to study Spanish colonial artifacts as they were found in good archaeological context. While Goggin, Smith, and the others were ultimately concerned with bringing their archaeological research to bear on the anthropological interests of culture change, ethnicity, and acculturation, it was Fairbanks who was first most explicitly concerned with these issues and, importantly, was the mentor of a number of archaeology students who have conducted important anthropological studies of the Spanish colonial period in Florida and the Caribbean (Baker 1968; Milanich 1972, 1978; Deagan 1978, 1987; Loucks 1979; Willis 1984; Marrinan 1985).

The 1976 and 1978 University of Florida excavations at Baptizing Springs (8Su65) (Loucks 1979) were the first fruit of the explicit anthropological approach to mission archaeology. The remains of four structures were uncovered in the investigations, two presumably "Spanish" meaning either church or convento, and two thought to be aboriginal. The types and frequencies of Spanish and aboriginal artifacts present in each structure were compared in the hope of drawing conclusions about the political, economic, and social structure of the community. Differences in the frequencies of Spanish and aboriginal ceramics and nonceramic "prestige" items such as pieces of brass and other metals were noted, particularly between the two aboriginal structures, and some indication of status ranking was inferred (Loucks 1979:241–68).

Florida mission archaeology was given a public showcase in 1983 when the San Luis de Talimali mission (8Le4) was purchased by the State of Florida through the Conservation and Recreation Lands (CARL) Trust Fund. Although something was known of the layout of the site through previous excavations, the first tasks of the long-term research design were to undertake an auger survey of the 50-acre San Luis property and to complete a topographical contour map over the same area (Shapiro 1987b:26). The purpose of this initial work was to be able to distinguish functional areas of the site on the basis of artifact distributions and regular topographical features. In the subsequent seasons of fieldwork, the mission church, cemetery, aboriginal council house, and possible Spanish residential areas were identified and partially excavated (Shapiro 1987a; Vernon and McEwan 1990). The San Luis project was the first to provide an archaeological and historical bird's-eye view of a Florida mission town, complete with a wattle-and-daub thatched-roof church, ball poles on the central plaza, and smoke rising through the opening in the council house roof (Shapiro 1987b:133).

A project of similar scale and intent has been directed since 1980 by David Hurst Thomas at Mission Santa Catalina de Guale on St. Catherines Island off the central Georgia coast. The original mission, founded in 1567 by Jesuit priests supported by Pedro Menéndez de Avilés was destroyed in the 1597 Guale rebellion. Early in the 1600s Franciscans returned to the site and reestablished a mission, which nearly lasted out the century. Despite its relative prominence in documents of the time, the site remained archaeologically unknown until Thomas began employing a combination of systematic shovel testing and remote sensing techniques (Thomas 1987). Work to date has focused on the excavation of the mission church, which contained hundreds of subfloor burials, many interred with glass beads, religious medallions, and other items.

Mission burials were also the focus of the Florida Museum of Natural History project at the Santa Maria and Santa Catalina missions on Amelia Island, part of the barrier chain of sea islands north of Jacksonville. The Santa Catalina mission is thought to have been inhabited by refugees from the Santa Catalina mission on St. Catherines Island after its abandonment in 1680 (Saunders 1988). A mission cemetery was located about 25 m south of the Santa Catalina convento, but burials at the nearby Santa Maria site were made through the floor of its church. This structure appears to have been constructed of wood rather than wattle and daub and may have in part rested above ground on shell-filled sleepers. Extremely detailed research is also underway at the Florida Museum of Natural History on plant remains found at this and other mission sites (Ruhl 1987, 1988).

The Significance of the Fig Springs Site

Mission archaeology of the 1980s had become not only increasingly sophisticated but also much concerned with archaeological context. It was no longer of primary interest what artifacts were present or absent at a given site but, instead, where at the site artifacts were found. The variability of artifact distributions across the site—meaning that types of artifacts might be found with greater frequency in specific structures, areas, or sectors of the site—could lead to inferences about the society, politics, and economy of the mission community, and this factor was clearly integral to the research at Baptizing Springs and San Luis.

Enough survey and testing had occurred and enough mission sites had been discovered to know that mission sites, however variable in overall plan, did have an archaeological signature. Thus they could be sought as predictable and important sources of information about the mission period. Unfortunately, most of the known sites already had been disturbed at the time of discovery or have since been obliterated. A few of the sites, like San Luis, had substantial intact components but also had a long history of subsequent use since the mission period and had been damaged to some extent. For some of the missions, particularly in Apalachee, the mission villages, the most sizable and arguably the most important part of the site, had never been located.

What was needed was a single site that was both undisturbed by human activity since the mission period and had all of its parts—the church-convento-cemetery complex and the mission village—intact and together on one piece of property. This was the hope for the Fig Springs site when the project began there in January 1988.

2

Beginnings

✣ ON JULY 13, 1949, JOHN GOGGIN
and a group of his students began a canoe trip down the Ichetucknee
River and soon, in Goggin's words, "decided to investigate a spring run
on the east side," pausing there long enough to find "lots of Spanish
pottery" (Goggin 1949) and sherds of Indian pottery strewn about on the
bottom and sides of the run. Goggin assigned three site numbers to these
underwater finds, although now they are grouped together as one site,
8Co1 (fig. 3).

John Goggin became fascinated with the Spanish majolica (tin-
enameled earthenware) from Fig Springs, unlike any he had seen before,
and returned to the site many times in the 1950s to increase his
collections of sherds. Eventually he was to pioneer the use of scuba gear
in underwater archaeology in deep dives made in Blue Hole, a large
spring just north of Fig Springs (Goggin 1960b). As the result of his
interest in the Fig Springs majolica, Goggin began test excavations of
Spanish colonial sites in Mexico, the Dominican Republic, and Nueva
Cadiz off the coast of Venezuela in the first archaeological investigation of
the occurrence of majolica in the New World (Goggin 1968).

Despite his sustained interest in Fig Springs, Goggin was never able to
locate the original archaeological site from which the artifacts in the
springs had come (fig. 4). Although he was fairly certain that the materials
had come from a nearby mission, he thought that he had found only the
refuse dump for that site.

Over the years Fig Springs gained a reputation as an excellent source
of artifacts, and the area where Goggin's finds were made was worked
over and over again. Russell Platt (fig. 5), a longtime resident of the area,
also amassed an impressive collection of Spanish and aboriginal artifacts
from the springs during this period, including a majolica plate of the type

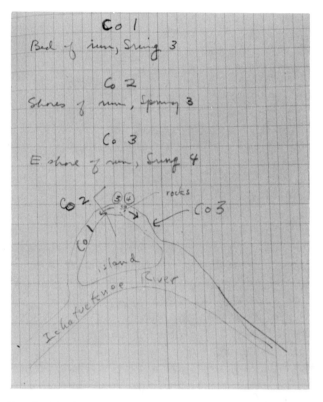

FIG. 3. *The sketch of Fig Springs in John Goggin's 1949 field book (P. K. Yonge Library of Florida History).*

Columbia Plain pictured in Goggin's monograph (Goggin 1968:pl. 3b). (Unfortunately the Platt collection was destroyed or dispersed after a fire burned Mr. Platt's house.) A large portion of the bank at Fig Springs was cut away and subsequently undermined by souvenir hunters in search of artifacts. A spoil pile produced from these diggings was itself dug in by later treasure seekers. Fortunately these activities, destructive as they were, were confined to a small area of the springs, since no one knew of the undisturbed archaeological site just up the hill. Neither Goggin nor Platt seems to have explored the wooded bank above the springs to any extent (fig. 6). One afternoon in 1970, B. Calvin Jones excavated some test pits in this area, but found only aboriginal pottery and lithic flakes attributed by him to the Deptford period. Most of the collecting stopped

FIG. 4. *John Goggin at Fig Springs, early 1950s.*

when Fig Springs became part of Ichetucknee Springs State Park in 1971. Through the 1970s and 1980s it became well known that a Spanish mission was once in the vicinity, partly because the area was named Mission Springs in the park brochure. Still, it was not known for certain if such a mission really existed, since the overgrown woods of the hillside overlooking the springs gave no visible or obvious clue that it did.

Ney Landrum, former director of the Florida Division of Recreation and Parks, deserves much of the credit for the events leading to the discovery of the mission site. As the five-hundredth anniversary of the Columbus landing approached, Landrum was looking for a way to bring

FIG. 5. *Russell Platt at Fig Springs, 1988.*

Florida's "lost" Spanish heritage to the forefront of public attention. Funding was made available to conduct archaeological and documentary research of the conquistador Hernando de Soto's route through the peninsula in 1539. There long has been a great popular interest in the de Soto route and the places and peoples encountered by the expedition. De Soto Trail research, much of it done under the direction of Jerald T.

Milanich of the Florida Museum of Natural History, paid almost immediate public dividends as new discoveries along the route came to light (Milanich and Milbrath 1989).

The second objective of the Landrum plan was to find and excavate a Spanish mission in one of Florida's state parks and ultimately complete an architectural reconstruction of the mission for public interpretation. Public interest in the Florida missions had already been amply demonstrated by the success of the San Luis project in Tallahassee (Shapiro 1987b). Other than San Luis, did a site exist capable of meeting Landrum's expectations?

In December 1986 mission artifacts, human burials, and a small patch of possible burned clay floor were unearthed in shovel test excavations on the bluff above Fig Springs by a field crew led by Kenneth W. Johnson and directed by Milanich in their search for the Indian town of Aquacalyquen visited by de Soto in August 1539 (Johnson 1987, 1990).

FIG. 6. *The area of Fig Springs where Goggin collected, as it appears today.*

This was the first sign of the mission from which Goggin's artifacts had come (eventually over 4,000 were collected; see Deagan 1972). Before moving on to other sites in their quest for de Soto (Milanich believed that some of the missions of Potano and Timucua were founded in or near villages earlier visited by de Soto), the Florida Museum of Natural History crew excavated 44 50-cm-by-50-cm shovel tests across the bluff and four 1-m-by-1-m units where the burials were found (Johnson 1987). The project was then turned over to the Florida Bureau of Archaeological Research, and plans were made to conduct a systematic power-auger survey of the 30 wooded acres immediately adjacent to the springs and including the area of the previous testing.

The Fig Springs auger survey began in February 1988, under my direction. The 16 months of subsequent fieldwork have made it certain that Fig Springs is a Spanish mission site dating to the first half of the seventeenth century. About 320 sq m of site area were excavated, including the remains of what are identified as a mission church, a convento, the mission cemetery, most of a large structure in the associated Indian village, and midden deposits dating to the mission period.

Of course, field archaeologists are well aware of the shortcomings of the archaeological record in reflecting the complex realities of the past and are justifiably reluctant to ascribe functional titles to excavated remains until all the facts are in. In reviewing the architectural information from the Fig Springs excavations, a great deal of time was spent comparing it to previous work done at other missions where the overall site plan was known, particularly work at San Luis and the Apalachee missions by Gary Shapiro and Calvin Jones, Loucks's work at Baptizing Springs, and the Mission Santa Catalina de Guale project directed by David Hurst Thomas. As these archaeologists have noted, broad similarities in site plan do emerge across the mission provinces, although each site presents the pattern in its own way. All share the concept of sacred and secular districts, with the religious buildings and cemetery in one area of the site and the mission village in another. Thus, the Fig Springs church, convento, cemetery, plaza, and aboriginal areas as described in chapter 5 are so named because of their general resemblance to the architecture and site plans of known sites. It should not be thought, however, that the excavated site plan as presented here is the only plan that ever existed at the Fig Springs mission. Fifty years is a long time for rather insubstantial wood frame buildings to occupy single locations;

indeed, it would be unusual if building sites did not change over a period of years in response to changing needs of the community. During episodes of remodeling or rebuilding, the inhabitants themselves may have done their best to salvage usable building materials and clean up former building locations, thus making the architectural history of the mission even more difficult to discern.

Environmental Setting

The Fig Springs site is located on a terrace approximately 8 m above Fig Springs and the low shoreline of the Ichetucknee River (fig. 7). The terrace was created by a combination of past human activity at the site such as leveling for building construction, as will be discussed, and erosion of deposits that has tended to remove surface irregularities.

Soils are sands of the Bonneau classification (USDA 1984) and clays developed from weathering of the limestone bedrock of the Suwannee formation, a fossil-bearing marine limestone dating to the Oligocene Epoch. The limestone and clay are quite shallow in places, particularly along the edge of the terrace at the drop down to the springs. There are several surface exposures of the limestone bedrock at the site, especially at the water's edge. One large limestone exposure is named Fig Island, which sits prominently at the source of the springs (Fig Springs being a collective name for a number of springs that originate here). Boiling out below this rock is the major spring in the system, with an estimated output of up to 25 million gallons daily.

Present vegetation in the area of the site is an oak-hickory forest with an understory of dogwood and maple. A few magnolias can be found, and several cedar trees grow on the slope to the springs. There are many cedar stumps along the banks of the run, the remains of trees logged in the 1930s. Several large slash pines and longleaf pines are present in the central and eastern area of the site, but most of the pine forest is on the high ground to the east of the site boundary. Pine forest, probably once the dominant vegetation type across the site, is the climax forest in this environmental setting. Pine lumber appears to have been used exclusively in the construction of the mission buildings. After the site was abandoned, hardwood species took over to the exclusion of pine. Besides oak hammock, other vegetation communities within walking distance of Fig

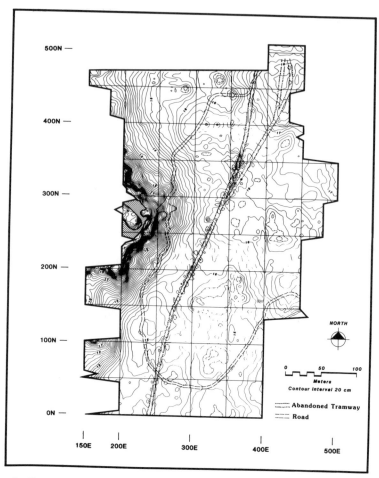

FIG. 7. *Topographical map of the Fig Springs site, produced after the first field season, 1988.*

Springs include the sandhills to the south and the cypress-maple river swamps along the narrow floodplain of the Ichetucknee River.

Animals typical of these vegetative communities can be found in the area of the site today. White-tailed deer, turkeys, bobcats, otters, squirrels, and beavers are all commonly observed in the vicinity. Several species of water turtle occur in the springs and river, and the gopher tortoise can be found in the sandy uplands. An informal bird count done by Roan McNab between February and May 1988 noted over 80 species, including four types of hawk, the Mississippi kite and swallow-tailed kite, the wood duck, and the sandhill crane. Fish include bass, sunfish, the bowfin or mudfish, and gar.

Climate is characterized by hot, humid summers with afternoon thundershowers. About one-half of the annual rainfall occurs in such showers between June and September (USDA 1984). Mild winters generally prevail, with an average daily temperature of about 55 degrees. Occasionally however it can get bitter cold, with daytime temperatures down into the teens (as we personally experienced during fieldwork in February and March 1989), and heavy rains can and do occur at any time throughout the year. In our field experience, September has been a particularly rainy month.

Fig Springs is part of the Gulf Coastal Lowlands physiographic province (USDA 1984). Drainage is via the Suwannee River into the Gulf of Mexico. Fig Springs is about one mile south of the headsprings of the Ichetucknee River, which flows for about five miles before joining the Santa Fe River. The confluence of the Santa Fe and Suwannee rivers is about six miles from this point, and then the Suwannee continues on its southerly course, emptying into the Gulf of Mexico about 12 miles north of Cedar Keys. Distance from Fig Springs to the Gulf by water is about 50 miles. Except in very dry periods, this route is entirely navigable by canoe or shallow draft vessel.

3

Culture and History

✛   Fɪɢ Sᴘʀɪɴɢs ɪs ʟᴏᴄᴀᴛᴇᴅ ɪɴ the North Florida archaeological culture area, as defined by Milanich and Fairbanks (1980:22–23, 32–33). The North Florida sequence begins with the Paleo-Indian period. Absolute dates are not available for the Paleo-Indian occupation of the region, but it is assumed to have been between about 12000 B.C. and about 6500 B.C., like the rest of Florida. Some of the best Paleo-Indian stone points and tools collected in the state have come from the Grassy Flats area of the Ichetucknee River and are in the possession of private collectors. These are the large Suwannee and fluted Simpson types (Bullen 1975:56–57). The extensive collections made by the Simpson family are curated at the Florida Museum of Natural History.

The Archaic period represents the cultural adaptation to the modern climate and environment that followed the Pleistocene Ice Age. Like the Paleo-Indians, Archaic peoples are best known by their stone projectile points and tools, a number of which have been found at Fig Springs (fig. 8). Sharpened bone tools of probable Archaic origin also have been found in the river, and other Archaic sites in Florida where preservation has been favorable have yielded artifacts of basketry or matting and wooden implements. Territories were large and populations still low and probably organized into bands of closely related families. No Archaic campsites are known at present for the Ichetucknee area. Dates for the Archaic are between 6500 B.C. and about 1000 B.C.

Pottery first appears near the end of the Archaic, in what archaeologists have called the Orange period. This fiber-tempered pottery, so named because organic fibers were mixed with the clay, is found in very small quantity along the Ichetucknee River but not from any single substantial site. Archaeologists assume that the introduction of pottery is generally

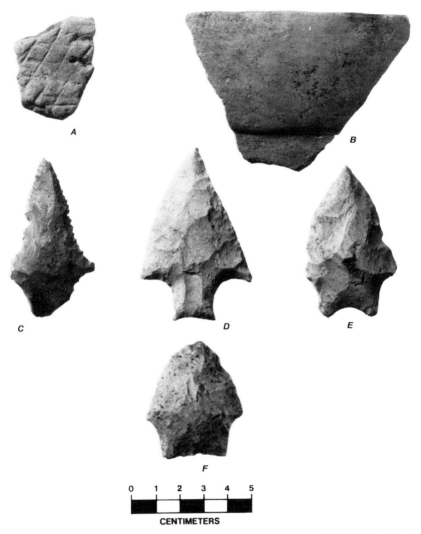

FIG. 8. *Prehistoric artifacts found at Fig Springs. (A) Keith Incised sherd, (B) Weeden Island Plain rim sherd, (C) Kirk Serrated projectile point, (D) Florida Archaic Stemmed, (E) Arredondo point, (F) Gilchrist point.*

correlated with changes in group size, residence pattern, and food habits, but these topics have been very difficult to study since relevant sites are difficult to identify and excavate. It is thought that the peoples using fiber-tempered pottery were transitional in their culture between nomadic Archaic cultures and cultures that eventually were to adopt permanent village life.

Small villages occupied on a seasonal basis are evidenced archaeologically in the Deptford period, dating between about 500 B.C. and A.D. 300. There appears to be a thin scatter of Deptford materials, primarily check-stamped pottery of hard, sandy clay, along the bluffs and river margins of the Ichetucknee. No discrete Deptford site has yet been located in the vicinity. Burial mounds and small earthworks, known for Deptford peoples elsewhere in Florida, have not been discovered in the Ichetucknee Springs area. It is possible that Deptford peoples spent most of the year on the Gulf coast, where Deptford period shell middens and burial mounds exist. Deposits of broken freshwater shells are found in several locations on the Ichetucknee River just south of Fig Springs, but these have not been definitely shown to have resulted from human activities.

The most visible archaeological remains in the area belong to the Weeden Island culture, with a beginning date of A.D. 200 (Milanich et al. 1984). Two small burial mounds in the park, one on the east side of the river near the Midpoint Tube Launch (8Co43) and the second on the west side due west of Devil's Eye Spring (fig. 9), have been attributed to the Weeden Island culture on the basis of collections of Carrabelle Punctated and Swift Creek Complicated Stamped pottery located there. As is the case with Deptford artifacts, only a thin scatter of Weeden Island pottery is present along the east bluff of the Ichetucknee River. A Keith Incised and at least one Weeden Island–style rim sherd were recovered in the 1988 auger survey (see fig. 8). Again, the lack of absolute dates poses a problem for a tight dating of the Weeden Island deposits. Terminal dates for Weeden Island cannot be fixed and may extend past A.D. 1000.

The Suwannee Valley Pottery Series

The problem of which (if any) archaeological culture existed at Fig Springs prior to the mission period has proved to be difficult to resolve. One difficulty is that European artifacts have so far been found only in archaeological contexts that suggest very late sixteenth or early to mid-seventeenth century dating. The aboriginal pottery associated with these European artifacts (presumably Spanish-derived) found at the Mill

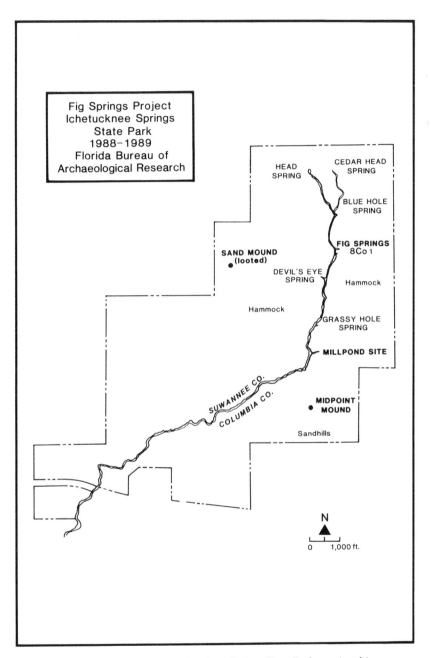

Fig Springs Project
Ichetucknee Springs
State Park
1988–1989
Florida Bureau of
Archaeological Research

HEAD
SPRING

CEDAR HEAD
SPRING

BLUE HOLE
SPRING

FIG SPRINGS
8Co 1

SAND MOUND
● (looted)

DEVIL'S EYE
SPRING

Hammock

Hammock

GRASSY HOLE
SPRING

MILLPOND SITE

SUWANNEE CO.
COLUMBIA CO.

MIDPOINT
● MOUND

Sandhills

N
▲

0   1,000 ft.

FIG. 9. *Archaeological sites in Ichetucknee Springs State Park mentioned in text.*

Pond and Fig Springs sites belongs to a "roughened" complex of surface treatment (scratched and brushed surfaces and heavy dragged punctations), cob-marked, cord-marked, and punctated ceramics related to the Alachua Tradition and the familiar complicated stamped ceramics of the mission period.

Suwannee Valley pottery is found in the southern end of the aboriginal village found at Fig Springs (excavation units 50N/295E and 70N/310E) in the absence of Spanish materials and complicated stamped mission pottery, suggesting that this complex may have been present before the mission was established. However, there is no indication from the excavations of exactly how early it is—that is, if Suwannee pottery developed out of Weeden Island and spans the centuries from A.D. 900 (the conventional date for terminal Weeden Island elsewhere in Florida) to the mission period or, instead, represents an influx of people into the north peninsula in the fifteenth or sixteenth centuries prior to European contact.

The single radiocarbon date from Fig Springs for the Suwannee complex of 360 ± 60 B.P. (with a calibrated age of A.D. 1490) (Beta 32577) from 50N/295E suggests that the second alternative is a real possibility. At the very least, the date alone does nothing to substantiate an in-situ developmental sequence connecting Weeden Island peoples to the inhabitants of the mission, as is the assumption based on the recovery of Suwannee ceramics in association with mission period sites at Baptizing Springs, Indian Pond, and elsewhere in North Florida (Loucks 1979; Milanich et al. 1984; Johnson 1987; Johnson and Nelson 1990). It is curious that the only burial mounds yet known in the Ichetucknee area contain only Weeden Island ceramics and lack the roughened, cord, cob, and punctated Suwannee series types.

The origin of Suwannee Valley ceramics (and thus the cultural origin of the founding population of mission Indians) must await the development of a well-dated archaeological sequence either coming forward in time from Weeden Island or backward from the mission period. A good stratigraphic column would be ideal but may not be possible given the rather thin prehistoric occupation of the area in general. A battery of radiocarbon dates from discrete components or sites is something that could be accomplished in further work without too much difficulty, especially given the positive results at Fig Springs in locating charcoal features in soil cores or auger borings as a guide to placing excavation units.

Although it is possible to see how, in theory at least, the roughened

Suwannee Series pottery may have devolved from incised, punctated, and even dentate stamped Weeden Island ceramics, it is also possible to argue for an Alachua Tradition affiliation (Milanich 1971). The types Alachua Cob Marked, Prairie Cord Marked, and Lochloosa Punctated are consistently present in the Ichetucknee assemblages, although in different ratios than those in the Alachua heartland area south of the Santa Fe River (Milanich 1971). Thus the sequence for Fig Springs may follow that developed for North-Central Florida—a migration of Alachua Tradition (presumably farming) peoples from South-Central Georgia by perhaps A.D. 700, displacing or assimilating the indigenous cultures (Weeden Island north of the Santa Fe, Cades Pond south of that river; see Milanich et al. 1976, Milanich and Fairbanks 1980:97). Unfortunately, there are no well-dated sites in the Ichetucknee area between A.D. 700 and the fifteenth century, when such a migration and displacement might have occurred, nor are there any mounds in the vicinity attributable to Alachua or Alachua-related peoples such as exist in the heartland area to the south. At present, pottery seriations are insufficient by themselves to confirm the existence of prehistoric cultures in the Fig Springs vicinity during this 900-year period. In short, there is little physical evidence to argue that the area was indeed inhabited by prehistoric peoples rather than abandoned during this time. Curiously, there is also a gap in the Alachua sequence between A.D. 1100 and A.D. 1400 (Milanich 1971:28).

The area was almost certainly abandoned following the final collapse of the Timucua missions by 1706 (table 1). The Spanish colonial government understandably felt uneasy about having the back door to their capital at St. Augustine unprotected by a human buffer, and they had a distinct political need to forge new alliances among the surviving southeastern Indians. By 1778 Creek Indians, called Seminoles after their move to Florida, had settled the village of Weechatooka near the confluence of the Ichetucknee and Santa Fe rivers (see fig. 2) and the abandoned mission fields had been given the name "Weechatookamee Old Fields" (Purcell 1778).

The relationship between the Weechatooka Seminoles and the better known Seminole inhabitants of Cuscowilla and Talahasochte (south of Weechatooka on the Suwannee River) is not known. The Weechatooka site has not been discovered, and there are only fragmentary remains at Fig Springs that can be attributed to an eighteenth-century Seminole occupation. This gap is reinforced by the reclassification of most of the

Table 1. Historical Summary of the Ichetucknee Springs Area

1841	Small American settlement established at Cedar Hammock, northeast of Ichetucknee Springs, consisting of 21 persons, 8 of whom were slaves.
1839	Limited activity during the Second Seminole War; Fort White established.
1778	Joseph Purcell maps North Florida at the request of Col. John Stuart. The "Weechatookamee" River is shown, as are the "Weechatookamee Old Fields" east of the river and Weechatooka village south at the confluence of the Santa Fe River.
1760(?)	Area first inhabited by Seminole Indians, possibly affiliated with the larger Seminole towns on the Suwannee River and Alachua prairie.
1685	First documented Yamassee Indian raid on interior Timucua; Santa Catalina mission attacked.
1677	Spanish cattle ranches established at several abandoned missions.
1657	Timucua briefly visited by Governor Rebolledo following the Timucua Revolt.
1656	The Timucua Revolt, centered at San Martín.
1656–1649	Disease epidemics decimate the mission Timucua.
1617–1614	Smallpox, measles, and typhus sweep the Timucua missions.
1616	Visitation of the Timucua Province by Fray Gerónimo Oré.
1608	First permanent Timucua missions founded by Martín Prieto.
1597	Baltasar López preached among the Timucua for three months.
1565	The North Florida Timucua have limited contact with the French outpost at Fort Caroline.
1539	Spanish conquistador Hernando de Soto passes through general vicinity en route to Apalachee.

brushed ware at the site—labeled previously in the interim site reports Chattahoochee Brushed (Weisman 1988a,b), as Fig Springs Roughened, part of the Suwannee Valley Series. This also raises the perplexing question of the cultural relationship between the roughened Suwannee pottery and Chattahoochee Brushed, a type associated with the historic Creek Indians of Georgia and Alabama. Several eighteenth- or early nineteenth-century artifacts have been collected at the site (fig. 10), as surface finds or from the modern humus. Notably lacking, however, are the quantities of European pearlware and creamware ceramics and faceted blue glass trade beads that characteristically mark Seminole settlements of this period (Weisman 1989).

The Ichetucknee River seems not to have been the scene of heavy Seminole occupation during the first or second Seminole wars. The outpost of Fort White was established in 1839, in the midst of the Second Seminole War, and by 1841 the settlement of Cedar Hammock had been founded. The latter had a population of 21 people, eight of whom were

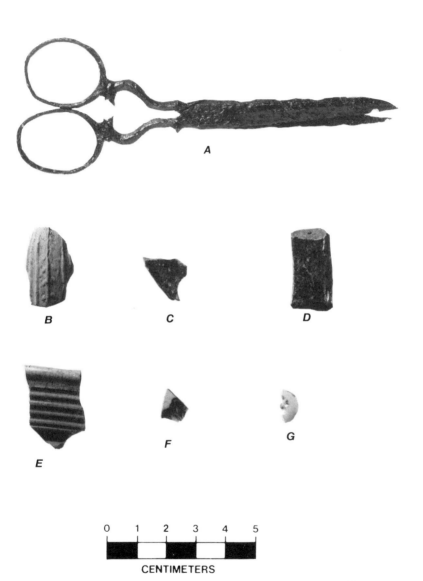

FIG. 10. *Eighteenth- and nineteenth-century artifacts found at Fig Springs. (A) iron scissors, (B) kaolin pipe bowl, (C, D) stoneware sherds, (E, F) refined earthenwares, (G) porcelain button.*

slaves. Permanent aboriginal habitation probably had ceased some decades before, possibly terminated by General Andrew Jackson's strike against Bowlegs and the Suwannee Seminole towns in 1818.

The Mission

After the failure of the Jesuit missions founded by Menéndez, mission activity was again taken up by the Franciscan priests. By 1597 priests had ventured well inland from the coast, carrying their word to Indians who previously had been well out of the mainstream of European contact. It appears from the documents that it was the Indians themselves who initiated the Franciscan presence. In July 1597, the brother of the *cacique mayor*, or head chief, of Timucua, a native polity west of the St. Johns River in what is now North Florida, traveled to St. Augustine to pledge obedience to the king and request that a missionary be sent to his village (Hann 1988a). For his reward, the man was given a shirt of Rouen linen, a doublet of Dutch linen, a pair of shoes, and a red hat for himself and several others to be distributed among the principal men of the village.

In September 1597, Fray Baltasar López came 50 leagues inland from the San Pedro mission on Cumberland Island, Georgia, to preach for three months among the Timucua. The 50-league distance from San Pedro to the head village of Timucua corresponds to the approximate distance between Cumberland Island and Fig Springs at 2.6 miles to the league, given the somewhat indirect route that must have existed. According to López, Timucua consisted of the main settlement and five satellite villages, with a combined population of about 1,500 people.

What sort of greeting López received and how seriously the Timucuans had prepared for his visit are not known. In the July trip to St. Augustine, the Indians had been given two iron axes and a hoe by Juan Ximénez, the "keeper of provisions," with which to build a church and "house" for the requested priest (Hann 1988a). The cacique understood that he was to keep the tools for his own use after the construction for the priest was complete. It seems that López's brief stay did not have a lasting effect on the natives, and in his absence Christianity lost its hold. In 1607 Fray Martín Prieto again traveled to the head village of Timucua, presumably the same site visited by López, again at the request of the principal chief (possibly the same man who had gone to St. Augustine in

1597, now having inherited the chieftainship from his brother). Timucua was at war with the Indians of Apalachee, and it was hoped that the priest would quell the hostilities and mediate the peace. Fray Martín was successful in his diplomacy and returned to Timucua confident that he would receive the "reward of heaven" (Oré 1936).

Martín Prieto stayed on in Timucua in 1608, which now consisted of 15 additional villages besides the five main satellites. The principal village was named San Martín (subsequently appearing on mission lists as San Martín de Timucua or San Martín de Ayacuto). In 1655, the distance between Mission San Martín and St. Augustine was given as 34 leagues (88.4 miles) (Geiger 1940:126), close to the 82 straight-line miles that exist today between St. Augustine and Fig Springs.

Prieto began a major task of converting (or reconverting) the Timucua Indians to Christianity. In the center of the plaza at San Martín, he burned 12 wooden images used in the native religion and then went to four other villages, burning six more images in each (Oré 1936). Returning to San Martín, he baptized about 100 Indian "boys and girls" (Oré 1936:110). Prieto's account of the founding of San Martín was recorded in 1616 by Oré during an official visitation of the Timucua Province. Another priest who was active at San Martín between 1610 and the 1620s was Juan Gómez de Palma (Geiger 1940). Fray Martín Prieto died sometime between 1624 and 1630 (Hann 1988b).

In 1630, Fray Alonzo de Jesus requested horses from the government for San Martín and the other Timucua missions so that travel and the movement of supplies from St. Augustine to the interior could be made less burdensome. The difficult movement of goods back and forth from St. Augustine continued to be a problem and was one of the causes of the Timucua Rebellion of 1656. In attempting to explain to the authorities what had gone wrong in the province to provoke the rebellion, priests were quick to point out that native caciques did not take kindly to carrying loads of mission-grown corn to St. Augustine on their backs (Hann 1987).

San Martín has been considered one of the centers of the 1656 rebellion (Swanton 1939:156), at which time it may have been destroyed. The Timucua Rebellion lasted for eight months and resulted in seven recorded deaths. In 1657 Governor Rebolledo (whose poor leadership was responsible for the uprising, said the priests) ordered the native population of Arapaha to resettle San Martín. The name disappears from the mission lists at this time, however, and it is unlikely that Rebolledo's order was carried out.

The certain identity of Fig Springs as Mission San Martín perhaps may never be made, despite the positive correlation between the archaeological and documentary evidence. The San Luis mission in Tallahassee and Santa Catalina de Guale on St. Catherines Island, Georgia, are among the few mission sites that can be given names beyond a shadow of doubt, because maps and later documentary sources can be, and consistently have been, accurately tied to modern locations. Based on the league measurements from St. Augustine given in the known mission documents, the geographical description provided in Peña's account, and the archaeological dating of the site to the period when San Martín was known to have existed, the association between Fig Springs and San Martín is as strong as can be hoped for in the absence of additional written descriptions or map depictions of the mission site. Previous identification of the site as Santa Catalina de Afuyca (or Ahoica) (Deagan 1972; Milanich 1978:75) can be abandoned, however, for lack of fit between documented dates of that mission, 1675–1685 (Geiger 1940; Bushnell 1988) and the pre-1650s dating of most of the known Fig Springs assemblage. This is not to say that the remains of the Santa Catalina mission in Timucua Province will not someday be unearthed in the vicinity of Fig Springs. If this occurs, the artifacts and architecture of this later site should provide an informative contrast to the remains of the presumed San Martín mission.

Dating the Site

Ceramic dating of Fig Springs as provided by Goggin's majolica collection clearly indicates occupation of the mission in the first half of the seventeenth century (Goggin 1968:74, Deagan 1987:5). Majolica types present with terminal production dates of 1650 include Mexico City White, Sevilla White, Sevilla Blue on Blue, Fig Springs Polychrome, Caparra Blue, Santo Domingo Blue on White, San Luis Blue on White, Ichtucknee Blue on White (Goggin's unique spelling of "Ichtucknee" preserved by later scholars; another Goggin spelling that appears in his notes is "Ischtucknee"), and Columbia Plain (all identifications and nomenclature follow Deagan 1987 and comparative collections at the

Florida Museum of Natural History, Gainesville). Of the many majolica types introduced after 1650, only Puebla Polychrome is known to occur at Fig Springs and is only represented by five sherds (two of which cross-mend). In fact, Fig Springs has been used as a type site for early Spanish colonial material culture in the Florida interior (Goggin 1953; Deagan 1972, 1987).

The results of the Fig Springs excavations indicate that the chronology of occupation at the site is actually quite complex. Whereas most of the occupation of the site certainly falls within the broad time period defined by the majolica dating, not all occupation of the site was contemporaneous. To refine the internal dating of site components, a study of the aboriginal pottery was begun, in the hope of identifying selected ceramic attributes that seem to have changed through time.

Two attributes appear to be measurable for chronological significance. The first is grog (crushed sherd) tempering in the pottery. Field observation noted that sherds from excavation contexts at Fig Springs

Table 2. Suggested Chronology of Aboriginal Occupation at Fig Springs

Dates	Representative unit	Association	Artifacts
1640s–1630s(?)	240N/295E	Aboriginal structure	70% ceramics are grog-tempered. Complicated stamping is 71% of decorated assemblage (n = 114). Spanish majolica, olive jar, and hardware present.
1630–1620	120N/250E	Midden	62% of ceramics are grog. Complicated stamping is 50% of decorated assemblage (n = 72). Olive jar and glass bead in vicinity.
1620–1610	Mill Pond	Structure(?), midden	4% of ceramics are grog; 35% of decorated assemblage is complicated stamped (n = 52). Olive jar is 28% of total ceramics by weight.
1610–1490	50N/295E	Structure(?), midden	No grog or complicated stamping present. Cord marked (35%), roughened (31%), and punctated (25%) dominate decorated assemblage (n = 160). No Spanish materials. Radiocarbon date of A.D. 1490.

which lack Spanish artifacts or any clear association with Spanish artifacts also lack grog-tempering. It was also noted that the percentage of grog tempering in the assemblage increases as the percentage of Spanish materials increases. Thus it was concluded that the presence/absence or percentage of grog in a given excavation context can be used to give that context a relative date in comparison to other excavation areas.

The second attribute is the presence of bull's-eye (concentric circle) complicated stamped pottery, first defined by Hale Smith (1948) from mission contexts in Leon and Jefferson counties and named by him the Jefferson Series. Excavation contexts with greater percentages of complicated stamped pottery relative to other types of decoration also have a later relative date. The utility of grog tempering and complicated stamping as measures of the timing and duration of the mission phenomenon in North Florida is further strengthened by the radiocarbon date of A.D. 1490 referred to earlier. This came from an excavation context at the south end of the Fig Springs site, which contained Suwannee series ceramics and lacked grog-tempered pottery, complicated stamped pottery, and Spanish artifacts. The first estimate of the chronology of the aboriginal occupation at Fig Springs is presented in table 2. This implies an early historic period aboriginal occupation at Fig Springs prior to the formal establishment of the mission early in the seventeenth century.

4

Field Survey and Excavations

✛   Fieldwork at Fig Springs
consisted of three phases of investigation. The first was the power-auger
survey of the 30 acres of woods adjacent to the springs, in which the size
and shape of the archaeological site and the pattern of artifact distribution
were revealed (Weisman 1988a) (fig. 11). The auger survey began on
February 1, 1988, and was completed on May 10. The first season report
was issued to the Division of Recreation and Parks in early June. Artifact
distribution and topographical maps compiled during the auger survey
have guided work at the site ever since. In fact, the basic pattern of the site
began to emerge within the first two weeks of the survey, after 208 auger
borings had been completed and 123 field specimens (hereafter FS)
analyzed.

In order to be able to maintain consistent horizontal and vertical
control of survey and excavation data, a permanent grid system was
established before any work began. A central point near the burials and
clay floor found in the previous Florida Museum of Natural History
testing, designated 300N/300E (meaning that it was 300 m north and 300
m east of an arbitrary 0 North/0 East point) was set with a concrete
monument. From this point, the grid was extended in all directions to
cover the area of the proposed survey and marked with a surveyor's hub
and nail at 50-m intervals. Concrete monuments were placed at 100-m
intervals on the 300E line and at grid points 100N/200E, 100N/400E,
100N/500E, 300N/400E, 300N/500E, 400N/500E, 500N/500E,
500N/200E, and 400N/200E. Elevations in meters above mean sea level
were calculated for the tops of iron rods set in the monuments by
surveying in from a fixed benchmark on U.S. 27 near Fort White.

The site, as understood after analyzing the auger results, consisted of
the following site areas. The first was the mission complex itself,
consisting of two and possibly three structures located at the south and

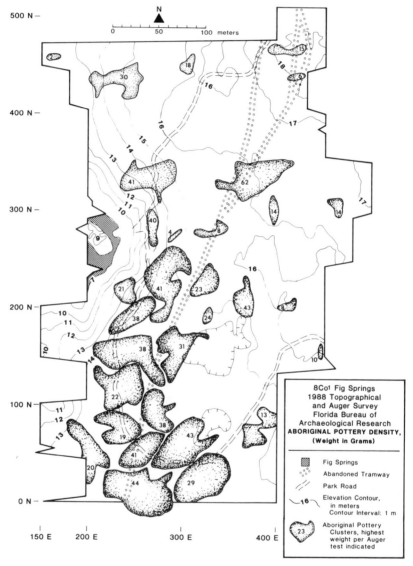

FIG. 11. *Areas of aboriginal pottery density, based on weights in grams of pottery collected in the auger survey.*

west sides of the probable mission cemetery. Estimated size of this area was about 3,500 sq m (over three-quarters of an acre). Wrought nails, Spanish majolica and olive jar sherds, and some burnt clay were recovered in the auger borings, but few sherds of aboriginal pottery were found. Consequently, this area showed as a virtual blank on the site map of aboriginal pottery distribution. In a 30-m by 50-m rectangular area south of the mission complex, almost no artifacts of any kind were found and the area was interpreted as the mission plaza.

South of the plaza, south of the 250 N grid line, aboriginal pottery and lithics were densely distributed across an area estimated to measure 280 m (N–S) by 150 m (E–W), containing about 10 acres (4 hectares) of deposits. This was interpeted as the aboriginal village associated with the mission. With the exception of a single piece of unidentified majolica (150N/240E), a green wire-wound glass bead (130N/250E), and several pieces of olive jar or coarse earthenware (200N/200E, 230N/330E), Spanish artifacts were not found in this broad area but seemed to be restricted to the mission complex itself. The broad outline suggested by analysis of the auger results generally resembled mission plans known or assumed for other sites (Jones and Shapiro 1987; Shapiro 1987b; Thomas 1987). To assist the park planners in their initial conceptual design of the proposed architectural reconstruction, a conjectural view of the Fig Springs mission was drawn up (fig. 12). Although many of the architectural details were shown to be incorrect by the subsequent excavations, the general layout of the site is thought to be accurate.

The next step was to start excavation of the buildings themselves. Funding for the second field season was provided by the Florida Division of Recreation and Parks. Work began on July 7, 1988, and finished on October 25. The second season report was filed early in December (Weisman 1988b). In planning for the excavation, it was realized that despite the tremendous value of the auger survey for discerning broad-scale patterning at the site, the results of the individual borings (augered at 10-m intervals) were not especially helpful for determining the specific placement of excavation units. Therefore, areas judged likely to contain architectural remains on the basis of the auger survey were gridded at 1-m intervals. Soil cores taken with a 20-mm stainless steel coring tool were then retrieved and carefully checked for the presence of burnt clay or clay rubble, charcoal flecking, or carbonized wood. The same area was then gone over with a metal detector, and all readings were

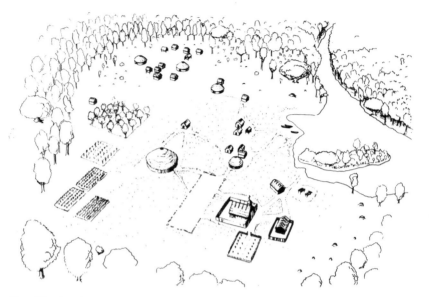

FIG. 12. *Artist's conception of the Fig Springs mission, based on the distribution of artifacts found in the auger survey. Foreground is the mission complex itself. Fig Island is to the right. View to the southwest. Drawing by Ian Breheny.*

flagged and recorded. Excavation units were then selected and staked out on the basis of these architectural indicators.

Unit size for the 1988 excavation was the 2-m square, partly because it was desirable to compare the Fig Springs results directly with those obtained at San Luis, where 2-m units had been used to sample the site (Shapiro 1987b), and partly because this was thought to be the minimum size required for properly recognizing, recording, and interpreting architectural features. All excavation units were designated and subsequently referred to in the notes by the coordinates of their southwest corner. Ken Johnson's field notes and report from the 1986–1987 testing were again consulted and checked against our auger results (Johnson 1987). It seemed likely that the prepared clay floor and the burials located by Johnson probably marked the location of the church, as he had also suspected. This was where we wanted to begin. By means of the coring tool, the clay floor was quickly relocated. Spring and early summer 1988 had been very dry seasons at Ichetucknee, and the cores also revealed that the soil in the vicinity of the church and across the terrace was extremely dry and nearly colorless. As a remedy, about 900 gallons of water were sprayed in the anticipated excavation area from a trailer-mounted water tank borrowed from the park rangers. Excavation unit 299N/314E was staked out on July 13, and by the next day the clay floor was coming into view (fig. 13).

Eleven church units were excavated in 1988 (fig. 14), and the basic floor plan (figs. 15, 16) was interpreted at that time. In addition, five units were excavated in the presumed convento location, two in the cemetery, one over a patch of possible burnt clay tentatively interpreted as the kitchen floor (fig. 17), two in a thin aboriginal midden east of the church, and five near 240N/295E, where dark soil cores were suggestive of an aboriginal dwelling (fig. 18).

Basic excavation procedures were established during the 1988 excavation. The main technique consisted of careful horizontal stripping of excavation units in natural or culturally deposited levels, or by dividing homogenous strata into arbitrary 10-cm levels. Soil from general level excavations was sifted through ¼-inch mesh tripod-mounted screens, although in some cases later in the dig modern humus was stripped and discarded without screening. Artifacts encountered in place and thought to be in their original context of deposition were mapped and given a map specimen (MS) number in addition to the field specimen (FS) number

FIG. 13. *Uncovering the previously excavated portion of clay floor of the church.*

FIG. 14. *Mapping the sill plate and door threshold. View to the north.*

assigned to each excavation lot. A total of 499 map specimens have been recorded in the Fig Springs excavations. Areas of regularly shaped dark or charcoal-stained soil or areas of obviously displaced soil or backfill were identified as *features*. Archaeological features are thought to represent discrete areas of past human activity, such as storage pits, hearths, or burial pits. For the most part, features, unlike artifacts, cannot be removed intact and must be studied and recorded fully in the field during excavation.

Before excavation, features were assigned numbers and then drawn in plan view. Excavation then began by removing one-quarter or one-half of the feature (depending on its size and type) so that a cross section of the fill could be drawn. The second half of the fill (or the remaining quadrants) was then excavated according to the strata recognized in the feature profile. Feature fill was either water-screened in the field through $^{1}/_{16}$-inch mesh screen or was bagged for flotation processing by the Zooarchaeology Lab at the Florida Museum of Natural History. The dimensions of the excavated feature were checked against the plan view and were redrawn, if necessary, in red pencil on the original map. A total of 112 features were recorded and excavated in the combined field seasons. Postholes and post molds, while technically archaeological features, were assigned separate numbers when it was possible to identify their function prior to excavation. In the 1988 season, nine post molds and five postholes were recorded, although some identifications changed after excavation. In the 1989 season, no attempt was made to designate postholes or molds prior to their excavation, and they were recorded along with the rest of the features.

Burial pit fill was excavated and screened separately from the general excavation matrix. Fill directly around the skeletons was water-screened through $1/16$-inch mesh screen. Measured drawings and photographs were made of all burials, and much of the Burial 8 excavation was recorded on videotape. All burials were backfilled in place, after first being covered with black plastic. Burial 8 was also protected before backfilling by a wooden box, wrapped in plastic.

All separate excavation episodes—that is, the excavations of natural or arbitrary levels in an excavation unit or feature—were recorded on a

FIG. 15. *Sill plate, door threshold, and vertical wall boards excavated in the 1988 season.*

FIG. 16. *The completed 1988 excavations in the church area. Sill plate at right. View to the north.*

FIG. 17. *Exposing the "clay floor" of the presumed kitchen, 1988 season.*

FIG. 18. *Dark soil cores in the area of the aboriginal structure, indicating the presence of features.*

standard form (fig. 19). Other field records include the daily journals kept by myself and the other excavators, plan view and profile maps of all excavation units (total of 232 maps), separate field specimen, map specimen, and soil sample logs containing cross-referenced provenience information, Polaroid prints of excavations in progress filed with the field notes, color slides and black-and-white prints of the excavation (some 700 of each), and approximately eight hours of videotape footage produced by University of Florida anthropology student Gardner Gordon during the 1989 season.

Test excavations during the 1988 season enabled us to evaluate the architectural integrity of the archaeological remains. Without question, the site existed in a remarkable state of preservation, given that the buildings were buried only slightly below the surface and apparently constructed mostly of wood and other perishable materials. But crucial architectural details were missing, or, in the case of the aboriginal structure, the basic configuration of the building had not been determined in the limited excavation. My field journal for September 27 includes this comment: "Somewhat perplexing—where are the postholes

EXCAVATION RECORD

FIELD SPECIMEN (FS) _1100_

Site __8-Co-1__   Grid Coordinates ___238___ (North)
                                      ___297___ (East)

Zone _____, Level _____, or Feature _43_, Level _North_

Provenience Type _03_ Sample Type _01_ Screen Size _16_

Recorder _JW_   Excavator _JW_   Excavated with Tr _✓_ Sh ____
                                 Other _space, core tuth, Consl_

DATUM ELEVATION ___16.95___ (MMSL)

Opening El.   Closing El.
  SE _2.315_ (BD) _14.635_ (MMSL)   _2.595_ (BD) _14.355_ (MMSL)

NE _____ _____   _____ _____

NW _____ _____   _____ _____

SW _____ _____   _____ _____

C _____ _____   _____ _____

STRATUM DESCRIPTION   Location Sketch

Short Title _light brown sand fill_

Stratigraphic Def. _a 28 cm deep_
aboriginal pit fill consisting of light brown
sand with frequent charcoal flecking, unburned
bone frags, shords, and shell. Tan sand
border's base
Feature Part of _____

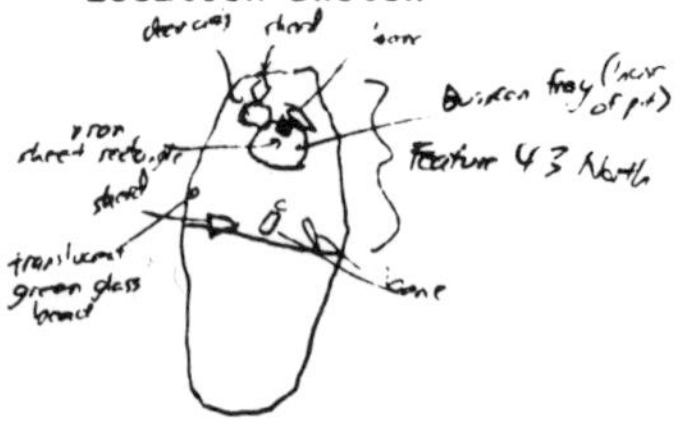

Artifacts (list F.S.) _#1100 ~ •Busycon extenar frag, also shords, loom, charcoal,_
green glass bead, iron rectangle Other Samples _____

Photographs _color / B-W_ Other Records _p.96, #144_

Interpretation _pit fill (poss. storage pit)_

FIG. 19. *The standard form filled out for each excavation provenience.*

associated with the [aboriginal] structure?" Clearly, this was more than just a detail. More excavation was necessary, and funding for a third season was kindly provided by Jerald T. Milanich with Division of Recreation and Parks money previously earmarked to study the early contact period in Florida.

On the first day of excavation for the third field season, January 9, 1989, three areas of the site were targeted for expanded excavation: the area of the presumed church, the general location of the convento, and the aboriginal structure discovered in 1988. The expanded units (or blocks) were of variable size, the purpose being not to compare artifact frequencies or percentages between units but to expose entire architectural elements and readily determine the relationships between elements. Students from the University of Florida participated in the 1989 excavations and, under my direction, earned archaeological field school credits. Members of a Smithsonian Research Expedition also assisted in the excavations between February 20 and March 2. Ann Kirking Post of the Smithsonian and Jerald T. Milanich of the Florida Museum of Natural History helped coordinate these activities. During this third season, additional testing was accomplished in the aboriginal village, in which more refuse areas and an additional structure were identified, and the Mill Pond and Midpoint Mound sites were partially excavated. The third season of investigation was completed on October 2, 1989, by which time all excavation areas of the Fig Springs site (fig. 20) had been lined with black plastic and backfilled.

FIG. 20. *The site after backfilling.*

In the remainder of this report the results and conclusions presented will be based on the 1989 excavations, which in most cases subsumed or expanded our knowledge of the site as gained from the 1986–1988 seasons. The reader is urged to consult the earlier reports of these investigations to see how the understanding of Fig Springs archaeology has evolved as fieldwork has progressed.

Stratigraphy

A considerable amount of time was spent trying to comprehend the stratification of the Fig Springs site. Although much of the stratification now appears to be simple and relatively straightforward, it did not always seem so during excavation. Described below is a "typical" section such as might be obtained in the aboriginal village outside the structural areas. Then, the modifications of this basic sequence, as they exist in the areas of the buildings proper, will be described.

Stratum 1—Modern Humus

A band of modern humus covers the site, variable in thickness from about 4 cm to 20 cm. In the convento and cemetery areas, the modern humus is from 6 cm to 20 cm thick. Humus over the church is about 4 cm (over some areas of prepared clay floor) to 10 cm thick. Humus covering the aboriginal structure area is generally about 10 cm thick and in the village area about 15 cm to 20 cm thick. This stratum consists of a dense band of root mat at the surface and an underlying gray, organic sand. The modern humus was excavated as Zone 1, and divided into Zone 1, Level 1 (the root mat), and Zone 1, Level 2 (gray sand) if the stratum was particularly thick or well developed.

Stratum 2—Original Humus and Mixed Cultural Deposits

Stratum 2 is the ground surface that existed before the site was occupied and subsequently was added to as a consequence of human occupation. It is directly below the modern humus and consists of brown sand mottled with tan sand of uniform 24 cm thickness across the site. This stratum had been scraped away for the construction of the church, convento, and aboriginal structure but is present as a mixed humus and midden deposit in other areas of the site. Burials in the cemetery were dug through the original humus stratum, and these intrusions in the cemetery profiles are evident.

Stratum 3—Old Root Zone or Subhumus

Stratum 3—tan, brown, and white mottled sand—is below the original humus and is derived from it. It contains root molds and root stains from trees and other vegetation that grew on the site during or before the period of occupation. The root stains are clearly evident in plan view and profile and are the best marker of this stratum. Unlike the original humus, the old root zone had not been stripped from the building areas prior to construction and is present in all areas of the site. Thickness is 15–20 cm. Intrusions through the old root zone are evident in the burial units and in pit features associated with the aboriginal structure.

Stratum 4—White Sand (Sterile)

Below the old root zone is white sand that contains no artifacts except those due to animal or root disturbances. In some areas the sterile sand is tan rather than white. In the eastern portion of the site, the sterile sand is quite thick (several meters at least, to judge from the sides of some recently active sinkholes). Along the edge of the terrace, where the convento, church, and aboriginal structures are located, this deposit is underlain by red to orange sticky clay. Beneath the church, the sterile sand is about 40 cm thick down to clay. In the area of the aboriginal structure, particularly just to the north and east of the building itself, the sterile sand is barely discernible as a stratum, with clay being encountered within about 24 cm of the present ground surface.

Stratum 5—Clay Subsoil

As mentioned, along the edge of the terrace above Fig Springs, a natural deposit of red to orange (and occasionally tan) clay can be found close to the surface. During the auger survey we thought that this shallow clay was just below the modern humus, not yet able to recognize the compressed stratigraphic relationship that really exists (see above). This belief led to the speculation, now thought to be false, that the clay represented a prepared surface for the mission plaza. It does not appear to be the same type of clay used for the prepared floor of the church, the latter probably having been obtained from the red sandy clays (or clayey sands) that can be found along the banks of the springs. The parent material for the clay is the limestone bedrock, as evidenced by the chunks of decomposing limestone often found in the clay stratum.

This is the generalized stratigraphic sequence of Fig Springs. However, building construction has altered this sequence in some interesting ways and has resulted in the existence of cultural strata (described below) derived from human activities that have replaced (and thus are stratigraphically equivalent to) natural soil deposits.

Stratum 6—Sand Cap

Stratum 6 is a 10–12 cm stratum of yellow sand found below modern humus in the area of the church only and appears to have been applied as a cap or mantle blanketing the church remains. Few artifacts were found in the stratum, but many were found just below it (and recorded as the map specimens described earlier) lying on the presumed floor of the structure. The cap is most noticeable in the central and eastern portions of the building and perhaps was not placed as thickly or has eroded from the west (downhill) half. Because the cap stratum exists only in the church area and seems to suggest some intentional concealment of the burnt structural remains, it has been a great curiosity. Archaeologists visiting the excavations have examined the church profiles with interest and have come to share the interpretation that the stratum postdates the building and does not itself appear to have been used for architectural purposes. The source of the yellow sand has not been located.

Stratum 7—Construction Fill

Like the sand cap, stratum 7 has been definitely identified only in the church. The construction fill is a 10–15 cm stratum of tan, brown, and orange mottled sand that replaced the original humus as a substrate for the building. It is underlain by the old root zone. Artifacts are found on top of the construction fill, especially in the northeast, east, and south-central areas of the church where the fill also served as the floor. Few artifacts are found mixed within the fill. The fill had the effect of creating a flat, regular surface for building construction, but in fact it was graded to slope slightly downhill to the west. The total difference in floor elevation from east to west is about 13 cm, but the breaks in elevation occur in a series of steps. A stepped church floor leading to the altar has also been noted in a late-sixteenth-century Catholic church at the Maya town of Tipu (Jones, Kautz, and Graham 1986). The prepared clay floor can be considered part of this stratum. It is clear that from the beginning the builders intended that parts of the floor be covered with clay and parts with sand and took care, by the placement of partition walls, to keep them separate. Although the clay floor was placed on construction fill, it is not stratigraphically above the sand floor in all areas of the building and is best thought of as a specialized type of flooring. Roof support posts for the building intrude the construction fill stratum but do not penetrate the old root zone.

Stratum 8—Occupation Stratum, Aboriginal Structure

Stratum 8 is the cultural stratum that has replaced the original humus as an occupation surface inside the aboriginal structure, as the inhabitants seem to have scraped away the old surface within the living area itself. It appears that this stratum resulted from cutting old root zone from the eastern portion of the structure and grading it out as fill for the western half. The stratum is heavily mottled with brown to tan to gray sand and contains charcoal flecking. It averages about 15 cm in thickness but is somewhat thicker when associated with feature intrusions. Artifacts are abundant and are concentrated in the upper 10 cm of the fill. The stratum is underlain by old root zone, with the break sometimes marked by patches of brown clayey sand presumably of natural origin. The occupation stratum accumulated through time but appears to have been lower than the outside grade, suggesting that the floor was slightly sunken.

5

Architecture and Site Plan

✝ AS THE PHYSICAL RECONSTRUCTION
of the Fig Springs mission complex was the ultimate objective of the
Division of Recreation and Parks, the emphasis in excavation was in
identifying individual buildings and determining their relationship to
one another. Methods of construction and architectural techniques and
styles, as they could be revealed through archaeology, were also of great
interest because of the desire for authenticity and historical accuracy in
the reconstruction. Described and discussed in this chapter are each of
the major excavation areas and their suggested placement in the overall
site plan. Figure 21 is a plan view of the excavation area of the main
mission complex.

The Church

The identification of this structure as the mission church is based on
several factors: the lack of internal features suggestive of domestic
use—artifacts, artifact scatter, food refuse debris, hearth and storage pits,
etc.; the special preparation of the building surface by the placement of
construction fill, resulting in the structure being elevated above the
surrounding grade; the shared alignment of building walls and floor plan
with associated Christian Indian burials interred along the north wall of
the building; and the general architectural similarity to other excavated
mission structures that have been interpreted as churches.

A total of 110 sq m was excavated in and adjacent to the church.
Procedures consisted of stripping and screening modern humus down to
the clay and sand floors of the structure. At floor level, 154 in-situ
artifacts were recorded as map specimens and were mapped in place.
Excavations were carried below the floor in three places, revealing the

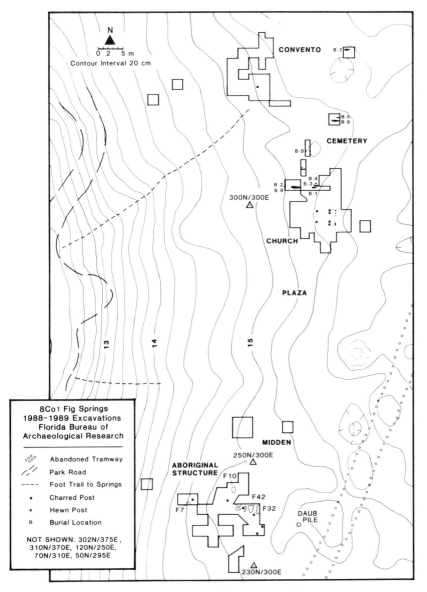

N

0 2 5 m

Contour Interval 20 cm

CONVENTO

B-7

B-5
B-6

CEMETERY

B-9

300N/300E

B-2 B-4
B-8 B-3
B-1

CHURCH

PLAZA

13   14   15

8Co1 Fig Springs
1988–1989 Excavations
Florida Bureau of
Archaeological Research

○°○ Abandoned Tramway

Park Road

---- Foot Trail to Springs

• Charred Post

▪ Hewn Post

B· Burial Location

NOT SHOWN: 302N/375E,
310N/370E, 120N/250E,
70N/310E, 50N/295E

MIDDEN

250N/300E

ABORIGINAL
STRUCTURE

F10

F42

F7   F32

DAUB
PILE

230N/300E

FIG. 21. *Site plan of the mission complex.*

basic construction sequence. Deep excavation in the southern area of the church (unit 303N/313E) had stratigraphy, from top to bottom, of modern humus, capping stratum, construction fill, old root zone, sterile white sand, and orange clay reached at a depth of 110 cm below present ground surface. The north profile of 301N/310E, on the west side of the church, contained the original humus stratum in the west half. In the east half, where the floor begins, this stratum is replaced by construction fill. Finally, excavations were taken deeper in the center of the structure, through an area of sand floor or subfloor (fig. 22). Profiles here also indicated that the construction fill was placed directly on the old root zone. Balks were left between units for profiling and then removed (fig. 23).

Estimated dimensions of the structure are approximately 10.5 m (N–S) by 8.5 m (E–W), based on measurements of verified floor area. Orientation of the presumed long axis is about 3° east of north.

Prior to construction, the original ground surface was stripped and

FIG. 22. *Profile showing the dark sand cap stratum and, below, sand fill on top of the old root zone in the church.*

FIG. 23. *Excavations on the church floor and drawing profiles.*

graded, then a 10–12 cm lift of sand fill was applied. This fill was not brought to a uniform level but was sloped down slightly to the west. The prepared clay floor was placed on the construction fill in the western portion of the building. The clay floor was repaired at least once during the use of the building. The floor was built in a series of steps, gaining in elevation from west to east. The overall difference in elevation between highest area of floor and the ground surface existing at that time is between 10 and 15 cm. Roof support posts, of hewn pine, were placed on clay support pads near the edge of the floor or were embedded in construction fill at the corners of an interior room. A hewn-pine sill plate, or grade beam, approximately 20 cm wide and 3 m long, was placed at the eastern end of this room. A hewn-pine step or door threshold was found at the southern end of the sill plate. Pine boards used as wall or room partitions were dug slightly into the ground. Construction materials consisted of packed sand and clay for flooring, clay used for chinking between boards on the east wall of the building, and hewn-pine posts, boards, and beams. There was no evidence for wattle-and-daub architecture.

The floor plan, as understood through archaeology, includes three rooms or activity areas (fig. 24). The first of these is an L-shaped room (long axis N–S, foot of the L pointing east) with a prepared clay floor. The total floor area is about 36 sq m. The clay pads for the roof columns are in this room and are set in about 1.7 m from the outside edge of the floor. No evidence for board walls or collapsed wattle-and-daub walls exists, and the room appears to have been open to the outside. At the west edge of the floor, there is a change in grade of several centimeters to raise the floor above the level of outside ground surface. At the line of clay support pads, there is another step of about 5 cm in elevation. Continuing east, there is another gradual step of about 3 cm, where the clay floor and the sand floor meet. Finally, the sand floor in the east part of the building was raised up to 5 cm above portions of the clay floor.

The second room is interior to the structure and has dimensions of 2.5 m (N–S) by 4 m (E–W). The west side and portions of the north and south sides of this room are bordered by the clay-floor room. At the east end is the hewn sill plate and door threshold (fig. 25). There are four wooden 10-cm-by-10-cm corner posts associated with this room. The function of the posts appears to have been roof support and anchoring of board partition walls (fig. 26) that separated the clay and sand floors. Actually, two of the corners contain double posts (Features 3 and 22) (fig. 27). The floor itself was of unconsolidated sand, which is probably best interpreted as subfloor beneath a raised wooden platform that extended from the sill plate to the west edge of the interior room (fig. 28). The raised wooden floor may have had two levels, with a step occurring at the double posts (thus explaining their existence, as additional support) back to the sill plate.

A third room or activity area is the sand floor east of the prepared clay floor, east of the sill plate, and south of the interior room (fig. 29). This is the area where the construction fill serves as a floor surface. Full-height partition boards evidently separated this room from the clay floor and interior platform on the east side. It is the only place where burnt-clay chinking was recovered in association with wall-board remains and wall lines. Full-height partitions may have been present at the south end of the sill plate across to the double post at Feature 3 but not extending the entire way to the corner at Feature 26. The sand-floor room probably was open to the outside.

Associated artifacts include fragments of olive jar, pale green bottle glass, and intact wrought-iron nails 2.5 cm to 10 cm in length found along

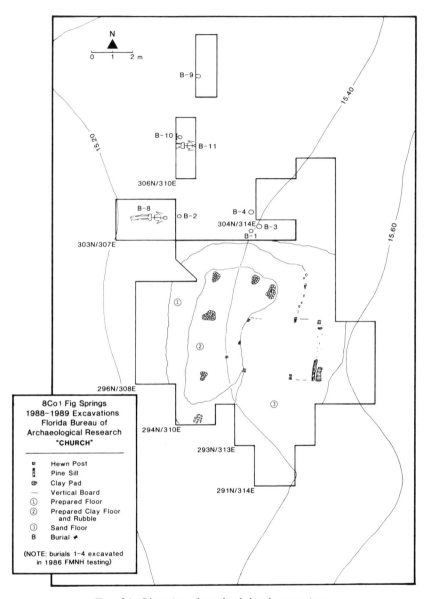

FIG. 24. *Plan view of completed church excavations.*

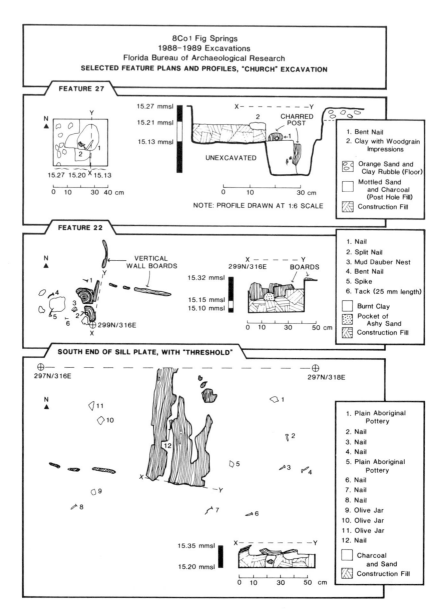

FIG. 25. *Selected architectural details of the church.*

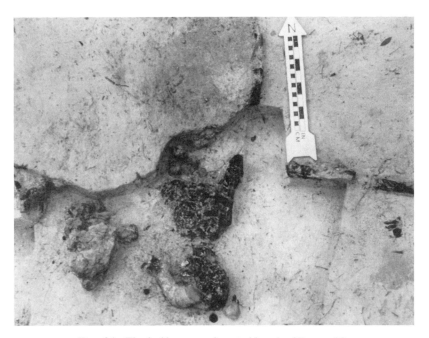

FIG. 26. *The double posts and vertical boards of Feature 22.*

the sill plate. Sherds of Mexico City White majolica were found on the prepared clay floor, and a sherd of San Luis Blue on White majolica was found in the construction fill south of the interior room. Brass or iron wire-wound straight pins were found associated with the interior room corner posts or on the sand floor south of this room (15 of 19 pins were found in the church). A lead curl "net weight" (South et al. 1988:180) was found (fig. 30), as was a single cobalt glass seed bead. A flattened lead shot was found next to charred post remains (Feature 27) on the west side of the interior room. Aboriginal artifacts include Jefferson Complicated Stamped ceramics and two new varieties (to be discussed), Jefferson Check Stamped, *var. Fort White,* and Lamar Check Stamped, *var. Fort White,* both with extremely broad checks, found primarily in the church. Plain aboriginal pottery and several sherds of St. Johns pottery have also been found. Other aboriginal artifacts are a limestone pipe bowl, recovered from the original humus just outside the northwest corner of the structure, and a piece of *Busycon* (conch) shell columella in the subfloor fill of the interior room.

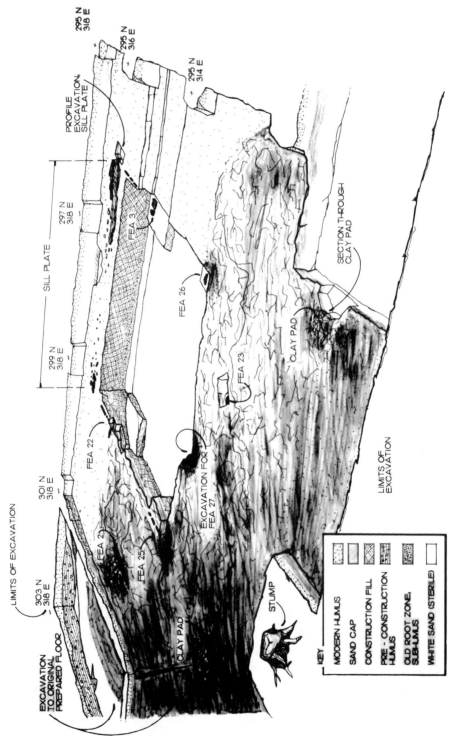

FIG. 27. *Block diagram of the church excavation. View to the northeast. Drawing by Todd Kurtzer.*

LIMITS OF EXCAVATION

303 N
318 E

EXCAVATION
TO ORIGINAL
PREPARED FLOOR

301 N
318 E

FEA 2

FEA 25

CLAY PAD

STUMP

FEA 22

EXCAVATION FOR
FEA 27

299 N
318 E

SILL PLATE

297 N
318 E

FEA 3

FEA 26

FEA 23

CLAY PAD

PROFILE
EXCAVATION,
SILL PLATE

295 N
318 E

295 N
316 E

295 N
314 E

SECTION THROUGH
CLAY PAD

CLAY PAD

LIMITS OF
EXCAVATION

KEY

MODERN HUMUS
SAND CAP
CONSTRUCTION FILL
PRE - CONSTRUCTION
HUMUS
OLD ROOT ZONE,
SUB-HUMUS
WHITE SAND (STERILE)

FIG. 28. *The interior room of the church, showing the sand fill below the presumed raised floor.* Lower left *is the sill plate.* Center left *and* center right *are the double posts of Features 3 and 22, respectively. View is to the west.*

Figure 31 is a conjectural reconstruction of the church structure provided by Keith Reeves of Architects Design Group, Inc., the architectural firm retained by the Division of Recreation and Parks to develop plans for the architectural reconstruction of the Fig Springs mission. The view is from the southwest. Shown is the stepped appearance of the clay and earthen pad on which the building sits, the hewn roof support posts, full-height board walls on a portion of the south wall of the interior room, and part of the board skirt around the interior raised platform. Roofing materials and style of construction are entirely conjectural. The fenced area indicates the mission cemetery, actually somewhat larger than depicted. In this interpretation, the main function of the chapel-like church was to provide shelter for the altar, sacristy, and pulpit. The congregation may have assembled for Mass outside the structure itself, on the lower ground to the west and southwest toward the springs. For how many years this open-air structure served the needs of the Fig Springs congregation has not been determined, although it was rebuilt at least once in the same location before its final abandonment. In

FIG. 29. *Completed church excavations, view to the east. See also fig. 27 for similar view.*

sixteenth-century Mexico, friars often built open chapels similar to the conjectural Fig Springs church to be used before the construction of the formal church could be accomplished (Kubler 1948:314).

The Convento

Over 30 percent of all wrought-iron hardware recovered in the total Fig Springs excavations came from the area of the convento excavation. S-bend type nails, thought to mark wooden architecture (Weisman 1988b), were found along a presumed wall line. A single charred hewn post (grid coordinates 301.5N/301.4E) was also uncovered and, together with the hardware, suggests that the building was of wooden frame. Artifacts of Spanish origin were found throughout the excavation area, including an iron chest lock (fig. 32) similar to one found at sixteenth-century Santa Elena (South et al. 1988:72) three straight pins (15 pins were found in church and one in the aboriginal area), glass beads (four total), and glass fragments. Majolica and olive jar sherds were also

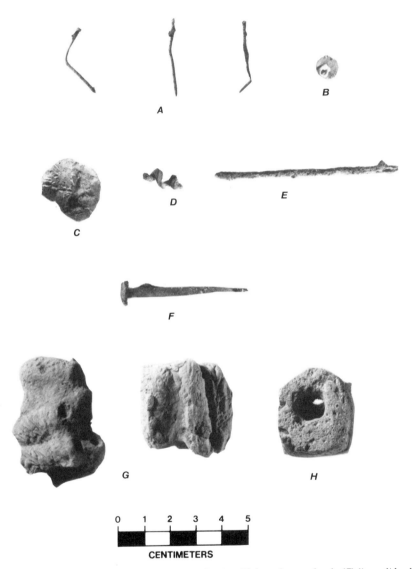

FIG. 30. *Selected church artifacts. (A) straight pins, (B) brass button shank, (C) "spent" lead shot found with Feature 27, (D) lead curl "net weight," (E) iron sewing needle, (F) burnt straight nail, (G) mud dauber nest, (H) stem portion of aboriginal limestone smoking pipe.*

FIG. 31. *Working drawing of conjectural reconstruction of the church based on 1989 excavations. View to the northeast, similar to fig. 27. Note stepped floor leading to the interior of structure and the placement of the interior room. Fenced area indicates general location of cemetery, although it is larger than shown. Drawing by I. S. K. Reeves V, AIA, of Architects Design Group, Inc.*

obtained, as were sherds of the aboriginal Suwannee and Jefferson ceramic series. With respect to the overall site plan, this structure is clearly associated with the mission church and cemetery. Approximately 52 sq m have been excavated in the presumed area of the convento (fig. 33). Soils appear to be heavily disturbed as the result of erosion and redeposition. Modern humus is up to 20 cm thick and contains many intrusions from recent roots and tree falls. Below the humus is a stratum of brown-to-red compact sand with red (raw) clay inclusions and containing artifacts. As this is the stratigraphic position naturally occupied by the original humus, this stratum is probably cultural in origin although it cannot be said definitely that it represents a floor. Maximum thickness is about 25 cm. Adjacent to the brown-to-red sand stratum in the west half of the excavation area is a deposit of tan-to-gray sand, which may be cultural in origin, may be the result of redeposited cultural materials coming from upslope areas in the direction of the cemetery, or else may be leached original humus. Artifacts are also found in this stratum. Below the cultural layer is a stratum of gray-and-tan sand with lenses of red clay

A

B   C

0   1   2   3   4   5
CENTIMETERS

FIG. 32. *Selected convento artifacts. (A) Iron trunk lock, (B, C) ornamental glass handles.*

FIG. 33. *View of the excavation area from the convento looking south. Left background is the church excavation. Convento "trail" to the springs is visible as a depression just to the left of the stump in right center.*

and large inclusions of decomposing limestone. In some cases this stratum is within 25 cm of the present ground surface and appears to have been penetrated by the overlying cultural stratum. The top elevation of the cultural stratum (about 15.12 mmsl) is the same as outside the church, although the top of the burned convento post (14.84 mmsl) is over 40 cm lower than tops of the church posts. The emphasis of the convento excavation was on the block excavation of areas around the charred post, mapping artifacts in place in the cultural stratum, and obtaining profiles of the stratigraphic sequence.

Estimated dimensions of the convento are 7 m (E–W) × 12 m (N–S) as a maximum or 5 m (E–W) × 9 m (N–S) as a minimum. The orientation of structure cannot be determined with accuracy, but the single excavated post is aligned with magnetic north.

This structure was almost certainly of wood-frame construction. As in the church, mud dauber nest fragments were recovered. Wattle-and-daub architecture is not in evidence, nor is there certain evidence of a prepared clay floor. There is some indication that original humus was stripped prior to construction, but the placement of a special construction fill is questionable. The occupation surface (or surfaces) seems to have been 25–40 cm below floor levels in the church. The single feature from this excavation is a charred hewn rectangular post (Feature 34) with measurements of 20 cm (E–W) by 10 cm (N–S).

Spanish artifacts associated with the convento excavation include one Mexico City White majolica sherd, three Ichtucknee Blue on White sherds, and a single Cappara Bluc sherd. Glazed and unglazed olive jar, cobalt and aqua seed beads (one each), a drawn Ichtucknee bead and a blue faceted (pre-eighteenth-century) bead, a pale green blown-glass handle (see Deagan 1987:140b, for a similar specimen), an iron chest lock, and a lead shot also are of Spanish origin. Three straight pins, two brass and one iron, were also found, as was an unidentified sheet-brass fragment. A total of 93 identifiable specimens of wrought-iron hardware were collected, most of which were nails, spikes, and tacks. Aboriginal artifacts include Jefferson Complicated Stamped and Jefferson Incised pottery (two sherds of the latter), Alachua Cob Marked and roughened Suwannee sherds, and sherds of the St. Johns series. Plain ceramics account for about 51 percent of the assemblage, and complicated stamped about 10 percent, by count. Ichetucknee and Pinellas projectile points were also noted.

A shotgun shell and several large sherds of a probable eighteenth-century green-glass bottle were found in humus, and two Archaic points were found in general level excavations. A total of 111 Map Specimens were recorded for the combined convento excavations.

The Cemetery

Adjacent to the north wall of the church and aligned with it is the mission cemetery, containing the remains of Christian Indians buried Christian-style in individual grave pits placed in rows.

A total of 11 burials has been discovered in an excavation area of approximately 26 sq m. Burials 1–4 were recorded in the December 1986 Florida Museum of Natural History survey, in an area now known to be adjacent to the north floor line of the church (Johnson 1987, 1990). Fragmentary human skeletal remains were encountered in the 1988 auger survey, at grid coordinates 330N/320E and 340N/330E. Two meter test units 316N/316E, near the center of the cemetery, and 329N/319E, in the northern area, were excavated in 1988 to provide additional information about the size of the cemetery and condition of the interments. Burials 5, 6 (316N/316E), and 7 (329N/319E) were recorded as the result of these excavations. In 1989, further information was required about the exact relationship between the burials and the church structure, since the question of subfloor burials had not been answered in 1988. It was also necessary to improve definition of the western limits of the cemetery, and in so doing obtain a continuous profile from the church area to the convento. Beginning outside the north wall of the church and working north, units 303N/307E (2 m × 3 m), 306N/310E (1 m × 4 m), and 310N/311E (1 m × 4 m) were excavated, and Burials 8 (303N/307E, fig. 34), 9 (310N/311E), 10, and 11(306N/310E, fig. 35) were recorded. Specific information on Burials 1–11 is presented in Appendix B.

Burials intruded the original humus stratum, which in most cases was replaced over the backfilled burial pit (fig. 36). Interments occurred in individual graves, between 45 and 80 cm below the present ground

FIG. 34. *Burial 8 excavation. Black plastic in right rear covers church excavation. View is to the east.*

FIG. 35. *Burials 10 and 11. Note the intrusion of Burial 10* (left) *on Burial 11 and clear outline of burial pit.*

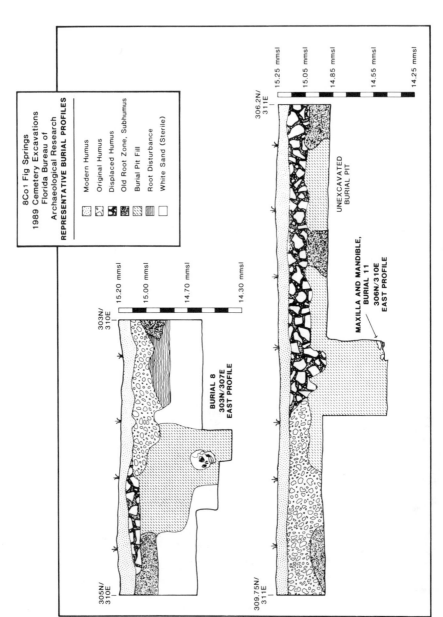

8Co1 Fig Springs
1989 Cemetery Excavations
Florida Bureau of
Archaeological Research
REPRESENTATIVE BURIAL PROFILES

Modern Humus
Original Humus
Displaced Humus
Old Root Zone, Subhumus
Burial Pit Fill
Root Disturbance
White Sand (Sterile)

BURIAL 8
303N/307E
EAST PROFILE

UNEXCAVATED
BURIAL PIT

MAXILLA AND MANDIBLE,
BURIAL 11
306N/310E
EAST PROFILE

FIG. 36. *Representative burial profiles.*

surface (about 30–65 cm below the seventeenth-century surface). Burial pits are well defined and contain tan-to-white sand fill mottled with displaced orange-to-red clay subsoil. Additional burial pits were mapped in plan and profile in 329N/319E, 306N/310E, and 310N/311E but were not excavated.

The cemetery is generally rectangular in shape, with estimated dimensions of 8.5 m (E–W) × 36 m (N–S), or 306 sq m. Using an estimated density of one burial per square meter, 300 interments in the cemetery is a conservative figure of the burial population. However, intrusive burials are present (Burial 8 intrudes on Burial 2, Burial 10 intrudes on Burial 11) (fig. 37), making a figure of 400 burials not unreasonable.

At least seven orderly rows of burials are evident, with intrusive burials occurring in or between these rows. The relationship between Burials 5 and 6 may represent the "ideal" arrangement. Here, the interments are about 1 meter apart, with the feet of one (Burial 5) in line with the head of the second (Burial 6). Thus, Burial 5 represents one row of interments,

FIG. 37. *Burial 8 intrusive on Burial 2, with legs of Burial 2 visible below Burial 8 pelvis and femurs.*

Burial 6 another. Burials are oriented approximately 3° north of east, parallel to wall and floor lines of the church. Heads are to the east, feet to the west. All burials are supine, generally with arms folded over the chest. Hands are clasped in front of the face in Burials 6 and 8. Burials 6, 7, 8, and 11 seem to have had their heads placed or propped against the wall of the burial pit, "as if the pit was too small" as I wrote in the field notes.

A single blue seed bead was recovered from soil screened from the neck region of Burial 7 and appears to be the only artifact directly associated with a burial found in the cemetery excavations. Eleven identifiable wrought nails and spikes were recovered from general excavations in the burial units, including a 26-cm spike found above Burial 6 (316N/316E). An iron cotter-pin hinge and a spherical gilded bead (FS 1028) were found in the matrix above Burial 8. Occasional aboriginal pottery sherds are found, most belonging to the original humus stratum. A root disturbance in 303N/307E has brought St. Johns Check Stamped and complicated stamped aboriginal pottery and a sherd of Sevilla White majolica in near association with Burial 8, but these artifacts are clearly not part of burial pit fill. With the exception of the bead found with Burial 7, artifacts are not found with the burials and do not appear to have been intentionally placed in the fill.

The graves were presumably marked by wooden crosses, slabs, or stakes, but this has not been verified archaeologically. Whether or not the iron hardware recovered indicates the existence of an arbor covering the cemetery or the presence of an earlier or later structure such as another church or convento are questions for further research. Deep excavations below the floor on the north side of the church (298N/308E, 301N/310E) indicate that burials were not placed below or intruded through the floor of that structure. The presence of the original humus stratum across the excavated area of the cemetery also suggests that no earlier building had been located here (over the burials), assuming the humus would have been removed prior to construction as in the church and other buildings. The cemetery area is not entirely free of artifacts (despite none having been recovered in the auger survey), indicating that some early postmission activity may have occurred here or, as is likely, debris from the church and convento areas was occasionally swept out and discarded on the surface. Fencing around the cemetery, as shown in the architect's drawing, is entirely conjectural.

Aboriginal Structure

Archaeological features excavated in this area, including cob-filled smudge pits and trash-filled pits, resemble similar features from other known or assumed aboriginal structures at San Luis (Shapiro and McEwan 1990), Baptizing Springs (Loucks 1979), and Richardson (Milanich 1972) and are not features typically associated with church or convento structures. There is also no evidence for hewn-wood architecture or the use of handwrought hardware, as appears to have been commonly used in the building construction of the central mission complex. This lack plus the fact that much greater percentages of aboriginal artifacts than Spanish artifacts were found within the building limits and associated midden together suggest that this structure was constructed and used by the mission Indians. In the overall site plan, the structure is located south of the plaza area, on the north side of which is the church-cemetery-convento complex. As the results of the auger survey indicate, the building is located at the north end of the Indian village associated with the mission.

Approximately 85 sq m of area have been excavated inside the structure and an additional 32 sq m excavated in sheet midden deposits to the north and west. Three units excavated in 1988, 240N/295E, 236N/298E, and 242N/287E are now recognized as being inside the building. Unit 244N/295E, reported on in 1988 as containing the large roasting or cooking hearth (Feature 10), is now recognized as lying outside the north wall of the building rather than in a central position, as was first proposed (Weisman 1988b). Unit size varied in the 1989 excavations, again with an emphasis on determining relationships between features identified in plan view (figs. 38, 39). Continuous long profiles through the structure east-west were obtained on the 236N, 238N, and 240N lines, generally along and just inside the north wall line. Nearly continuous north-south profiles were compiled from sections on the 295E, 297E, 299E, 301E, and 302E lines, generally in the central and eastern areas. Taken together, the profiles indicate a break in the original humus stratum at the limits of the building (fig. 40). Inside the structure, the humus is replaced by a cultural stratum of compacted tan, brown, and gray mottled sand approximately 20 cm thick. The occupation surface inside the structure and the ground surface outside were active surfaces,

FIG. 38. *Excavations along the north wall line of the aboriginal structure, 1989. View to the southwest.*

FIG. 39. *Zone and feature excavation along the north wall of the aboriginal structure, 1989. The unexcavated area in right rear is the presumed plaza. View to the northeast.*

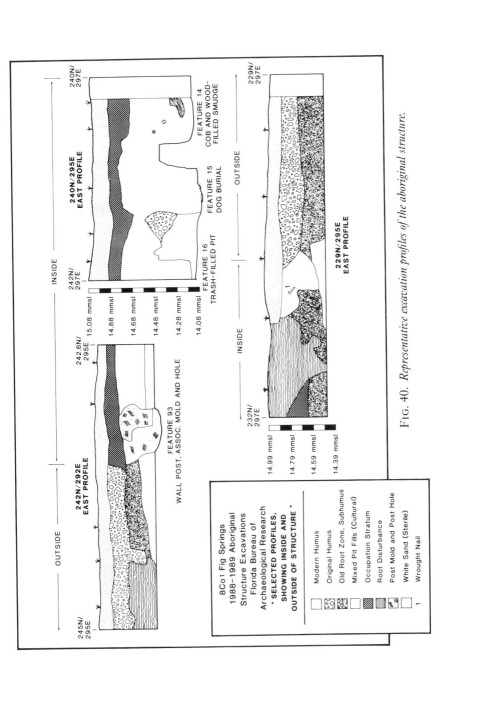

FIG. 40. *Representative excavation profiles of the aboriginal structure.*

increasing in thickness through time as the result of human activity, so it is difficult to determine if the floor of the structure was slightly sunken or recessed in relation to the outside surface, beyond the difference that would have resulted from stripping it of humus. The fact that the cultural deposits are somewhat thicker around the inside edges of the building than in the center might indicate a sunken or swept floor, but the first set of features encountered during excavation, both inside and outside the structure, have about the same opening elevations.

Differences in depth to sterile subsoil from east to west across the building site indicate that fill dirt may have been spread out across the building area prior to construction. At the northeast corner of the structure and along the eastern wall, sterile sand is encountered about 32 cm below surface (hereafter cmbs), or at an absolute elevation of 14.80 mmsl. In the center, sterile is about 45 cmbs, or an elevation of 14.60 mmsl. In the western portion of the structure, sterile is encountered approximately 32 cmbs, with an elevation of 14.58 mmsl. Clearly, modern erosion has been at work, removing cultural deposits in the western half of the building, at least the upper 5 cm or so. But there is a 22-cm drop in elevation for the top of sterile sand in the 14-m east-west dimension of the structure, suggesting that the ground itself was sloping down to the springs prior to the construction of the building. Next, it was observed that the old root-zone stratum was absent or weakly developed on the east side of the structure, but seemed to be very thick from the center to the west. In fact, the tops of features were often very hard to recognize in this area of the excavation because the associated soil matrix was extremely mottled. In looking back at the features that had been profiled in our excavation sections, it also appeared that features in the east half of the structure were dug directly through sterile (and thus were easy to recognize in plan) (fig. 41) whereas features in the center and west were dug through a mottled old root zone stratum before penetrating sterile. An explanation that accounts for all these observations is that the old root zone had been stripped from the east side of the building (the top of the slope at the time) and graded out as fill to the west to form a flat surface on which to construct the building.

Archaeological excavation was attempted according to natural and cultural levels. There was some difficulty in keeping the displaced old root zone separate from the undisturbed old root zone stratum that was below it. The cultural stratum was divided into arbitrary 10-cm levels for

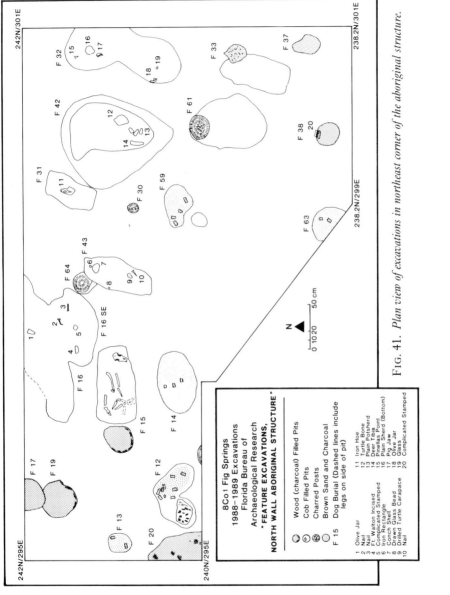

FIG. 41. *Plan view of excavations in northeast corner of the aboriginal structure.*

vertical control, but the levels do not now seem to be analytically significant. Most of the artifacts within the building were recovered in Zone 2, Levels 1 and 2, and were particularly concentrated between about 14.83 and 14.68 mmsl (20–35 cmbs). The thicker cultural stratum in the northeast corner of the building had a number of artifacts recorded at 14.96 mmsl or higher (15 cmbs), which may represent a final occupation of the structure plus extra accumulation of materials against the wall. There are occasional artifacts in the modern humus stratum in this area, which most likely date to the late eighteenth or early nineteenth centuries.

The usual excavation procedure consisted of stripping a large area until a number of features could be recognized and mapped in plan. It was noted very early in the excavations that features tended to occur together in clusters. Selected features from each cluster were chosen for the first phase of detailed excavation, so that the type of cluster and its function and placement in the overall floor plan could be identified. Eventually, however, nearly every feature was sectioned and recorded in profile. At first, all feature fill was water-screened through $1/16$-inch mesh screens until it was recognized that certain types of features (posts, postholes, smudge pits) contained little in the way of small artifacts or plant and animal remains. Screen size was then changed to $1/4$-inch, also used for general level excavation. All material from trash-filled pits was either water-screened or saved for flotation processing. The entire excavation area (fig. 42) was lined with black plastic and backfilled on September 28, 1989 (fig. 43).

Estimated dimensions of the structure are 9 m (N–S) by 14 m (E–W). The northwest corner and south wall line of the building were not fully exposed in the excavation but were confirmed through coring. The long axis of structure is oriented approximately 45° west of north.

Individual wall posts were placed about 2.7–3 m apart and approximately 30–35 cm deep (up to 60 cmbs). Posts typically are rounded, about 20 cm in diameter. As in the church and convento, fire-hardened mud dauber nests were found in the fill around charred posts. There is no hard evidence that wrought nails or spikes were used as fasteners, and no direct evidence of wattle-and-daub architecture. There is a pile of daub rubble about 8 m east of the excavated structure, but based on the results of soil cores taken between the structure and the daub pile it appears that the two belong to different episodes of occupation. The existence of thatched roof and thatched or plank walls is inferred but not archaeologically substantiated.

FIG. 42. *Completed excavation of aboriginal structure.* Top, *view to the southeast showing Features 10 and 60 in left foreground and wall post (Feature 93) at right center.* Bottom, *view to the west.*

FIG. 43. *Backfilled aboriginal structure, view to the southwest.*

The floor plan of the aboriginal structure is rectangular (fig. 44), possibly with rounded corners. Sleeping benches may have lined the inside walls, as is postulated for the San Luis council house (Shapiro 1987a) and the aboriginal structure at the early seventeenth-century Richardson site, south of Gainesville (Milanich 1972). Below the benches were cob-filled and wood-filled smudge pits. Estimated bench width is 1.7 to 2 m. There appears to have been an interior room, lacking benches and smudge pits. Dimensions of this room are up to 8 m E–W, 3.5 m N–S for the major portion, and 5.5 m in an expanded area on the west side. Numerous hearth/firepit features found in this room indicate that it may have been a central area for producing heat and light for the structure and may have served as a public area. Possible entrances are indicated near the northwest corner and on the east wall where smudge pits (and presumably benches) are absent.

Outside the north and west walls and aligned perpendicular to them are linear trash-filled pits. These pits actually may have been under the eaves of the building. Two deep, oval to linear cooking or roasting pits (Features 10, 61) are located outside the north wall and may have been covered by an extension of the roof or by a simple light framework.

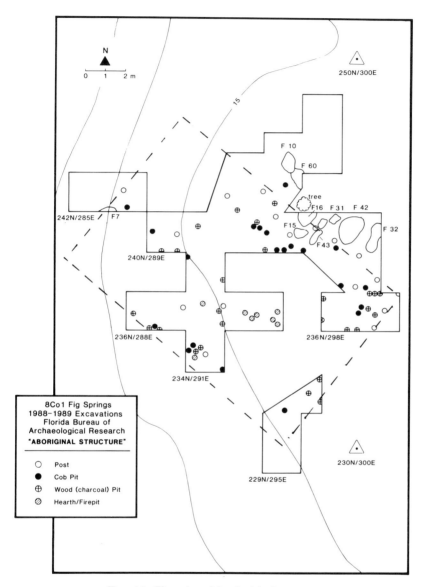

Fɪɢ. 44. *Floor plan of the aboriginal structure.*

The 78 archaeological features excavated in and around the aboriginal structure were the most interesting and significant aspect of the investigations in this area. The fact that 69 percent of total features excavated in the Fig Springs project were associated with this structure helps explain why six months were spent in its excavation. Features were classified into five broad types on the basis of form as determined in profile and the kind of fill contained within the feature (fig. 45).

The first type of feature is the bell-shaped pit, which accounted for 53.9 percent of all aboriginal features excavated. Bell-shaped pits were found to be cob-filled (24.4 percent of all aboriginal features) or wood-filled (29.5 percent of all aboriginal features). Cob-filled pits include Features 8, 9, 11, 12, 13, 14, 45, 48, 49, 50, 51, 59, 63, 67, 77, 78, 82, 106, and 111. Pit fill typically consists of brown sand with lenses of charred corncobs usually lining the bottom and sides of pit. A dozen or more cobs per feature were often found (see Appendix E). The cobs were either intact or fragmentary, but kernels were not found (fig. 46). Cob-filled pits average 30–35 cm in depth, and are first observed about 40 cmbs. Differences in top and bottom elevations indicate that not all features were in use at the same time (table 3).

Aboriginal pottery and lithics are occasionally found in the fill but not with any frequency. The inferred placement of the cob pits under or at the edges of benches around the inside wall of the structure may help explain the general lack of artifacts. Regular spacing between features of about 1 m is suggested.

Similar features in the San Luis council house (Shapiro 1987a) have been interpreted as smudge pits for insect control, and that function is inferred here. Experimental cob-filled and wood-filled bell-shaped pits dug during the excavations in the back-dirt pile produced a thick smoke and a relatively slow burning fire. A handful of fuel kept the fire burning for 1–2 hours.

Wood-filled bell-shaped pits include Features 19, 20, 47, 57, 58, 65, 68, 69, 70, 73, 76, 80, 83, 87, 92, 95, 100, 101, 102, 104, 105, 110, and 112. Here the fill is brown sand with charcoal flecking, with lenses of charcoal frequently lining the pit (fig. 47). Wood-filled pits are typically 30–40 cm deep and are first seen about 40 cmbs. A Jefferson Complicated Stamped sherd was found in the bottom of Feature 70, but as with the cob pits artifacts were generally scarce.

In the floor plan, wood-filled pits are closely associated with cob-filled

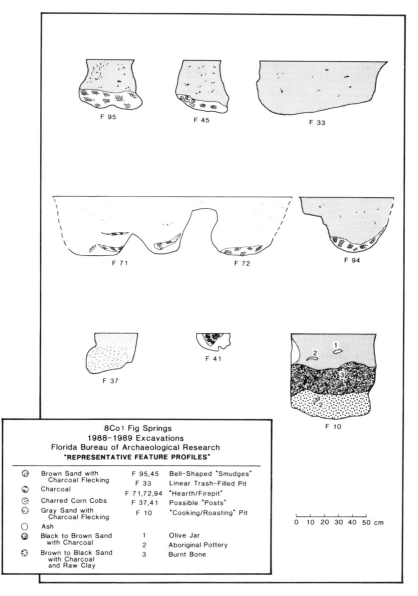

FIG. 45. *Representative feature profiles, aboriginal structure excavation.*

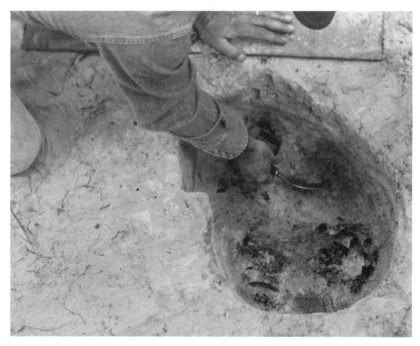

FIG. 46. *Excavating a cob pit (Feature 11). Note mass of charred cobs in bottom of feature.*

pits. Due to lack of artifacts and domestic refuse in the pit fill and the association between these features and other features interpreted as possible bench-support posts, wood-filled pits are thought to have been underneath or at the edges of sleeping benches, as at the Richardson site (Milanich 1972). The function of these pits may have been as insect smudges or as a source of heat in the fall and winter months. Most of the wood identified from these features is of the hard-pine group.

The second type of feature is the circular, straight-sided pit, which comprise 23 percent of the total aboriginal features. Features of this type include 17, 30(?), 37(?), 38(?), 41, 46, 61, 64, 66, 74(?), 79, 88, 91, 93, 97, 99, 108, and 109. Fill consists of gray-to-brown sand with charcoal and charcoal flecking. The actual remains of burnt posts are found in these features, in posthole fill of tan-to-brown mottled sand. Charred wall posts exist in Features 61, 64, and 93. These features are up to 45 cm deep and are first observed between 25 and 30 cmbs.

Few artifacts are found in these features besides an occasional sherd or lithic flake. Features 30, 37, 46, 61, 64, 66, 91, 93, 109, and 113 are

Table 3. Top and Bottom Elevations of Aboriginal Features (mmsl)

Feature no.	Top	Bottom	Feature no.	Top	Bottom
7	14.68	14.36	69	14.63	14.38
8	14.68	14.59	70	14.67	14.10
9	14.65	14.40	71	14.68	14.23
10	14.70	14.30	72	14.68	14.23
11	14.70	14.46	73	14.48	14.13
12	14.65	14.28	74	14.61	14.28
13	14.65	14.33	76	14.61	14.21
14	14.65	14.21	77	14.66	14.16
15	14.78	14.03	78	14.48	14.00
16	14.63 (?)	14.15	79	14.48	14.28
17	14.55	14.40	80	14.51	14.26
20	14.55	14.20	82	14.51	14.10
30	14.82	14.70	83	14.73	?
31	14.83	14.76	87	14.47	14.17
32	14.74	14.56	88	14.57	14.25
33	14.72	14.37	91	14.46	14.18
37	14.68	14.40	92	14.66	14.25
38	14.70	14.35	93	14.79	14.40
41	14.70	14.51	94	14.63	14.28
42	14.67	14.42	95	14.47	14.14
43	14.65	14.40	96	14.48	13.98
44	14.68	14.62	97	14.48	14.33
45	14.68	14.34	98	14.50	14.22
46	14.68	14.41	99	14.46	14.21
47	14.68	14.38	100	14.42	14.22
49	14.55	14.40	101	14.65	14.40
50	14.50	14.35	102	14.65	14.30
51	14.58	14.33	103	14.56	14.38
52	14.67	14.57	104	14.48	14.21
53	14.67	14.48	105	14.48	14.21
54	14.67	14.49	106	14.48	14.18
56	14.55	14.33	107	14.47	14.27
57	14.55	14.27	108	14.48	14.38
58	14.55	14.47	109	14.60	14.25
59	14.58	14.44	110	14.49	14.16
60	14.77	14.30	111	14.49	14.23
61	14.59	14.39	112	14.54	14.24
63	14.58	14.37			
64	14.52	14.49			
65	14.55	14.38			
66	14.55	14.40			
67	14.49	14.39			
68	14.53	14.33			

Notes: Elevations compiled from multiple sources, including plan view and profile maps and excavation records. UID and features in south aboriginal village not included.

FIG. 47. *Cross section of a wood-filled pit (Feature 97), aboriginal structure. Note bell shape.*

thought to be posts on the outside wall line. Features 17, 38, 41, 97, 99, and 108 are possible bench or inner roof supports. Features 79, 74, and 88 are inner roof-support posts.

Basin-shaped pits are the third type of feature and account for 7.7 percent of all aboriginal features excavated. Basin-shaped pits include Features 56, 71, 72, 94, 98, and 107. Fill is typically gray "ashy" sand with charcoal flecking and inclusions, mottled sand fill with charcoal flecking, or lenses of ash and charcoal. These pits average 35–45 cm in depth and are first observed at about 40 cmbs. Shell-tempered cord-marked pottery was found in Feature 94, but otherwise artifacts are not common.

All basin-shaped pits except Feature 107 appear to be part of the central space of the structure. Features 71, 72, and 94 are about in the middle of the floor. Features 98 and 56 are in the west-central and west floor area. Feature 107 is associated with the cluster of cob- and wood-filled pits on the presumed south wall of the structure. These features are assumed to have been hearths or fire pits providing heat and light and as points of gathering for social or public activities. As such, they are the functional equivalents of the central hearths in public and domestic buildings in Apalachee and the lower Southeast, of the late prehistoric–early historic period (Knight 1985, Hally 1988). However, the Fig Springs examples lack the characteristic clay lining and the clay lip or rim around the basin (a beautiful example of which is preserved as the central feature in the Earth Lodge at Ocmulgee National Monument, Macon, Georgia).

The fourth type of feature is called the linear pit. There are two categories of linear pits: charcoal-filled (accounting for 2.6 percent of all aboriginal features) and trash-filled (9 percent of total aboriginal features excavated). Charcoal-filled linear pits include Features 96 and 103. Fill is brown, gray, and tan mottled sand with charcoal flecking. Feature 96 is about 50 cm deep, Feature 103 about 20 cm deep. Feature 103 was first noted at 40 cmbs and Feature 96 at 25 cmbs.

An olive jar sherd, a sherd of complicated stamped pottery, and a sherd of shell-tempered pottery were found in the upper fill of Feature 96. A single plain aboriginal sherd and a few lithic fragments were found in Feature 103 fill. The long axis of Feature 96 (measuring about 1.1 m) parallels the south wall of the building and appears to be about 1 m inside. Feature 103 is oriented approximately 45° to the presumed north wall of the building, and is located 1.0–1.5 m inside. Both are near clusters of cob- and wood-filled smudges, but their function or functions remain unknown.

Trash-filled pits are the archaeologically richest excavation contexts encountered at Fig Springs. Features 7, 16, 31, 32, 33, 42, and 43 (figs. 48, 49) are trash-filled pits. Quantities of Spanish and aboriginal artifacts and animal remains are found in a light-to-dark-brown sand fill. Charcoal flecking is sometimes present in the fill, but the artifacts and food remains generally are not burnt or charred. Trash-filled pits average 35 cm in depth and are first noted about 40–45 cmbs.

Artifacts found in trash-filled pits include Spanish glass beads, iron hardware and implements, aboriginal pottery, projectile points, lithic flakes, and mammal, reptile, and fish remains (fig. 50) (see Appendix E).

The trash-filled pits appear to have been outside the north and west walls of the structure and are oriented to it perpendicularly. The original function of these pits is unknown. They seem too small to have been intended for food-storage pits and as such would have required some sort of lining and cover, since they fill with water from the sides during heavy rains. Original excavation of the pits (except in Feature 7) stopped when clay subsoil was encountered. Feature 7 was dug to about the same depth but into sterile sand subsoil, since clay subsoil was not present in this area of the site. It is possible that the pits were dug to cache items of value or to store personal possessions, then were later filled with household trash when the pits were no longer needed or functional.

A fifth feature type is the oval pit, which accounts for 3.9 percent of all aboriginal features excavated. Oval pits have two kinds of fill, either refuse mixed with charcoal (Features 10 and 60, accounting for 2.6 percent of the features), or tan sand placed over the burial of a dog (Feature 15). A great deal of time was spent excavating Feature 10, which was first identified in the 1988 testing and subsequently completely excavated in 1989. Appendix E contains a detailed identification and analysis of the plant and animal remains obtained from this feature.

Fig. 48. *Trash-filled pits outside northeast corner of aboriginal structure. Feature 32 in left foreground, Feature 33 is linear pit in left background. Excavators are Gardner Gordon (front) and Kristen Smith (rear).*

FIG. 49. *Quarter section of Feature 16, a large trash-filled pit, showing density of artifacts and biological remains encountered.*

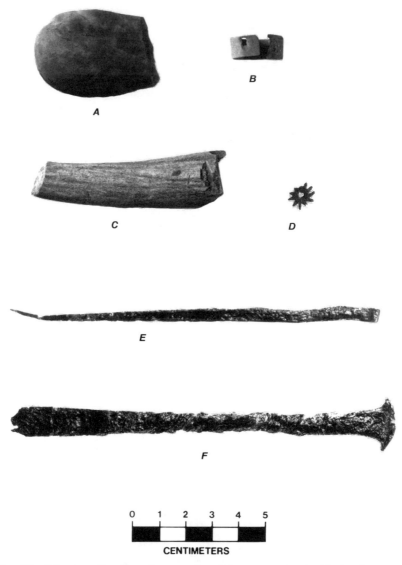

FIG. 50. *Selected artifacts from the excavation of features associated with the aboriginal structure. (A) Quartzite pottery burnishing stone (Feature 16), (B) sheet brass "ring" (Feature 16), (C) cut antler tine (Feature 16), (D) copper star (Feature 10), (E) iron awl (Feature 16), (F) iron chisel or knife (Feature 16).*

Feature 10 contains stratified fills consisting of (top to bottom) gray-to-brown compact sand with numerous charcoal inclusions (a possible hearth), mixed fills of brown-to-black sand with charcoal, burnt bone and numerous artifacts, and a basal stratum of brown to black clayey sand, charcoal, and artifacts. A pocket of ash and gray homogeneous sand is intrusive. Feature 10 has a maximum depth of 60 cm and was first noted at 14.78 mmsl (25 cmbs). The bottom of the pit was dug through a thin stratum of sterile sand down to the clay subsoil but does not substantially penetrate it.

Feature 60 has a maximum depth of 40 cm and was first recorded at 14.77 mmsl (about 30 cmbs). Feature fill consisted of very packed brown-to-black sand with charcoal inclusions and a few lumps of raw clay. Strata were not discernible, and, in contrast to Feature 10, few artifacts or food remains were present. This feature was also dug to the clay substrate and stopped.

Feature 10 contained many artifacts, many of them burnt. The feature was excavated according to the layers of fill identified in a profile recorded in the 1988 season (Weisman 1988b; figs. 51, 52). In a reversal of the situation seen in the general level excavations, complicated stamped ceramics are found in higher percentage (45.8 percent of total aboriginal pottery, by count) than plain (33.6 percent). Several burnt Pinellas projectile points and an Ichetucknee point were also recovered. Spanish materials include glazed and unglazed olive jar, a burnt and unidentifiable sliver of majolica, a burnt wrought-nail fragment, and an eleven-point copper star, 1 cm in diameter, similar to specimens found in a refuse pit at sixteenth-century Santa Elena (South et al. 1988; South personal communication October 21, 1989; see fig. 50). Olive jar comprises 8.5 percent of total ceramics (by count) from Feature 10 (table 4). Feature 60 contained several small plain aboriginal sherds and unidentified fragments of burnt bone.

Features 10 and 60 are located about 1.5 m north of what is presumed to have been the north wall of the aboriginal structure. Both appear to have originated in the humus and mixed-cultural stratum that is present outside but not inside the building. Feature 10 evidently intrudes on the northern portion of Feature 60. It cannot be determined at present if the features were covered by a roof; the presumed "posthole fill" intrusion near the center of Feature 10 cannot be interpreted with confidence. The most logical function of these features is that of roasting or cooking pits.

Fig. 51. *The excavation of Feature 10, the cooking or roasting pit.* Top, *John Worth removing distinct layers of fill for botanical and zooarchaeological analysis.* Bottom, *the completed excavation, view to the south.*

FIG. 52. *Profile of Feature 10 as recognized in 1988, showing hearth and ash fills. "Post" designation is questionable.*

Feature 10 shows clear evidence of cooking activities around a hearth (or hearths) and repeated use as a fire pit. The function of Feature 60 is less clear, because intact hearths and large quantities of artifacts and burnt-food remains were not found, but its overall appearance is similar to Feature 10.

The dog-burial pit (Feature 15) (fig. 53) had a fill of tan sand mottled with brown and gray. The fill generally appears homogeneous although weak lensing is evident. Feature 15 originates about 30 cmbs (14.78 mmsl) and bottoms at 14.08 mmsl (100 cmbs) on sterile clay subsoil. The sides of the pit slope inward toward the bottom, and the back legs of the dog actually rest on the sloping south wall of the pit (see fig. 53).

Few artifacts were found in the pit fill, and those that were, near the top of the feature, were probably intrusive from Feature 16. A plain Jefferson sherd was found embedded in the fill on the south wall of the pit about 25 cm above the burial. No artifacts were found in direct association with the skeleton.

The skeleton was first uncovered near the end of the 1988 season, but unfortunately the head extended into an unexcavated unit and could not be exposed. However, the skeleton was tentatively identified as dog at that

Table 4. Comparison of Artifacts from Selected Features and General Level Excavation, Aboriginal Structure

| Artifact | Feature no. and est. vol. (cu. m) | | | | | 240N/295E[c] (14.82–14.61, .8 cu. m) |
	F10[a] .7	F32 .16	F42 .23	F43 .07	F16[b] .03	
olive jar, glazed	2	0	0	0	0	0
olive jar, unglazed	5	1	0	0	0	0
wrought nail	2	0	0	0	0	4 (frag.)
spike	0	0	0	0	1	0
chisel	0	0	0	0	1	0
awl	0	0	0	0	1	0
tack	0	0	0	0	0	1
metal frag.	7	1	2	2	0	1
brass frag.	0	0	1	0	0	0
drawn bead	0	3	1	1	1	0
seed bead	0	3	1	1	1	0
wire-wound bead	0	1	0	0	0	0
bone bead	0	0	0	0	1	0
shell bead	0	0	0	0	1	0
glass frag.	0	1	0	0	0	1
comp. stmpd. pottery	20	0	3	1	1	1
plain	17	4	32	12	1	39
cord marked	1	1	0	0	0	0
cob marked	0	0	0	0	0	1
punctated (Lochloosa)	0	0	0	0	0	1
St. Johns	0	1	0	0	0	0
UID pottery	9	1	1	0	12	11
UID stamped	14	0	0	0	0	0
UID incised	1	0	1	0	0	0
Pinellas points	5	0	0	0	0	2
UID points	0	2	0	1	0	0
lithics	184	50	69	1	27	59
flakes w/cortex	0	3	0	0	2	3
cortex	0	0	1	1	0	4
utilized flakes	1	0	0	0	0	2
shatter	57	0	0	0	4	19
lead shot	0	1	0	0	0	0
clay ball	0	1	0	0	0	0
shell	0	0	0	1	0	2 (?)
mud dauber nest	0	0	0	0	0	1

Note: Plant and animal remains are not included in table 4.
a. Feature 10 materials are from FS 885, bulk sample excavated in 1988.
b. Feature 16 materials are from FS 892 only, excavated in 1988.
c. Materials from 240N/295E are combined from Zone 2, Levels 1 and 2.

time. In the 1989 season this identity was confirmed by Irvy Quitmyer through direct comparison of the skeleton to Florida Museum of Natural History Zooarchaeology Range specimen #2238, a German shepherd collected in the early 1960s by Stanley Olsen. The skeleton was removed on August 31. The size of the skeleton and the condition of bones and teeth nearly match the modern specimen, and it is concluded that the animal was the size of a typical German shepherd and was in middle age.

The skeleton was slightly flexed and was lying on its left side. The front legs were pulled back and tucked below the rear legs, which as mentioned actually rested on the side of the pit. Caudal vertebrae and the sacrum were twisted sharply to the right. Terminal digits (claws) are present. There are no obvious signs of disease or trauma. It appears that the animal was buried wholly intact after the time of death. On stratigraphic grounds, the burial occurred during the mission period occupation of the site, as the pit intrusion is capped off by an undisturbed artifact-bearing stratum that dates to this time. The current interpretation is that the interment took place early in the history of the structure, thus explaining why the backfill is relatively free of debris.

The dog burial appears to be about 1 m inside the north wall of the structure. Feature 16, a trash-filled pit that intrudes the burial pit in the northeast corner, may have been on the wall line. Features 12, 14, and 19, cob- or wood-filled smudges just south and west of Feature 15, are definitely inside the structure. Burial may have been made below a sleeping bench, although which came first has not been determined.

Six features (52, 53, 54, 55, 81) recorded in the aboriginal area excavations cannot be attributed to any of the five described categories and actually may not be of cultural origin. Most of these features are just outside the presumed north and south walls of the structure.

In excavations in and around the aboriginal structure, 191 map specimens were recorded. Spanish artifacts include olive jar and Mexico City White, Fig Springs Polychrome, and Caparra Blue majolica, and in the associated midden, two sherds of Puebla Polychrome (total of 10 majolica sherds altogether). Over 91 percent of the total glass beads recovered from the Fig Springs excavations came from the aboriginal structure (149 of 164). Seed beads, aqua, cobalt, brown, and amber in color, account for about 76 percent (n = 125) of the bead assemblage. Ichtucknee drawn beads account for about 12 percent of the total beads

FIG. 53. *Excavation of the dog burial. (A) The dog burial exposed in its burial pit. Unexcavated pedestal to the left is the southeast quadrant of Feature 16. (B) Irvy Quitmyer comparing dog burial with modern skeleton of German shepherd. (C) The location of the dog burial inside the north wall of the aboriginal structure. Circular charcoal mass in right center is charred wall post (Feature 64). (D) Keith Terry preparing the dog burial for removal.*

(n = 19), 78 percent of which were found in general level excavation and 22 percent in features. Iron artifacts include an iron hoe, chisel, spike, and awl, all from feature contexts, and 22 identifiable nails from general level and midden associations. None of the nails appears to have been used in the construction of the building. A small gold religious medallion, associated with an early seventeenth-century cult of the Virgin Mary (Mueller 1972; Deagan, personal communication, July 24, 1989) was found in general level excavation in 238N/293E, the interior room. A small gold petal-shaped ornament, possibly part of a rosary (Deagan 1987:176a), was found in general level excavations in the floor area possibly beneath a sleeping bench about 4 m northeast of the medallion find.

The trash-filled pits outside the structure were a particularly rich source of artifacts (see table 4). Typically they were filled with large sherds of aboriginal pottery and well-preserved food remains, but projectile points, fragments of Busycon shells, and the occasional Spanish artifact (in Feature 16 iron tools mentioned above and a piece of rolled brass resembling a finger ring, in Feature 43 a sheet-iron rectangle). A single straight pin was found in the fill of Feature 41, a possible bench-support post.

The aboriginal structure was generally rectangular in shape, with major roof support posts of pine set at intervals of 2.75–3 m around the outside wall. There is some evidence for smaller posts in between, which may have helped secure whatever wall materials were in use or else helped anchor interior partitions. Roofing and wall fabric are conjectural, but some parallel may exist with the rectangular Timucua chief's house described by Le Moyne for the sixteenth-century Outina as being "lightly thatched with palm branches" (Lorant 1946:94). Walls may have been thatch, cane mats suspended or secured to the posts or the roof plate, or board planks. However, if the latter, nails were not commonly used to hold them in place. Despite the fact that there is a small pile of burnt daub 7 m east of the structure (approximate grid coordinates 238N/ 309E), there is no evidence for wattle-and-daub architecture in the excavated structure.

Other Site Areas

In addition to the major excavations carried out in the mission church, convento, cemetery, and aboriginal structure, limited testing or subsurface investigations was conducted in other areas of the site thought to be important in the overall site plan (fig. 54).

The Mission Plaza

The plaza is the area between the church and aboriginal area, where few artifacts were recovered in the auger survey. On the basis of the auger borings, it was initially thought that the plaza consisted of a packed-clay surface that either had been specially prepared by the inhabitants or else was a natural occurrence taken advantage of in the layout of the site. It is now known that the clay substrate occurs only along the western edge of the plaza and is a natural deposit close to the surface. The plaza substrate itself, as revealed in a series of soil cores taken north-south through the area, is primarily a clean (meaning free of artifacts) white sand that is bounded by the church construction on the north and a sheet midden associated with the aboriginal structure to the south. The southern limit of the plaza corresponds approximately to the 270N grid line, about 25 m north of the aboriginal structure. It is likely that erosion has removed the true southwest corner of the plaza. There is some indication that debris accumulating on the plaza surface was swept to the southeast corner, where a light distribution of aboriginal pottery is found.

The mission plaza represents an integral part of the site plan because of its function as a buffer separating the sacred and secular domains of the community and because it probably served as a point of assembly for community events.

The Mission Kitchen

In the 1988 test excavations, a patch of what appeared to be burnt-clay floor was found in unit 245N/280E, about 5 m west of the presumed west wall line of the aboriginal structure. As this was in the general area where the kitchen was thought to be (based on the recovery of olive jar, bottle glass, and faunal remains in the auger survey) and because a prepared-clay floor seemed to be a signature of Spanish architecture, the excavation area was interpreted as the mission kitchen. It was recognized that the floor (at 14.61 mmsl) was significantly lower than other building surfaces at the site—10–15 cm lower than the aboriginal structure nearby and 60 cm lower than the church.

Soil cores and metal detector sweeps of the surrounding area failed to

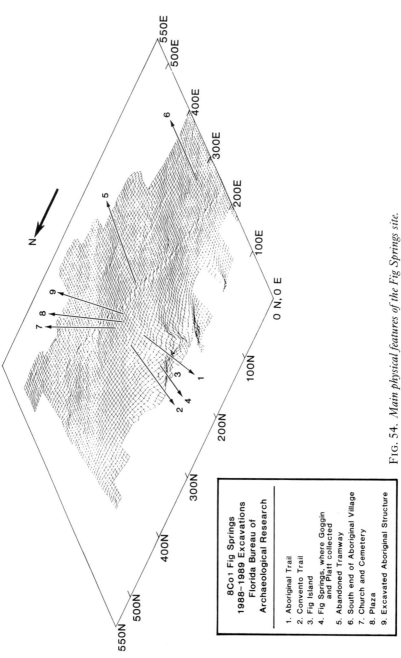

N

550N   500N   400N   300N

550E   500E   400E   300E   200E   100E   0 N, 0 E   100N   200N

6
5
9
7 8
3
1
2
4

8Co1 Fig Springs
1988–1989 Excavations
Florida Bureau of
Archaeological Research

1. Aboriginal Trail
2. Convento Trail
3. Fig Island
4. Fig Springs, where Goggin
   and Platt collected
5. Abandoned Tramway
6. South end of Aboriginal Village
7. Church and Cemetery
8. Plaza
9. Excavated Aboriginal Structure

FIG. 54. *Main physical features of the Fig Springs site.*

reveal any additional evidence for the building, and it was concluded that the structure had eroded downslope to the springs. Erosion would thus account both for the absence of additional structural remains and for the "kitchen-related" artifacts that continued to turn up on the access road just west (and downslope) of this spot after a heavy rain. No new information was gathered in 1989 pertaining to the identification of this area as the location of the mission kitchen except to take note again of the erosion that was occurring. However, in light of the fact that much food preparation (and perhaps consumption) was taking place in Feature 10 (the cooking/roasting pit), in clear association with the aboriginal structure, a large doubt is cast on the previous interpretation of the burnt floor as representing the remains of the kitchen. What mission building the clay floor represents, if any, is open to conjecture, since both its identification and certain placement in the mission period cannot at present be archaeologically investigated.

Footpaths to the Springs

As familiarity with the site increased during the project and additional areas were cleared of underbrush, two foot trails were discovered, apparently leading from the areas of the convento and the aboriginal structure to the springs. The convento trail can be seen from the convento area for a distance southwest about 75 m to where it intersects with the aboriginal trail and continues downslope to the water. The aboriginal trail can be seen at about 252N/269E, just west of the modern jeep access road, where it plunges downslope to the springs (see fig. 54). Exactly where this trail intersected the aboriginal structure cannot be determined because of erosion, but presumably it was on the north side of the structure.

Both trails are well-worn paths that were heavily overgrown at the start of the project and were not in use (or apparently known about) by the park rangers and current users of the springs. Sediments move down the trails during heavy rains, and a fanlike deposit containing mission artifacts is present at the base of the aboriginal trail where it ends at the stream bank. It is likely that a number of the artifacts found in the springs by Goggin and in recent years were deposited there by runoff down the trails. Soil cores and an auger boring (270N/240E) were placed in the area at the base of the aboriginal trail, and a profile of the convento trail (which, unfortunately, failed to show it as a discrete stratum) was obtained near its northern terminus (west profile of unit 321N/300E).

The "Well"

Unit 255N/296E (4 m × 4 m) was staked out over a depression in the ground about 10 m north of the excavated aboriginal structure. At the bottom of the depression, thinly buried beneath modern humus accumulation, was an iron ring or band. The ring was discovered in the metal detection survey of the area, and was partially exposed to get a better look. From what could be seen, the object appeared to resemble a barrel hoop or band, not unlike the kind used on barrels in the famous barrel wells of St. Augustine and Santa Elena. After a period of meticulous excavation (fig. 55), the level of the band was finally reached, and it was exposed in its entirety. To our surprise (and chagrin) an iron axle was found buried in the soil in the center of the ring, and it quickly became apparent that we had excavated an iron rim and axle from a heavy wheelbarrow or cart, such as were in use in the early part of this century. The matrix above the wheel (around the depression) is the dark soil midden associated with the aboriginal structure. Several glass beads, a sherd of Puebla Polychrome majolica (which cross-mends with a sherd found in midden closer to the building), rusted nails, and a spike were among the Spanish items recovered in this stratum.

It is not known if the depression is part of a sinkhole or other natural phenomenon or is the result of some past human activity. In the field notes it is referred to as the "construction pit" and the soil within the depression as "construction pit fill," because of the appearance of having been purposely excavated, but the natural clay substrate is very close to the surface in the east half of the unit and may have been subject to serious erosion in the past.

Aboriginal Village/Midden

In the 1988 and 1989 seasons, a total of six test units was excavated in the aboriginal village midden to provide collections of aboriginal pottery and other artifacts from areas that seemed (on the basis of sherds recovered in the auger survey) to date to slightly different time periods of occupation. We hoped to use these excavations to develop an outline of the history of aboriginal habitation at Fig Springs. Was there a village in existence before the founding of the mission (as Prieto's account indicates)? If so, what effect did the placement of the mission complex itself have on the subsequent settlement pattern of the village? Although

FIG. 55. *Excavating the "well." Note deposit of raw clay in background. Keith Terry is pointing to the iron axle and rim.*

entire projects can be (and hopefully will be) derived from these questions, we hoped to gain at least a glimpse at what was happening in the village beyond the pale of the mission.

The excavations (fig. 56) indicate that the village midden is actually a mixed deposit found in the original humus stratum, the first stratum encountered when the modern humus is stripped away. Unit 256/306E, a sheet midden associated with the excavated aboriginal structure, and units 302N/375E and 310N/370E, in a midden area east of the mission church, clearly belong to the mission period occupation of the village. Unit 256N/306E contains a number of Spanish-derived items, including a brass finger ring, found with the stone setting still in place (fig. 57), in addition to complicated stamped and shell-tempered aboriginal pottery. Context of this unit is a sheet midden directly associated with the aboriginal structure located about 14 m to the south. Unit 120N/250E also dates to the mission period (olive jar found, and a wire-wound glass

FIG. 56. *Excavation in 50N/295E, south end of the aboriginal village. The radiocarbon date of A.D. 1490 was to come from charred cob samples from a feature in this unit.*

FIG. 57. *Artifacts found in the excavation of the aboriginal midden. (A) brass ring with stone setting, (B) stone tool, (C) shell disc. All from unit 256N/306E.*

bead from auger test 130N/250E), but may be slightly earlier than the excavated aboriginal structure.

Units 50N/295E and 70N/310E, near the south end of the village, appear to predate the founding of the mission and may represent one area of the site where this earlier component has not been obscured by the later mission occupation. Suggested dating for these units is late fifteenth century to mid-sixteenth century. The basis for this dating, besides the fact that no Spanish material, complicated stamped, or grog-tempered pottery occurs, is a radiocarbon date discussed previously, yielding a calibrated date of A.D. 1490 obtained from charred cobs in a pit (Feature 85) associated with the cultural stratum in 50N/295E. At the two sigma level (95 percent confidence), the date range is A.D. 1430–A.D. 1650. Pottery is exclusively of what is called here the Suwannee Series. Averaged between the two units, plain pottery accounts for about 15 percent of the assemblage, roughened about 27 percent, cord-marked 16 percent, punctated 16 percent, and cob-marked 3.4 percent.

While the date range of the radiocarbon sample does not unequivocally place the Suwannee Series in premission times, doing so allows for a sensible ordering of components at Fig Springs and nearby sites so that the timing of the mission influence (the introduction of complicated stamping and Spanish materials in aboriginal domestic contexts) can be paced in archaeological terms.

The Mission Dump

Goggin was probably correct that the cultural deposits in and around Fig Springs itself represent a refuse dump for the mission. In conversation, Jerry Milanich has suggested that the large sherds found by Goggin (and several near-complete vessels) indicate that Fig Springs was an embarcadero, where canoes or other shallow-draft vessels would load and unload goods for further transportation inland. Certainly, in seasons of high water, water commerce via the Ichetucknee, Santa Fe, and Suwannee rivers with larger vessels anchored in the Gulf of Mexico could have been accomplished with relative ease. However, artifacts found in the springs are also being carried there downslope by erosion. Most of this portion of the site has been dug and disturbed by Goggin, Russell Platt, and others. Soil cores taken through the existing peninsula show it to be redeposited spoil.

Relationship of Site Areas

Together the church and cemetery areas are higher in elevation than any adjacent site area. The convento floor has about the same elevation as that of the aboriginal structure, and both are some 50 cm lower than the highest areas of the church. If the vertical relationship between building areas reflects the deliberate use of space to convey meaning about the relative importance of sacred areas versus secular areas, the conclusion is clear that the church was purposely raised above the surrounding area.

Further investigations at Ichetucknee Springs, at Mill Pond in particular, will likely reveal additional and possibly earlier Spanish components than those excavated at the Fig Springs site, perhaps remains directly traceable to the visit of Father López in 1597. It is certain that the internal history of the mission community—as one hopes will eventually be revealed through the archaeological study of settlement patterns—will show a complex pattern of alternating population nucleation and dispersal through time.

6

Artifacts

✛   MORE THAN ARCHITECTURE
and stratigraphy are needed to tell the story of an archaeological site. To
flesh out the human activities at the site and to understand what went on
there, artifacts must be recovered from good archaeological context—that
is, in such a way that the spatial relationships between artifacts are
measured and recorded, and the occurrences of artifacts within discrete
soil strata are recognized. On the basis of the context of recovery and
ethnographic parallels, archaeologists can then ascribe some function to
the items they have found. The need for context at Fig Springs was
particularly acute, since the interpretive potential of the thousands of
artifacts previously collected from the springs (see Appendix A) by
Goggin and others was limited because they could not be traced to
specific site areas.

There are of course many ways to classify artifacts, depending on the
goals and objectives of the research. For the study of the Fig Springs
artifacts a functional approach is chosen, to try to use what has been
learned about the artifacts from their excavation context to get an idea of
how they functioned in the mission community. Each of the artifact
categories contain items that are thought to share a similar function or
functions. For example, Spanish majolica and aboriginal pottery are
treated together in the category "food preparation and storage," because
this reflects the interpretation from archaeological context of how these
artifacts were used at Fig Springs.

The five artifact categories—architecture and furnishings, food
preparation and storage, tools and weapons, adornment, and religious
items—are discussed below. Unidentified artifacts, those for which no
function can be reasonably provided, comprise a sixth category.

Architecture and Furnishings

Most of the artifacts in this category are wrought-iron nails and spikes
used in construction of the church and convento. A total of 106 intact

wrought nails was found, plus an additional 154 iron fragments that were large enough to be identified as nails. A total of six intact spikes (defined here as being more than 10 cm in length) were recovered (three others were mapped in place associated with post features in the church and not removed), plus an additional nine identifiable spike fragments (fig. 58) (see table 5 for combined spike and nail fragment totals). Because the 1988 seasons were focused on the discovery and identification of specific buildings, a typology of nails and spikes was developed on the basis of their archaeological utility to mark building sites. For this purpose, all nails and spikes were further divided into straight, bent, or unidentified (UID) types.

Straight nails and spikes have not been altered in any way by use. While these artifacts *may* have been used (and in most cases probably were) in construction, they may also have been lost, discarded, or stored away from a specific building site for later use. Straight nails and spikes comprise the largest category of iron hardware and are found in all areas of the mission complex. In the aboriginal structure, several straight nails and a spike 133 mm in length were recovered from Feature 16, a trash-filled pit, and a straight nail (55 mm in length) and spike fragment (69 mm in length) were mapped in place along the north wall line. A total of 20 intact nails was found in the aboriginal structure (17.8 percent of the total intact nail collection, table 6), and five more were found in contexts in the aboriginal midden.

Straight nails are also found along the wall line of the interior room in the church and associated with the posts at the room corners. One of their functions appears to have been for nailing the vertical wall boards to (now vanished) horizontal supports. Average nail length in the church, including spikes, is 64 mm, with a range of 30 mm–134 mm (table 7). Four wrought tacks (two of 22 mm length, one 26 mm, and one 29 mm) were found on the sand floor in the southern area of the church at an elevation of 15.24 mmsl. Nails and spikes found in the convento, most in a broad area north and east of the charred post, also had an average length of 64 mm and accounted for 38.4 percent of the total intact collection (table 8).

Bent nails and spikes were further subdivided according to the kind of bend. "Gentle bend" hardware exhibited a slight arching bend across the entire length (see fig. 58), such as would occur if the nails or spikes had been pulled out of lumber for reuse. Therefore gentle-bend nails, by themselves, are not good indicators of specific building sites. Gentle-

FIG. 58. *Selected hardware from the Fig Springs excavations. (A) spike from Feature 16, (B, C) S-bend nails, (D–F) gentle-bend nails, (G) clinched nail, church, (H) secondary use nail, midden, (I) L-head nail, (J) headless nail from Feature 22, church.*

Table 5. Spike and Nail Fragments from Excavation Areas

	Total	% total	Range (mm)	Average length (mm)
Cemetery	4	2.5	20–44	35
Church	61	37.4	12–95	35
Convento	50	30.7	18–127	38
Aboriginal structure	46	28.2	12–98	36
Aboriginal midden	2	1.2	37–59	48

Note: Included in the totals for each area are one spike fragment (35 mm) from the cemetery, four spike fragments (27, 60, 38, and 95 mm) from the church, three spike fragments (35, 111, and 127 mm) from the convento, and one spike fragment (98 mm) from the aboriginal structure.

bend hardware is most commonly found in the church but is also distributed across the rest of the mission complex and occurs in the aboriginal area. Clinched nails were those with a right-angle bend produced by hammering over the end (see fig. 58). A related category is "secondary-use hardware," meaning nails and spikes with ends that have been bent at angles greater than 90°, possibly for use as hinges or hooks. Clinched and secondary-use nails are rare at Fig Springs and have a limited distribution. Three have been found in the church, three in the cemetery, and one in Feature 16 outside the aboriginal structure.

The type of hardware that is the best marker for the location of structures is of the "S-bend" type. S-bend nails and spikes result when a knot is encountered during nailing; these nails cannot have been pulled out of their original location and used again, or else the characteristic S-bend would necessarily have been straightened out. Of the eight S-bend nails found in the excavations, seven came from the church and one from the convento. Association of the S-bend nails appears to be with posts or wooden elements at room corners. Several S-bend nails in the church were not rusted, and probably were embedded in the structure when it burned (viz., South et al. 1988:53).

Attributes of nail form were also recorded, and L-head, T-head, and rose-head types noted at Santa Elena (South et al. 1988) and other Spanish colonial sites (Lyon 1988) are present. T-headed and L-headed nails are thought to have been used in flooring, because their heads could be countersunk, whereas rose-heads were used in joining (South et al. 1988:40–41). Curiously, rose-head nails have only been found in the church excavation (see table 7). Six L-head nails and one T-head nail

Table 6. Intact Nails and Spikes from the Aboriginal Area

FS no.	Length (mm)	Excavation unit	Elevation (mmsl)	Comments
878	75	244N/295E	14.73–14.68	T-head
892	133	240N/295E	14.47–14.15	Fea 16
892	83	240N/295E	14.47–14.15	Fea 16
1002	67	244N/297E	14.94–14.81	L-head
1101	69	236N/298E	14.90–14.83	
1027	69	238N/297E	14.86–14.78	
1070	73	238N/297E	14.86–14.76	
1099	83	238N/297E	14.78–14.68	T-head
1120	108	240N/289E	14.97–14.89	
1125	89	240N/289E	14.87–14.76	
1125	82	240N/289E	14.87–14.76	
1125	53	240N/289E	14.87–14.76	
1128	99	240N/289E	14.77–14.63	L-head
1128	86	240N/289E	14.77–14.63	
1132	57	242N/292E	14.92–14.78	
1139	83	242N/292E	14.79–14.67	
1142	55	242N/292E	14.69–14.57	
1158	73	234N/291E	14.88–14.79	
1162	89	234N/291E	14.29–14.20	
1181	82	238N/297E	14.63–14.47	

Total = 20   % total nails = 17.8   Average length = 80 mm

Nails and spikes from aboriginal midden

840	83	310N/370E	15.65–15.55	
993	27	255N/296E	14.88–14.49	
993	86	255N/296E	14.88–14.49	
993	106	255N/296E	14.88–14.49	Spike
993	80	255N/296E	14.88–14.49	

Total = 5   % total nails = 4.5   Average length = 75 mm

Note: Elevations are given in meters above mean sea level (mmsl).

were identified in the convento area. Two L-head nails and two T-head nails were recorded in the aboriginal area. Most of the S-bend nail heads are mutilated, as might be expected. Architectural hardware other than nails and spikes is not commonly found at Fig Springs, and is only associated with the church. These include an object resembling an iron staple from the sand floor on the south side of the structure and a bent-iron "cotter pin" from the original humus stratum above Burial 8 at

Table 7. Nails and Spikes from the Church Excavations

FS no.	Length (mm)	Excavation unit	Elevation (mmsl)	Comments
820	32	304N/314E	15.24–14.80	
820	36	304N/314E	15.24–14.80	
820	40	304N/314E	15.24–14.80	
766	34	297N/316E	15.38–15.29	Rose head
766	34	297N/316E	15.28–15.39	
784	51	297N/316E	15.31–15.06	in post mold
733	48	299N/314E	15.40–15.29	Rose head
733	35	299N/314E	15.40–15.29	Fea 22 (post)
809	55	295N/312E	15.35–15.25	Rose head
810	50	295N/314E	15.35–15.25	Fea 3 (post)
810	61	295N/314E	15.35–15.25	Fea 3 (post)
790	42	295N/316E	15.44–15.31	
790	54	295N/316E	15.44–15.31	
790	82	295N/316E	15.44–15.31	
790	47	295N/316E	15.44–15.31	Rose head
790	134	295N/316E	15.44–15.31	Spike
753	78	299N/316E	15.36–15.30	
779	86	291N/314E	15.33–15.22	
904	18	297N/312E	15.40–15.30	
904	49	297N/312E	15.40–15.30	
905	81	297N/312E	15.32–15.27	
919	85	293N/313E	15.30–15.07	
922	83	293N/313E	15.20–15.06	
924	36	293N/313E	15.10–15.00	T-head
933	52	301N/314E	15.26–14.99	Fea 21 (post)
949	77	299N/314E	15.27–15.08	Fea 22 (post)
949	83	299N/314E	15.27–15.08	Fea 22 (post)
957	82	303N/316E	15.16–15.08	
957	30	303N/316E	15.15–15.08	
958	45	295N/312E	15.24–15.04	Fea 26 (post)
966	47	298N/308E	15.24–15.07	
975	49	297N/312E	15.27–15.13	
978	54	295N/314E	15.28–15.10	
1013	31	297N/312E	15.32–15.19	
1013	33	297N/312E	15.32–15.19	
1013	50	297N/312E	15.32–15.19	
1028	80	303N/307E	15.13–14.98	

Total = 37   % Total nails = 33.3   Average length = 64 mm

Note: Elevations are given in meters above mean sea level (mmsl).

Table 8. Intact Nails and Spikes from the Convento Area

FS no.	Length (mm)	Excavation unit	Elevation (mmsl)	Comments
776	33	327N/298E	14.97–14.84	
789	50	327N/298E	14.86–14.75	
789	33	327N/298E	14.86–14.75	
791	83	327N/298E	14.75–14.67	
786	90	325N/296E	14.77–14.67	L-head
787	62	327N/296E	14.85–14.73	
928	63	329N/303E	15.24–15.12	
928	23	329N/303E	15.24–15.12	
947	84	331N/303E	15.33–15.20	L-head
959	80	321N/300E	15.09–14.90	
965	94	320N/304E	15.18–15.04	
971	55	320N/304E	15.07–14.95	
980	88	320N/304E	14.98–14.83	
981	86	322N/300E	15.18–14.90	
981	36	322N/300E	15.18–14.90	
981	20	322N/300E	15.18–14.90	
992	99	322N/300E	15.18–14.82	
992	67	322N/300E	15.18–14.82	
992	55	322N/300E	15.18–14.92	
992	31	322N/300E	15.18–14.92	
992	54	322N/300E	15.18–14.92	L-head
1005	20	322N/300E	14.93–14.80	
1005	23	322N/300E	14.93–14.80	
1005	25	322N/300E	14.93–14.80	
1005	40	322N/300E	14.93–14.80	
1005	96	322N/300E	14.93–14.80	
1005	92	322N/300E	14.93–14.80	
1005	27	322N/300E	14.93–14.80	
1005	91	322N/300E	14.93–14.80	L-head
1005	95	322N/300E	14.93–14.80	T-head
1005	124	322N/300E	14.93–14.80	Spike
1008	92	329N/298E	15.25–15.01	
1008	55	329N/298E	15.25–15.01	L-head
1020	32	329N/298E	14.91–14.79	
1020	92	329N/298E	14.91–14.79	
1021	26	329N/298E	14.97–14.87	
1022	70	322N/296E	14.93–14.83	T-head
1022	58	322N/296E	14.93–14.83	L-head
1022	73	322N/296E	14.93–14.83	
1022	80	322N/296E	14.93–14.83	
1031	89	322N/296E	14.84–14.71	
1031	85	322N/296E	14.84–14.71	
1031	83	322N/296E	14.84–14.71	

Total = 43   % Total nails = 38.4   Average length = 64 mm

Note: Elevations are given in meters above mean sea level (mmsl).

Table 9. Intact Nails and Spikes from the Cemetery Excavation

FS no.	Length (mm)	Excavation unit	Elevation (mmsl)	Comments
797	70	316N/316E	15.34–15.25	general level
800	99	316N/316E	15.25–15.15	general level
802	55	316N/316E	15.15–15.05	general level
802	260	316N/316E	15.15–15.05	general level
808	36	316N/316E	14.85–14.75	T-head
815	82	329N/319E	15.30–15.20	general level
817	59	329N/319E	15.20–15.10	general level
Total = 7	% Total nails = 6.3		Average Length = 94 mm	

Note: Elevations are given in meters above mean sea level (mmsl).

the northwest corner of the building. Table 9 is a summary of intact nails and spikes from the cemetery area.

The evidence for furnishings is slim. An iron chest lock similar to one found at Santa Elena (South et al. 1988:72) was found on the presumed floor stratum of the convento (see fig. 32) and is interpreted as part of a wooden chest or trunk belonging to the priest (see Manucy 1985:51, for the placement of such a chest inside a structure).

Food Preparation and Storage

Artifacts pertaining to food preparation and storage are the most common objects found at Fig Springs. Food preparation and storage artifacts include Spanish majolica, olive jar, aboriginal pottery sherds, and sherds of bottle glass. Of the total Spanish and aboriginal pottery obtained in the combined Fig Springs survey and excavations (5,451 sherds, 40,288.2 g), aboriginal pottery accounts for 96.1 percent of the assemblage by count (5,237 sherds) and 92.9 percent by weight (37,414.3). Majolica comprises 1.0 percent of the total by count (57 sherds) and .4 percent by weight (151.1 grams). Olive jar accounts for 2.9 percent of the total recovered pottery by count (157 sherds) and 6.7 percent by weight (2,722.8 grams). Combined, Spanish ceramics make up less than 4 percent of total Fig Springs ceramics by count and about 7 percent by weight. Majolica is present in the church, convento, aboriginal structure, and midden (and, of course, in the springs where Goggin collected) and occurs in plate, pitcher, and shallow-bowl forms.

Table 10. Glass Fragments from the Mission Period Component at Fig Springs

FS no.	Excavation unit	Area	Count	Weight	Color
787	327N/296E	Convento	1	0.2	clear
766	297N/316E	Church	1	1.8	pale green
796	295N/314E	Church	1	1.0	pale green
753	299N/316E	Church	1	1.9	pale green
814	296N/308E	Church	1	1.7	pale green
852	236N/298E	Aboriginal	3	3.6	clear
877	242N/287E	Aboriginal	1	0.4	pale green
886	240N/295E	Aboriginal	1	0.2	clear
905	297N/312E	Church	1	0.3	pale green
907	301N/314E	Church	1	1.6	pale green
916	301N/310E	Church	1	0.7	pale green
928	329N/303E	Convento	1	0.7	pale green
930	303N/316E	Church	1	0.8	pale green
932	331N/303E	Convento	1	1.4	clear
947	331N/303E	Convento	1	0.2	clear
947	331N/303E	Convento	1[a]	2.8	pale green
947	331N/303E	Convento	1[a]	4.8	pale green
947	331N/303E	Convento	1	0.3	clear
947	331N/303E	Convento	1	0.3	clear
973	301N/314E	Church	1	1.8	pale green
973	301N/314E	Church	1	0.6	pale green
973	301N/314E	Church	1	0.6	pale green
973	301N/314E	Church	1	0.5	pale green
973	301N/314E	Church	1	0.7	pale green
992	322N/300E	Convento	2	0.6	pale green
1002	244N/297E	Aboriginal	1	0.7	pale green
1010	329N/298E	Convento	1	0.5	pale green
1014	329N/298E	Convento	1	0.3	pale green
1017	329N/298E	Convento	1[b]	0.9	pale green
1020	329N/298E	Convento	1	0.3	clear
1022	322N/296E	Convento	1	0.1	pale green
1032	303N/307E	Church	1	0.5	clear
1043	303N/307E	Church	1	0.4	pale green
1046	298N/308E	Church	1	1.0	pale green
1074	238N/297E	Aboriginal	1[c]	0.9	pale green
1085	238N/297E	Aboriginal	1	0.1	pale green
1094	301N/314E	Church	1	0.1	clear
1098	244N/297E	Aboriginal	1	2.0	pale green
1120	240N/289E	Aboriginal	2	12.0	green
1125	240N/289E	Aboriginal	1	0.3	green
1131	240N/289E	Aboriginal	1	0.5	green
1132	242N/292E	Aboriginal	2	1.9	clear
1150	242N/295E	Aboriginal	2	7.1	clear
1158	234N/291E	Aboriginal	3	1.9	clear
1174	236N/291E	Aboriginal	1	0.5	clear

(continued)

Table 10. *Continued*

FS no.	Excavation unit	Area	Count	Weight	Color
1174	236N/291E	Aboriginal	1	7.7	dark green
1176	236N/293E	Aboriginal	1	0.2	clear
1185	236N/285E	Aboriginal	2	2.6	clear
1185	236N/285E	Aboriginal	1	1.0	clear
1192	229N/295E	Aboriginal	2	1.2	clear
1220	242N/292E	Aboriginal	1	4.4	clear

| | | Total | 61 | 78.6 grams | |

	Count	Weight
% Total glass in church	27.9	20.4
% Total glass in convento	24.6	16.0
% Total glass in aboriginal area	47.5	63.6

a. Fragments of a glass handle.
b. 13-mm diameter glass disc.
c. Latticinio glass rim found in Feature 32.

Aboriginal pottery is also present in all site areas, but occurs in greatest number and diversity of types in the aboriginal structure. Here, complicated stamped sherds account for 11 percent of all aboriginal pottery found. Complicated stamped pottery in the church accounts for about 14 percent of all aboriginal pottery, and in the convento this figure is 10 percent.

Glass is found in all three excavation areas but almost one-half (47.5 percent by count of the total 61 sherds) was found in the aboriginal structure (table 10). In the convento area most of a heavy "wine" bottle (Hume 1972:60) came from the bottom of the modern humus stratum, which probably postdates the mission. In the church, glass was found resembling the delicate pale aqua-green vial collected by Goggin in the springs, pictured in Deagan 1987:138). An ornamental handle (see fig. 32, and Deagan 1987:140) found in the convento suggests a drinking glass, vase, or decanter form. In the aboriginal area, glass sherds were found in Feature 32, a trash-filled pit (one a green "wine" bottle rim, the other a delicate rim with white striping or "latticinio" decoration, Deagan 1987:141), in Feature 38, and in general level excavations.

Majolica

The roster of majolica types recovered in the Fig Springs excavations is presented in table 11. Identifications follow the type collection housed

Table 11. Majolica from the Fig Springs Excavations

Mexico City White. Pink to red to off-white paste. Enamel is gray or greenish white. In Florida, dates to 1600–1650. Total sherds = 15.

FS no.	60	330N/260E	(auger test)	984	255N/296E	aboriginal
	747	316N/297E	church			midden
	753	299N/316E	church	1002	244N/297E	aboriginal
	814	296N/308E	church			midden
	966	298N/308E	church	1091	244N/297E	aboriginal
	917	293N/313E	church			midden
	972	294N/310E	church	996	244N/297E	aboriginal
	736	299N/312E	church			midden
	1045	298N/308E	church	1116	244N/295E	aboriginal
	1105	238N/297E	aboriginal			midden
			midden (pit)			

Fig Springs Polychrome. Pink to red to off-white paste. Gray blue enamel with animal or floral designs in yellow. Cracking and crazing of enamel evident. Can be difficult to distinguish from Mexico City White. In Florida, dates to 1550–1650. Total sherds = 12.

FS no.	1094	301N/314E	church	930	303N/316E	church
	779	291N/314E	church	966	298N/308E	church
	844	299N/314E	church	1002	244N/297E	aboriginal
	905	297N/312E	church			midden
						(2 sherds)
	906	301N/314E	church			
	910	301N/310E	church	1175	236N/293E	aboriginal
						structure
						(2 sherds)

Sevilla White. Cream paste with thick white glossy enamel. Some crazing. In Florida, dates to 1530–1650. Total sherds = 6.

FS no.	47	320N/290E	(auger)	957	303N/316E	church
	946	303N/316E	church	1043	303N/307E	church
	868	242N/287E	aboriginal	1174	236N/293E	aboriginal
			structure			structure

Puebla Polychrome. White paste with glossy white enamel. Blue scroll-like designs overpainted with black lacy pattern. In Florida, dates to 1630(?)–1725. Total sherds = 5.

FS no.	982	303N/316E	church	1002	244N/297E	aboriginal
	990	255N/296E	aboriginal			midden
			midden	1091	244N/297E	aboriginal
						midden (2)

(continued)

at the Florida Museum of Natural History, Gainesville, and Kathleen Deagan's 1987 publication. It should be noted that sherds listed as Panama Plain in the 1988 excavation report are correctly reclassified here as Mexico City White. Mexico City White is the most numerous type found, and accounts for 29 percent of the assemblage (15 of total 51

Table 11. *Continued*

Ichtucknee Blue on White. Cream paste, painted with floral or geometric designs. In Florida, dates to 1600–1650. Total sherds = 3.

FS no.	981	322N/300E	convento	1031	322N/296E	convento
	1005	322N/300E	convento			

Santo Domingo Blue on White. Soft cream paste with off-white enamel, overpainted with blue naturalistic designs. In Florida, dates to 1550–1650. Total sherds = 2.

FS no.	31	310N/340E	(auger)	1032	303N/307E	church

Cappara Blue. Soft cream paste with blue enamel. Fig Springs sherds are painted on both sides. In Florida, dates post-1492 to 1600. Total sherds = 3.

FS no.	793	291N/314E	church	1019	238N/297E	aboriginal
	979	322N/300E	convento			structure

San Luis Blue on White. Off white or red paste. Gray enamel painted with blue floral designs, often raised from surface. In Florida, dates to 1550–1650. Total sherds = 1.

FS no.	924	293N/313E	church

Sevilla Blue on Blue. Cream paste, light blue enamel painted with dark blue designs. In Florida, dates to 1550–1640. Total sherds = 1.

FS no.	129	270N/240E	(auger)

Columbia Plain. Cream paste with off-white or gray enamel. In Florida, dates post-1492 to 1650. Total sherds = 2.

FS no.	930	303N/316E	church	1172	236N/288E	aboriginal
						structure

16th-Century Lead-Glazed Coarse Earthenware. Red paste with dark green enamel. Total sherds = 1.

FS no.	927	293N/313E	church

UID Blue on White. Total sherds = 4.

FS no.	1000	256N/306E	aboriginal	1022	322N/296E	convento
			midden	1151	242N/295E	aboriginal
	1003	321N/300E	convento			midden

UID White. Total sherds = 2.

FS no.	52	320N/280E	(auger)
	1015	297N/312E	church

Total identifiable majolica sherds	51
Unidentified	6
Total	57

---

identifiable sherds). Majolica is found in all three excavation areas, and there are no types (in some cases, because of small sample size) that can reliably be said to occur in one area and not another. Selected Fig Springs majolica is depicted in figure 59.

Except for the type Puebla Polychrome (total of five sherds, four of

FIG. 59. *Majolica and olive jar sherds from the Fig Springs excavations. (A) middle-style olive jar neck, (B) Fig Springs Polychrome, (C, D) Sevilla White, (E, F) Santo Domingo Blue on White, (G) San Luis Blue on White, (H) Caparra Blue, (I) Ichtucknee Blue on White, (J) Puebla Polychrome.*

which are from the aboriginal midden and one from a midden outside the church) all majolica types are good temporal indicators of early to mid-seventeenth-century occupation (Goggin 1968:25–27, Deagan 1987:28–29). Beginning dates for Puebla Polychrome have not been definitely established but may be sometime in the several decades before 1650 (Goggin 1968:180). However, the types Mexico City White, Sevilla White, Sevilla Blue on Blue, Ichtucknee Blue on White, Caparra Blue, Santo Domingo Blue on White, San Luis Blue on White, and Fig Springs Polychrome seem to have been out of production by 1650 and were replaced by other types not present at Fig Springs.

With the exception of a single burnt and unidentified majolica fragment from Feature 10 (the roasting pit), majolica is not found in features or contexts that suggest special use or function as a status marker. Perhaps the sociological importance of majolica will become clearer when aboriginal structures not in direct association with the mission complex are excavated, but for now little can be said except that majolica plates, pitchers, and bowls were probably used to serve food to at least some of the residents of the site. Obviously, finding majolica in middens in and around the central mission complex says nothing about status, only function. By count, majolica comprises about 27 percent of the total Spanish ceramic assemblage from the site, but by weight this figure is just over 5 percent.

Olive Jar

As others have noted, olive jar is a ubiquitous find at Florida mission sites. At Fig Springs, olive jar sherds comprise about 73 percent of total Spanish ceramics by count and about 95 percent by weight. Olive jar is also found consistently in the church, convento, and aboriginal areas. Of the total 145 unglazed olive jar sherds collected, 10.3 percent by count came from the convento (33.6 percent by weight), 36.5 percent by count from the church (24.1 percent by weight), 47.5 percent from the aboriginal structure (56.3 percent by weight), and 5.5 percent from the midden (2.8 percent by weight). Olive jar sherds with light green or thin yellow glaze were also recorded. Of the total 12 glazed olive jar sherds, 58.3 percent by count came from the aboriginal structure (38.3 percent by weight), 16.6 percent came from the convento (33.1 percent by weight), 8.4 percent from the church (0.3 percent by weight), and 16.6 percent from the aboriginal midden (28.3 percent by weight). Glazed sherds in the aboriginal structure have a thin yellow glaze on the interior, whereas the convento sherds have a green glaze on both inside and outside. Almost 5 percent of total olive jar by weight was recovered from the Feature 10 (cooking/roasting pit) excavation outside the aboriginal dwelling.

The average weight for olive jar sherds is around 17 grams (although many were two to three times this weight), compared to less than 5 grams on the average for majolica sherds, thus the large and heavy nature of olive jar vessels is indicated. In the few cases where necks have been found (see fig. 59), the middle-style olive jar (dating between 1570 and 1770) is indicated (Deagan 1987:31–33). Olive jars were designed to store liquids for ease of transportation. They appear to have been used for food storage at the Fig Springs mission, or at least no other function is suggested. In the church, olive jar sherds were concentrated along the wall line defined by the charred sill at the east end of the interior room, and several sherds were found on the sand floor at the north and south ends of the building. In the convento, several large sherds were found along the presumed south and east walls. Olive jar is also found in association with the aboriginal structure and, as was mentioned, accounts for 8.5 percent (by count) of total ceramics recovered from Feature 10. This is a little more than twice the frequency with which Spanish ceramics are found in the aboriginal structure itself, but approximately the same frequencies seen in the church and convento areas. However, olive jar is present in the refuse fill of the cooking feature, not in the hearth area or ash deposits. A few olive jar sherds, glazed and unglazed, are also found in the trash-filled pits. At the bottom of the construction fill stratum below the sand floor at the south end of the church, a dark green lead-glazed coarse earthenware sherd with red paste was found. By comparison to the FMNH type collection, this sherd has been identified as a sixteenth-century type.

Aboriginal Pottery

Aboriginal pottery is the most common type of food-related artifact found at Fig Springs and accounts for about 96 percent of all ceramics recovered by count. Large bowl and jar sherds are typically found in the trash-filled pits outside the aboriginal structure. Other pottery concentrations occur along the south and east walls of the building, presumably where they were swept or dropped beneath the sleeping benches. Aboriginal pottery is also found in the church and convento and in midden deposits associated with the main mission complex.

A number of pottery types are found at Fig Springs, but these types are not evenly distributed across the site. A typological summary of sherds obtained in the test and block excavations from the church, convento, and cemetery areas is presented in table 12. Table 13 is a summary of excavated pottery from the aboriginal structure, the midden in the aboriginal village, and the two 2-m units in the south end of the village. An additional 4,524 grams of pottery less than ½ inch in diameter was

Table 12. Aboriginal Pottery from the Church, Convento, and Cemetery Excavations

	Church (ct/wt)	Convento (ct/wt)	Cemetery (ct/wt)
Jefferson Plain	187/1287.1	143/1051.5	31/210.9
Jefferson Complicated Stamped *var. Early*	47/518.8	28/411.1	3/24.5
Jefferson Complicated Stamped *var. Baptizing Springs*	1/3.5	—	—
Jefferson Roughened *var. Ichetucknee*	3/7.8	1/2.5	—
Jefferson Roughened *var. Santa Fe*	5/52.9	2/16.4	1/28.8
Jefferson Roughened, unspecified	1/5.2	2/6.3	—
Jefferson Cob Marked	5/48.6	3/84.2	1/11.6
Jefferson Check Stamped *var. Fort White*	9/99.0		
Jefferson Incised *var. Ocmulgee Fields*	—	1/17.5	—
Jefferson Incised *var. Columbia*	—	1/18.5	—
Lamar Complicated Stamped *var. Early*	1/4.7	—	2/5.1
Lamar Check Stamped *var. Fort White*	8/59.4	—	—
Lamar Check Stamped *var. Leon*	2/15.7	—	—
Lamar Incised *var. Ocmulgee Fields*	1/1.3	—	—
Fig Springs Roughened *var. Ichetucknee*	1/10.8	1/9.4	—
Fig Springs Roughened *var. Santa Fe*	1/12.7	1/26.3	—
Fig Springs Roughened, unspecified	—	1/6.0	—
Lochloosa Punctated *var. Lochloosa*	1/11.8	1/17.6	—
Prairie Cord Marked	1/2.6	1/1.9	—
Alachua Cob Marked	—	3/32.7	—
St. Johns Plain	2/7.0	6/20.0	1/5.7
St. Johns Check Stamped	2/6.7	4/11.4	3/8.5
Goggin Cord Marked	1/3.8	—	—
UID Aboriginal	48/261.2	65/316.9	16/88.5
UID Stamped	11/131.2	11/199.0	1/34.5
UID Check Stamped	2/50.1	1/6.9	—
UID Incised	3/27.4	—	—
UID Simple Stamped	3/8.9	—	—
Red Filmed	—	2/9.4	—
Total	346/2638.2	278/2265.5	59/418.1

Table 13. Aboriginal Pottery from the Aboriginal Structure, Midden, and South Village Excavations

	Structure (ct/wt)	Midden (ct/wt)	South Village (ct/wt)
Jefferson Plain	1961/14427.9	187/1085.2	—
Jefferson Complicated Stamped var. Early	336/3450.6	36/333	—
Jefferson Complicated Stamped var. Fig Springs	3/38.3	—	—
Jefferson Complicated Stamped var. Jefferson	—	1/3.5	—
Jefferson Check Stamped var. Fort White	1/12.0	—	—
Jefferson Check Stamped var. Leon	9/90.3	—	—
Jefferson Roughened var. Ichetucknee	7/129.5	—	—
Jefferson Roughened var. Santa Fe	18/267.9	3/25.9	—
Jefferson Roughened, unspecified	19/150.9	7/47.1	—
Jefferson Cob Marked	26/217.3	2/27.5	—
Jefferson Punctated var. Lochloosa	2/31.6	1/2.9	—
Jefferson Incised var. Columbia	2/7.4	2/25.5	—
Jefferson Incised var. Ocmulgee Fields	2/11.8	1/2.1	—
Lamar Complicated Stamped var. Early	9/103.5	—	1/8.6
Lamar Plain	50/652.6	—	—
Lamar Incised var. Columbia	1/5.9	1/13.0	—
Lamar Incised var. Ocmulgee Fields	5/16.3	—	—
Lamar Check Stamped var. Leon	2/15.7	—	—
Alachua Plain	4/28.0	—	39/173.0
Alachua Cob Marked	3/37.1	—	9/109.3
Prairie Cord Marked	43/306.9	15/145.1	42/266.1
Prairie Fabric Marked	1/5.7	—	2/7.2
Fig Springs Roughened var. Santa Fe	21/213.9	—	3/21.2
Fig Springs Roughened var. Ichetucknee	10/97.9	2/9.6	37/349.6
Fig Springs Roughened, unspecified	16/130.5	—	32/176.1
Lochloosa Punctated var. Lochloosa	4/60.7	1/2.9	26/145.6
Lochloosa Punctated var. Grassy Flats	6/24.3	1/13.1	15/143.9
St. Johns Plain	13/63.5	5/8.6	2/25.2
St. Johns Check Stamped	11/34.7	4/35.6	—
Red Filmed	3/15.5	—	—
Fort Walton Incised	9/207.5	—	1/6.1
Goggin Plain	19/81.2	4/87.0	—
Goggin Cord Marked	30/70.6	3/24.6	—
Goggin Incised	—	1/11.7	—
Gainesville Linear Punctated	—	—	1/11.5
Keith Incised	—	—	3/23.2
UID Aboriginal	254/1759.6	62/318.5	47/215.5
UID Stamped	199/1516.9	24/129.5	—
UID Incised	5/40.6	—	—
UID Simple Stamped	4/29.0	2/8.2	2/26.6
UID Dentate Stamped	—	—	3/14.1
Total	3108/24353.6	365/2360.1	265/1722.8

recovered, weighed, and discarded without attempts at typological identification. Pottery greater than ½ inch in diameter that could not be further identified to type was classified as "UID Aboriginal" and is tabulated accordingly for each excavation area. Frequencies of occurrence of each type in the individual excavation areas (as percentage of total count) are presented in table 14.

Most of the aboriginal pottery found at Fig Springs can be classified in five series, with types in each series arguably sharing a common archaeological culture. The pottery typology used in the third excavation season and subsequently used to reclassify sherds from the first two seasons is described in Appendix D.

The first series is called Suwannee Valley, because Suwannee types seem to represent the native aboriginal complex present in the Suwannee drainage when the missions were first established in the late sixteenth and early seventeenth century. The roster of types in the Suwannee Series at Fig Springs includes Alachua Cob Marked, Prairie Cord Marked, and Lochloosa Punctated—Alachua tradition types first defined in the Alachua area to the south in what would become the Potano mission province and dominant in that area (Goggin 1948, 1953; Milanich 1971)—and varieties of the type Fig Springs Roughened, ceramics with a roughened surface treatment (fig. 60) that are clearly associated with the cob-marked, cord-marked, and punctated types (fig. 61). Fig Springs Roughened appears to be a minor part of the typical Alachua Tradition assemblage in central Florida, where Prairie Cord Marked and Alachua Cob Marked are dominant (Milanich 1971).

There is an area in the south end of the Fig Springs village (the location of excavation units 50N/295E and 70N/310E) where the Suwannee Series exists in a pure form, that is, without intrusion or overlapping of the later mission ceramics. This is interpreted as an intact portion of the original premission village, which may have been dispersed along the banks of the Ichetucknee River farther south. The radiocarbon date of A.D. 1490 (discussed previously) obtained from charred corncobs in exclusive association with Suwannee ceramics in 50N/295E strengthens this interpretation. In a comparison of the distribution of roughened ceramics (including Jefferson Roughened and Fig Springs Roughened) across the site areas, 46.6 percent of the total roughened sherds recovered (223) came from the aboriginal structure by count, 42.1 percent from the aboriginal village, 5.4 percent from the convento, 4.9 percent from the church, and .90 percent from the cemetery, suggesting that the mission

Table 14. Frequency of Aboriginal Pottery in Excavation Areas

	Church (346)	Convento (278)	Cemetery (59)	Structure (3108)	Midden (365)	South End (265)
Jeff. Plain	54.1	51.5	52.5	63.1	51.3	—
Jeff. Comp. Stamped	13.6	10.1	5.1	10.9	9.9	—
Jeff. Comp. Stamped *var. Fig Springs*	—	—	—	.1	—	—
Jeff. Comp. Stamped *var. Bapt. Spgs.*	.3	—	—	—	—	—
Jeff. Comp. Stamped *var. Jefferson*	—	—	—	—	.3	—
Jeff. Check Stamped *var. Fort White*	2.7	—	—	.1	—	—
Jeff. Check Stamped *var. Leon*	—	—	—	.3	—	—
Jeff. Rough. *var. Ich.*	.9	.4	—	.3	—	—
Jeff. Rough *var. Santa Fe*	1.5	.8	1.7	.6	.9	—
Jeff. Rough unspec.	.3	.8	—	.7	2.0	—
Jeff. Cob Mkd.	1.5	1.1	1.7	.9	.6	—
Jeff. Punct. var. Loch.	—	—	—	.1	—	—
Jeff. Incised *var. Columbia*	—	.4	—	.1	.6	—
Jeff. Incised *var. Ocmulgee Fields*	—	.4	—	.1	.3	—
Lamar Plain	—	—	—	1.7	—	—
Lamar Comp. Stmpd.	.3	—	3.4	.3	—	.4
Lamar Check *var. Ft. White*	2.3	—	—	—	—	—
Lamar Check *var. Leon*	.6	—	—	.1	—	—
Lamar Incised *var. Ocmulgee Fields*	.3	—	—	.2	—	—

(continued)

area itself may not have been a heavily occupied portion of the site in premission times. Suwannee ceramics are sand-tempered and, where vessel form can be determined, appear to exist in both bowl and jar forms (see table 15). Most Suwannee rim sherds are of the simple type, meaning that they are the same thickness as the vessel itself and have not been modified (see table 16). Relative percentages of types present in the Suwannee Series are Fig Springs Roughened, about 27 percent, Prairie Cord Marked about 16 percent, Lochloosa Punctated about 15 percent, and Alachua Cob Marked about 3 percent. Plain ceramics account for about 13 percent of the total assemblage. Suwannee ceramics, with a total of 525 sherds weighing 3,943.2 grams, account for some 10 percent of the total aboriginal pottery found in the Fig Springs excavations.

Table 14. *Continued*

	Church (346)	Convento (278)	Cemetery (59)	Structure (3108)	Midden (365)	South End (265)
Lamar Incised *var. Columbia*	—	—	—	.1	.3	—
Fig Springs Rough. *var. Ich.*	.3	.4	—	.4	.6	14.0
Fig Springs Rough *var. Santa Fe*	.3	.4	—	.7	—	1.2
Fig Springs unspec.	—	.4	—	.6	—	12.1
Alachua Plain	—	—	—	.2	—	14.8
Alachua Cob Marked	—	1.1	—	.1	—	3.4
Prairie Cord Mkd.	.3	.4	—	1.4	4.2	15.9
Prairie Fabric Mkd.	—	—	—	.1	—	.8
Loch. Punct. *var. Loch.*	.3	.4	—	.2	.3	9.9
Loch. Punct. *var. Grassy Flats*	—	—	—	.1	.3	5.7
St. Johns Plain	.6	2.2	1.7	.5	1.4	.8
St. Johns Check Stamped	.5	1.5	5.1	.4	1.1	—
Goggin Plain	—	—	—	.7	1.1	—
Goggin Cord Marked	.3	—	—	1.0	.9	—
Goggin Incised	—	—	—	—	.3	—
Fort Walton Incised	—	—	—	.3	—	.4
Red Filmed	—	.7	—	.1	—	—
Gainesville Linear Punctated	—	—	—	—	—	.4
Keith Incised	—	—	—	—	—	1.2
UID Abo.	13.9	23.4	27.1	8.2	17.0	17.8
UID Stamped	3.2	4.0	1.7	6.5	6.6	—
UID Check Stamped	.6	.4	—	—	—	—
UID Incised	.9	—	—	.2	—	1.9
UID Simple Stamped	—	—	—	.2	.6	.8
UID Dentate Stamped	—	—	—	—	—	1.2
Total[a]	100.0	100.0	100.0	100.0	100.0	100.0

a. Totals equal 100 percent when rounded from the third decimal place.

The second series, called Lamar, conforms to descriptions of Lamar types in northwest Florida and the Georgia-Alabama region. Paste for Lamar sherds is coarse sand or crushed sand "grit." Lamar ceramics are not well represented at Fig Springs, consisting of a few bull's-eye complicated sherds around the aboriginal structure, several plain pinched rims in the same area, incised sherds from the convento and aboriginal areas, and two varieties of a check-stamped type (fig. 62). Total count of Lamar sherds is 84 (901.8 grams), accounting for almost 2.0 percent by count and 2.7 percent by weight of total excavated aboriginal pottery. This of course is a much lower figure than reported in the two interim field

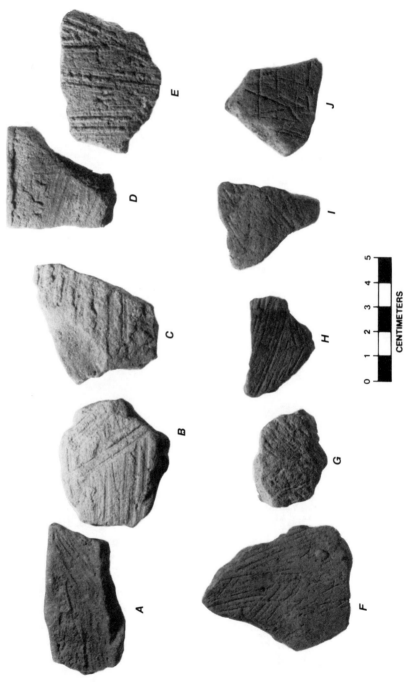

CENTIMETERS

0 1 2 3 4 5

FIG. 60. *Suwannee Series pottery*. *(A–E) Fig Springs Roughened* variety Ichetucknee, *(F–J) Fig Springs Roughened* variety Santa Fe.

Fig. 61. *Alachua tradition pottery. (A–D) Lochloosa Punctated* variety Lochloosa, *(E–G) Lochloosa Punctated* variety Grassy Flats, *(H) cob marked and cord marked, (I–K) Prairie Cord Marked, (L, M) Alachua Cob Marked.*

reports, when all complicated stamped pottery was called Lamar regardless of paste, in keeping with the San Luis typology (Scarry 1985; Shapiro 1987b). The idea that Lamar complicated stamping preceded and was the source of the well-known complicated stamped mission ceramics could not be confirmed in our stratigraphic excavations. In no

Table 15. Inferred Vessel Forms by Category of Surface Treatment

	Total rims	No. Excurvate (jar)[a]	No. Incurvate (bowl)[b]
Plain	176	11	16
Complicated Stamped	40	3	3
Cord Marked	16	—	3
Cob Marked	7	3	1
Roughened	12	1	4
UID Stamped	44	—	2
UID pottery	49	2	3
Total sherds	344	20	32

a. Jar form based on identification of the rim sherd as **excurvate restricted**, meaning that the vessel orifice is restricted below the rim (Shapiro 1987a:188).
b. Bowl form is based on identification of the rim sherd as **incurvate restricted** or from an **unrestricted bowl** (Shapiro 1987a:188), meaning that there are no restrictions in the orifice of the vessel below the rim.

case were Lamar sherds unquestionably lower in the stratigraphic column than grog-tempered ceramics of similar surface treatment.

The next series is named here Jefferson, to express similarity and continuity with the mission-period Leon-Jefferson ceramics first described by Hale Smith (1948). Although Smith acknowledged that a certain (unspecified) percentage of his Jefferson ceramics was grog-tempered, Jefferson is meant here to include only grog-tempered sherds. It is without question the dominant ceramic series of the mission period at Fig Springs (3,218 sherds with a total weight of 25,298.0 grams), accounting for about 61.4 percent of the total assemblage (including pottery from the auger survey) by count and 67.6 percent by weight. In the aboriginal structure, about 77 percent of the sherds are of the Jefferson Series.

A variety of surface treatments are exhibited on Jefferson sherds. The most common is the familiar bull's-eye stamp (fig. 63), which, together with minor stamping styles (fig. 64), make up about 70 percent of the total decorated ceramics. It is interesting to note that the Jefferson correlate of Alachua Cob Marked represents less than 3 percent of the ceramics in the mission complex itself and Jefferson Punctated is entirely absent (see table 14). The type Jefferson Plain (fig. 65) makes up 79.3 percent of the entire Jefferson Series and is therefore the most common type of pottery found at the site. Bowl and jar forms are represented in the Jefferson Series, and simple, folded, and pinched rims are present.

Table 16. Summary of Rim Types of Aboriginal Pottery from the Fig Springs Excavations by Surface Treatment

	Plain	Comp. Stamped	UID Stamped	Roughened	Cord	Cob	UID
Simple	107/962.4	15/71.6	14/110	8/71.3	15/139.9	6/51.4	30/181.1
% total	60.8	35.8	31.82	66.67	93.75	85.7	61.22
Flattened	51/316.9	15/239.8	13/178.6	3/22.9	1/9.1	1/4.1	12/68.3
% total	29.0	35.8	29.6	25.0	6.25	14.3	24.5
Folded	1/3.1	5/73.8	3/14.0	1/10.5	—	—	3/12.1
% total	.57	12.0	6.8	8.33	—	—	6.12
Impressed	9/61.9	—	—	—	—	—	—
% total	5.11	—	—	—	—	—	—
Ticked	2/20.7	—	—	—	—	—	—
% total	1.13	—	—	—	—	—	—
Pinched	1/7.9	—	9/57.9	—	—	—	—
% total	.57	—	20.45	—	—	—	—
Folded							
Pinched	2/4.0	5/73.8	—	—	—	—	—
% total	1.13	12.0	—	—	—	—	—
Folded							
Cane							
Punctate	3/10.0	—	—	—	—	—	—
% total	1.70	—	—	—	—	—	—
Flattened							
Notched	—	2/5.1	—	—	—	—	1/3.6
% total	—	4.8	—	—	—	—	2.04
Folded							
Stamped	—	—	4/15.0	—	—	—	—
% total	—	—	9.10	—	—	—	—
Punctated	—	—	1/3.3	—	—	—	—
% total	—	—	2.27	—	—	—	—
UID Rim	—	—	—	—	—	—	3/3.5
% total	—	—	—	—	—	—	6.12
Total	176/958.3	42/410.7	44/378.8	12/104.7	16/149.0	7/55.5	49/273.6

Shell-tempered ceramics comprise the fourth pottery series at Fig Springs (fig. 66) and are called the Goggin Series to commemorate John Goggin's discovery of shell-tempered pottery in his early explorations in the springs. With the single exception of a small cord-marked sherd found in the church, Goggin ceramics occur only in the aboriginal structure and associated midden. Almost 57 percent of the Goggin sherds are very fine cord-marked, with thicknesses of only 4–5 mm. Incised and incised with punctation styles are also known. Most of the known rims are

FIG. 62. *Lamar pottery. (A) Lamar cane punctated rim, (B, C) Lamar Complicated Stamped* variety Early, *(D, E) Leon Check Stamped* variety Leon, *(F) Lamar Incised* variety Columbia, *(G, H) Lamar Incised* variety Ocmulgee.

from plain vessels (none, unfortunately, from cord-marked vessels) and typically have a notched appliqué fillet strip on the rim, neck, or shoulder. Vessel form is the jar. One strap handle is present in Goggin's collection. In terms of surface treatment, Goggin Cord Marked appears to replace Prairie Cord Marked, which in frequency decreases through time from about 16 percent of the premission component to an average of just under 1 percent for mission period areas (see table 14). Goggin Cord Marked accounts for about 10 percent of the decorated mission-period aboriginal assemblage. Shell-tempered ceramics (plain and decorated combined) comprise about 1 percent of the total assemblage by count and about 0.7 percent by weight. The origin of the shell-tempered ceramics at Fig Springs is not known with certainty, but ties to the lower Chattahoochee River drainage are considered possible (Worth 1989). Goggin's initial collections from the spring were later classified into the Pensacola Series (Deagan 1972:33), but significant differences are now recognized between the Fig Springs pottery and that of the Pensacola Series as originally defined (Willey 1949:463–66) in terms of vessel form, surface treatment, stylistic execution, and rim treatment (Worth 1989, and see Appendix D). It is also curious that no cord-marked ceramics have yet been identified for the Pensacola Series. The Goggin Series appears to have a limited distribution and has not yet been reported from other mission-period sites in North Florida (Johnson and Nelson 1990). However, the Fox Pond site in Potano contains unnamed shell-tempered pottery as about a 1 percent component of the overall assemblage (20 sherds out of 1,889) (Symes and Stephens 1965:69).

FIG. 63. *Jefferson Complicated Stamped pottery. (A–D)* variety Early. *Sherd (B) is shown in fig. 41 (20).*

FIG. 64. *Jefferson stamped and incised pottery.* (*A, B*) *Jefferson Complicated Stamped* variety Fig Springs, (*C, D*) *Jefferson Complicated Stamped* variety Suwannee, (*E*) *Jefferson Complicated Stamped* variety Early *with overstamping,* (*F, G*) *Jefferson Check Stamped* variety Leon, (*H*) *Jefferson Check Stamped* variety Baptizing Spring, (*I, J*) *Jefferson Check Stamped* variety Fort White, (*K*) *Jefferson Incised* variety Ocmulgee, (*L*) *Jefferson Incised* variety Columbia.

FIG. 65. *Jefferson Plain and folded pinched rims. (A) plain vessel from Feature 16, aboriginal structure, (note large pieces of grog protruding through vessel surface), (B–D) folded pinched rims.*

The final series is the well-known St. Johns pottery (fig. 67) (Goggin 1948), consisting of types with a sponge spicule paste and characteristic chalky or greasy feel. The types St. Johns Plain and St. Johns Check Stamped are present and together account for 1.5 percent of the total mission assemblage by count and 0.92 percent by weight. St. Johns

FIG. 66. *Goggin Series pottery. (A) Goggin Cord Marked, (B) Goggin Plain with notched appliqué strip, (C) Goggin Cord Marked, (D) Goggin Incised, (E) Goggin Plain with notched appliqué strip, (F) Goggin Cord Marked.*

pottery is also found in the presumed original mission village portion of the site where Suwannee ceramics dominate and here accounts for less than 1 percent of the total assemblage. The wide temporal range of St. Johns ceramics has been amply demonstrated from other sites in peninsular Florida, and its recovery in sixteenth- and seventeenth-century contexts at Fig Springs is not surprising. The absence of St. Johns Check Stamped from the presumed premission component is more difficult to explain (see tables 13, 14), since this pottery type is thought to be a marker for the period after about A.D. 800 (Vernon 1984:110). A few St. Johns sherds were excavated from Feature 34, a trash-filled pit associated with the aboriginal structure, and several have come from general level excavation in the convento area. Of the structural areas of the site, St. Johns Series sherds were found most frequently in the convento (3.7 percent of total aboriginal convento pottery) followed by the church at just over 1.0 percent (see table 14).

That most of the cooking in the mission community was done with aboriginal vessels is certain, but the relative role of Spanish versus aboriginal ceramics in serving and storage has not been determined. Foods were stored in olive jars in the church, convento, and aboriginal areas, but aboriginal pottery jars were used for this purpose as well. Of a total of 344 aboriginal rim sherds from the entire excavation, 20 sherds evidently were from jars, 32 from bowls (table 15).

It is probable that even the largest aboriginal vessel at the site (with a

FIG. 67. *Miscellaneous pottery. (A, B) Fort Walton Incised, (C, D) pottery appendages (from aboriginal structure), (E) St. Johns Check Stamped.*

Table 17. Pottery Appendages from the Fig Springs Excavations

FS no.	Unit	Area	Type	Ct/wt	Description
838	310N/370E	Midden	UID	1/1.3	UID appendage
866	242N/285E	Abo.			
		Structure	Jeff. Plain	1/.9	UID appendage
1005	322N/300E	Convento	Jeff. Plain	1/2.6	lug
1031	322N/296E	Convento	St. Johns		
			Plain	1/15.7	foot
1192	229N/295E	Abo.			
		Structure	Jeff.Plain	1/24.4	handle
1193	229N/295E	Abo.			
		Structure	Jeff.Plain	1/29.8	handle (?)

diameter of about 50 cm) was smaller in volume than the typical olive jar, and aboriginal copies of the olive jar form have not definitely been identified. Actually, Colono-Indian vessel forms of any description are rare unless certain vessel appendages (table 17) such as feet (see fig. 67) can be considered copies of the Spanish *escudilla*, or cup, form (Goggin 1968:119). This is in contrast to assemblages from St. Augustine and the San Luis mission, where the resident Spanish populations made European vessel forms in demand.

Minority Types

Several large sherds of Fort Walton Incised pottery (see fig. 67) were found in general level excavations in the aboriginal structure and in Feature 16, in clear mission-period context. At least one carinated bowl is represented. A smaller sherd of probable Fort Walton Incised was found in the south end village excavations (50N/295E), associated with Suwannee ceramics. A total of 10 Fort Walton sherds was recovered in all.

Weeden Island pottery is poorly represented and appears to belong to a thin scatter of prehistoric artifacts distributed across the bluff above Fig Springs. A single Keith Incised sherd was recovered in the auger survey in the village midden (120N/250E), and a large plain sherd from a probable village area (auger test 340N/390E) with a flattened folded rim probably dates to this period. The Weeden Island component at Fig Springs is part of a broader settlement pattern that includes similar artifact scatters on both sides of the Ichetucknee River and two known burial mounds in the general vicinity.

Tools and Weapons

Recovered items relating to hunting and defense are mostly of stone, evidently of local manufacture from available sources of chert. A total of 233 intact or nearly intact stone projectile points were collected in the auger survey and combined excavations. Over 70 percent of the

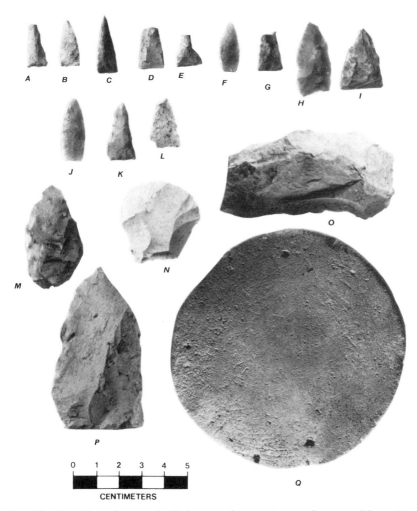

FIG. 68. *Projectiles and stone tools. (A–L) points from mission period contexts, (M) possible knife, (N) possible tool, (O) core, (P) possible tool, (Q) limestone disc (from south end of village).*

identifiable points are the small triangular Pinellas type (n = 92) (fig. 68), and a few Ichetucknee and Tampa points were also found. Most (about 86 percent) of the projectiles were found in and around the aboriginal structure. A total of 15 points were recovered in general level excavations along the north wall of the structure (unit 238N/297E) in the occupation stratum at approximately 14.83 mmsl. This stratum also contained the most lithic shatter noted for the site, with a total of 767.9 grams recorded. Seven projectiles were found in levels above and below this. Intact and fragmentary projectiles were also found in the fill of the trash-filled pits outside the structure, and seven points (some of which were burnt or charred) were recovered in the fill of the cooking/roasting pit (Feature 10). The convento excavations yielded five mission-period projectiles, three of which are Pinellas and two unidentified, and a Pinellas point came from the stratum overlying (but not associated with) Burial 6. No projectile points were found in the church proper, but one point was found in the small sheet midden on the north side of the building.

The use of firearms at the mission is indicated by the recovery of 12 lead shot and 2 gun flints (fig. 69). One lead shot was found in the auger survey of the aboriginal village (170N/320E), nine in general level excavations in the aboriginal structure, one in a cultural stratum in the cemetery overlying Burial 7, and one flattened specimen associated with a charred post in the church (Feature 27) that may have struck the standing post. Shot diameters (table 18) suggest .69 caliber and .54 caliber weapons, with buckshot loads in the .69 caliber guns (Clausen 1970:16). Gun flints are of the "honey-colored" flint of probable French origin (Hume 1972:220). One flint was surface collected near the convento; the second was found in what appears to be a midden stratum mixed with original humus just beyond the north wall of the church.

Stone tools other than projectiles are rare. Scrapers and knives were recovered in several instances and utilized flakes were occasionally noted. A scraper and possible expended core were found in the convento area (320N/304E) (see fig. 68) but may date to the prehistoric occupation (two Archaic points were also found in the general area). A stone knife was found in the subfloor construction fill in the church. A large flake that may have functioned as a scraper was excavated in the fill of Feature 42, a trash-filled pit north of the aboriginal structure. A smoothed quartzite burnishing stone was recovered in an adjacent trash-filled pit (Feature 16), and a limestone disc 11 cm in diameter and 1 cm thick came from excavations in the south end of the aboriginal village (50N/295E) (see fig. 68). One surface of the disc is slightly concave, with a small hole in the center, about 1 mm deep. Circular and linear striations are vaguely evident on both surfaces.

Iron tools found in the Fig Springs excavations attest to agricultural, woodworking, and leatherworking or tailoring activities. An iron hoe was found in a shallow feature outside the north wall of the aboriginal structure (fig. 70). The hoe is in better condition but virtually identical to one collected in Goggin's time from the springs and reported by Kathleen Deagan in 1972. Although comparative specimens are rare, hoes of this type appear to date to the seventeenth century (Hume 1972:275; B. Calvin Jones, personal communication, September 5, 1989). What

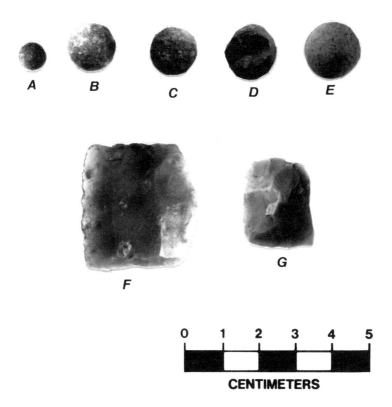

FIG. 69. *Lead shot and gun flints. (A–E) lead shot, (F–G) gun flints.*

Table 18. Lead Shot from the Fig Springs Excavations

FS no.	Excavation Unit	Diameter (mm)	Area	Comments
325	Auger Test 170N/320E	15	Village	
813	329N/319E	15	Cemetery	
866	242N/285E	8	Aboriginal structure	
866	242N/285E	8	Aboriginal structure	
975	297N/312E (Fea 27)	24	Church	Flattened
1034	238N/297E (Fea 32)	7	Aboriginal structure	
1120	240N/289E	15	Aboriginal structure	Flattened
1125	240N/289E	14	Aboriginal structure	Spent
1125	240N/289E	14	Aboriginal structure	Spent
1139	242N/292E	13	Aboriginal structure	
1139	242N/292E	7	Aboriginal structure	Flattened
1158	234N/291E	13	Aboriginal structure	

Total = 12

appears to be an iron chisel and awl were recovered together from Feature 16 (see fig. 50). An iron "sewing" needle, 7.1 cm in length, was found on the sand floor in the southeast portion of the church (see fig. 29). Wrought nails and probable Fig Springs majolica sherds were found in association.

Adornment

Artifacts of adornment include items of jewelry, clothing, and ornaments made from shell. European glass beads were the most common artifacts of adornment recovered in the Fig Springs excavations (fig. 71). A summary description of the bead assemblage is presented in Appendix C. Some beads were found in the church, convento, and aboriginal excavation areas, but most of the assemblage was recovered from

0 1 2 3 4 5

CENTIMETERS

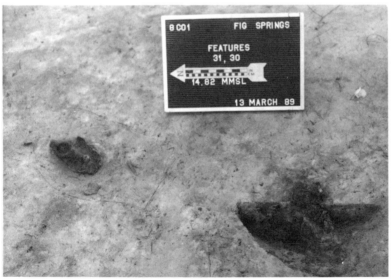

FIG. 70. *The iron hoe and the hoe in situ in Feature 31. Note heavy use of top edge of hoe as in hammering or pounding. Hoe is also shown in fig. 41 (11).*

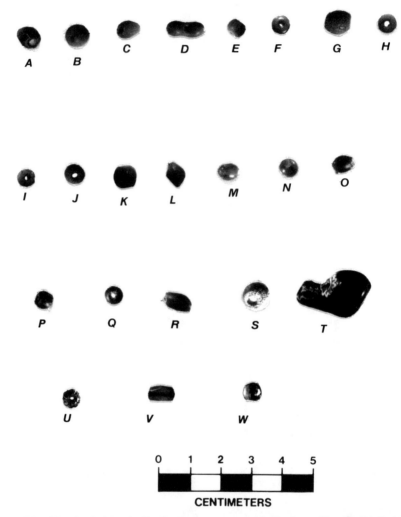

FIG. 71. *Glass beads from the Fig Springs excavations. (A) IIa drawn blue, (B–D) IIa40 Ichtucknee Blue, (E) IIa, (F–L) IIa40 Ichtucknee Blue, (M) IIa green drawn, (N) WIb green wire wound, (O) IIa blue drawn, (P) IIa burnt(?), (Q) WIb green wire wound, (R) IIa green oval heat-altered, (S) heavily patinated burnt spherical, (T) 5-layered heat-altered chevron, (U) gilded fluted, (V) WIIc or WIc blue faceted oval, (W) IIb gilded or amber spherical.*

trash-filled pit features and general-level excavations in the sheet midden associated with the aboriginal structure (table 19). The single heaviest occurrence of beads is Feature 16, a trash-filled pit adjacent to the dog burial, by virtue of the recovery of a cluster of 106 seed beads from the southeast quadrant of the excavation. In general, glass beads are of two types, the well-known seed bead and the drawn Ichtucknee type, both commonly reported from seventeenth-century Spanish colonial sites (Deagan 1987:174–75). Many of the Ichtucknee beads show evidence of heat altering, and resemble the previously described drawn beads from the Fox Pond site (Deagan 1987:175, Fig. 7.10). Of the total 19 Ichtucknee beads recovered, 78 percent were found in general level excavations, 22 percent in features.

Ichtucknee Blue beads are aqua in color and occur in oval (possibly the "barrel shape" of Kathleen Deagan's descriptions, see Deagan 1987), spherical, and doughnut shapes. Oval is most common. Seed beads come in oval, doughnut, and ring shapes. There is the possibility that the oval and doughnut shapes represent heat altering. The most common seed bead color is cobalt, followed by aqua, amber, and brown (the last two colors found only in the aboriginal area). Seed beads presumably were used here, as elsewhere, as necklace or embroidery beads. Use in a necklace is suggested by the recovery of a single blue seed bead from the neck area of Burial 7 (the only item of adornment found with any of the burials).

Table 19. Summary of Glass Bead Distribution

Type	Church	Convento	Cemetery	Abo. Structure	Abo. Midden
Ichtucknee	1	1	—	12	5
Seed	1	1	1	122	—
Other drawn	—	—	—	9	—
Tube	—	1	—	1	—
Wire wound	—	—	—	1	1
Faceted	—	1	—	—	—
Chevron	—	—	—	—	1[a]
Gilded	—	—	1	1	—
Other	—	—	—	3	—
Total	2	4	2	149	7

a. The chevron bead was found in auger test 420N/300E in a probable but not certain village context. No associated artifacts were found.

Two round green wire-wound beads were found, which most likely date to the mid-seventeenth century (Deagan 1987:175). One specimen came from a trash-filled pit outside the aboriginal structure (Feature 32), a feature, curiously, that contained no grog-tempered pottery. The second came from auger test 130N/250E, in the probable vicinity of another mission-period structure located in the aboriginal village. A possible wire-wound faceted oval blue bead was found in the convento area.

Other miscellaneous beads include a drawn gilded fluted bead from general level excavations in the southeast corner of the aboriginal structure, a gilded round amber bead from the fill over Burial 8, and a heat-altered (possibly two or three beads melted together), 5-layered chevron bead from auger test 420N/300E, north of the identified mission complex. Soil cores taken around the auger hole indicated a soil profile not containing a cultural stratum, with no associated architectural or cultural features evident. A spherical bead from the cooking/roasting pit feature (Feature 10) is burnt and heavily patinated, giving it an unusual gold-colored appearance.

All in all, given the wide range of bead types and varieties known to occur on seventeenth century Florida and Caribbean sites (Deagan 1987), a relatively restricted bead assemblage seems to be present at Fig Springs. However, in the context of the total artifacts recovered in the excavations, glass beads cannot be considered rare items—that is, they seem to occur with some regularity in virtually all mission-period proveniences.

In addition to the glass beads, two beads of probable aboriginal manufacture were recovered from the excavation of Feature 16. One is a spherical brown bone bead 5.5 mm in length, the other an oval shell bead 10.5 mm in length.

The second most numerous of the adornment artifacts are straight pins. A total of 19 brass or iron straight pins were found, a number of which had wire-wound heads and were completely intact (see figs. 29, 32). The pins closely resemble those recovered at sixteenth-century Santa Elena and pictured in South et al. 1988:152 (see also photograph of the same pins in the March 1988 *National Geographic,* p. 345). Table 20 is a summary of descriptive and provenience information pertaining to the Fig Springs pins. Of interest is the fact that most pins were found on the sand floor of the church or associated with the posts and board-wall lines of the interior room. Several were found in the convento area, and only

Table 20. Straight Pins from the Fig Springs Excavations

FS no.	Length (mm)[a]	Excavation unit	Elevation (mmsl)[b]	Association
766	17	297N/316E	15.37–15.29	church
810	16	295N/314E	15.33–15.25	church
803	23	295N/314E	15.31–15.26	church (Fea 3)
803	12	295N/314E	15.31–15.26	church (Fea 3)
753	32	299N/316E	15.36–15.30	church
905	13	297N/316E	15.32–15.27	church
907	31	301N/314E	15.39–15.24	church
919	23	293N/313E	15.30–15.07	church
919	23	293N/313E	15.30–15.07	church
922	21	293N/313E	15.20–15.06	church
927	23	293N/313E	15.00–14.90	church
927	9	293N/313E	15.00–14.90	church
947	19	331N/303E	15.33–15.20	convento
947	9	331N/303E	15.33–15.20	convento
949	30	299N/314E	15.27–15.08	church (Fea 22)
962	20	295N/314E	15.24–15.14	church
1003	14	321N/300E	14.96–14.83	convento
1013	30	297N/314E	15.32–15.19	church
1103	13	238N/297E	14.71–14.53	aboriginal structure (Fea 41)

a. Length of pins (some of which are fragmentary) is given in millimeters.
b. Elevations refer to top and bottom elevations of excavation level in which pins were recovered. Elevations are given in meters above mean sea level (mmsl).

one was found in the aboriginal excavations, here from the fill of Feature 41, a probable bench or intermediate roof-support post. The pins were presumably used in clothing of some kind, although their specific function and the reason for their apparent concentration in the church are open to speculation. Use of burial-shroud pins in the church is one suggestion, but if this was the case the shrouds probably were removed from the deceased prior to burial. At Santa Elena, a similar unequal distribution of pins from excavation contexts was noted, with more pins being found in the fort compound than in the domestic refuse associated with a Spanish structure (South et al. 1988:154).

Other clothing artifacts include a brass button back with shank attached (see fig. 29), found in the presumed sand cap over the clay floor in the church (and therefore, possibly postmission), and the 11-point copper star described previously from Feature 10. At Santa Elena, such stars are thought to have been decorative items sewn on clothing or horse tack or inlaid on furniture and may have been invested with Christian symbolism (Radisch 1988:149).

One of the most appealing adornment artifacts is a simple brass finger ring (see fig. 57) recovered from the sheet midden on the edge of the plaza about 16 m north of the aboriginal structure. This specimen looks identical to a ring collected from the springs in Goggin's time (and shown in Deagan 1972:38). The excavated ring was found with its small turquoise stone setting still in place. Provenience of the ring was fairly deep in the midden deposit (14.88 mmsl, about 36 cmbs), with some indication that the ring and other debris were thrown as refuse into a small depression in the existing ground surface. A piece of rolled sheet brass from Feature 16 may also have been used as a finger ring, probably as a secondary use of brass obtained from some other source.

Items of shell comprise a minor but interesting set of adornment artifacts. Although most of the recovered shell artifacts do not appear to be finished products, it is apparent from their regularities that certain types of end results were desired. The first of these is the shell disc or "gorget" form, as represented by a specimen found in association with the brass finger ring in the aboriginal midden. This artifact is round, with a diameter of about 7.4 cm, and was cut from the whorl of a large conch. No suspension holes, decoration, or other modifications are evident.

Cut-whorl pieces in triangular to rectangular to oval shapes are the second type of shell-adornment artifact. Artifacts of this type may have been intended for use as pendants. One such piece, with measurements of 9.5 cm x 7.5 cm, came from Feature 43, a trash-filled pit associated with the aboriginal structure. Four other examples were found in general level excavation inside the structure (fig. 72).

The third type is represented by elongate pieces cut from small sections of whorl or columella. One example, from the occupation stratum in the east end of the aboriginal building, had measurements of 4 cm × 1.4 cm, with a contour bend conforming to the curvature of the body whorl. A second example, and the only shell artifact from the excavation not to have come from a strictly aboriginal context, is a columella "plummet" about 9 cm in length, found in the fill along the west wall of the interior room of the church, between Features 25 and 27. The exact function of these artifacts is unknown, although they appear to have been purposely cut and worked and were not debris from the manufacture of other shell tools or ornaments. In fact, none of the shell

FIG. 72. *Shell artifacts. (A–C) cut whorl (C is from Feature 43, aboriginal structure), (D–F) cut whorl, (G, H) unidentified. All are from excavations in aboriginal structure. Shell (C) also is shown in fig. 41 (7) and fig. 19.*

artifacts appears to have been parts of shell tools or the biproduct of shell-tool manufacture, nor do they seem to represent any portion of the famous and historically documented shell dippers or drinking cups. However, a Busycon dipper is reported in the Florida Museum of Natural History collections from the springs.

A total of 11 shell artifacts was recorded in all, and, with the exception of two pieces from the church, all came from features, midden, or occupation strata associated with the aboriginal structure.

Religious Artifacts

Despite Goggin's recovery of a lead cross from the springs and the identification of Fig Springs from the beginning as a probable mission site (Goggin 1953), no other artifacts of certain religious function were found in subsequent collecting or in the first seasons of test excavation. However, late in the third season excavations, inside the aboriginal structure, we found what appeared to be a cast-gold medallion, consisting of a stylized crown resting on the interlocked letters "MA" (fig. 73). A field slide and sketch of the artifact were quickly sent to Kathleen Deagan

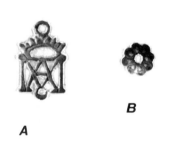

B

A

FIG. 73. *Religious artifacts. (A) gold venerra pendant or medallion, (B) possible rosary ornament of gold. Both from aboriginal structure.*

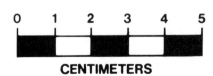

0   1   2   3   4   5

CENTIMETERS

at the Florida Museum of Natural History, who promptly replied (Deagan personal communication July 24, 1989) that the object resembled a *venera* pendant (Mueller 1972:118–21), associated with a cult of the Immaculate Conception popular between 1600 and 1650. According to Deagan, the interlocked M and A and the crown are cult symbols of the Virgin Mary, "Queen of Heaven and Immaculate."

The pendant was found in the occupation stratum (14.88 mmsl) associated with the interior room of the aboriginal structure. Artifacts found nearby in the stratum include a large sherd of Fig Springs Polychrome majolica, a drawn blue Ichtucknee bead, olive jar sherds, a charred peach pit, and plain and complicated stamped Jefferson pottery. The pendant is 2 cm in length, and numerous file marks are visible on both surfaces.

In the occupation stratum several meters northeast of the medallion was found a gold-plated petal-shaped perforated ornament approximately 8 mm in diameter. Again, in Deagan's opinion, this ornament could have been affixed to a rosary, as depicted on page 176 of her Spanish colonial artifact book from the San Juan del Puerto mission on the St. Johns River. There is the possibility that the pendant, perforated ornament, and gilded bead recovered from the aboriginal occupation stratum in the 1988 excavation were together part of a rosary lost or abandoned by an occupant of the aboriginal building during mission times. It is not out of the question that Goggin's lead cross also belongs to this association.

Unidentified Artifacts

The final category of unidentified artifacts consists of objects for which no reasonable function can currently be assigned, resulting from either a lack of known comparative material or ambiguities in the archaeological context of recovery. Many of these artifacts are nonetheless intriguing and not without considerable interest for further research. Selected unidentified artifacts are shown in figure 74. These include a small lead cylinder found in a midden area outside the church and a lead "curl" found on the church floor (see fig. 29), the latter identical to specimens found at Santa Elena and called lead line weights (South et al. 1988:180). An iron ring found in the auger survey (grid coordinate 180N/280E, in the aboriginal village) is similar to one found previously in the springs (and shown in

FIG. 74. *Unidentified artifacts. (A) glass disc, (B–H) clay balls, (I) iron piece, (J) iron ring, (K) iron "cotter pin," (L) iron "tooth," (M) iron ring similar to one found by Goggin in springs and pictured in Deagan 1972. Note apparent stamping on clay ball (G).*

Deagan 1972:37). A brass grommet found in the modern humus zone on top of the 1988 "kitchen floor" has the same kind of rectangular perforation as the sheet brass ring found in Feature 16. In the convento excavation, a 1.69-cm diameter pale green glass disc was found, with the same degree of patination seen on thin glass fragments from the church and convento areas.

Perhaps the most unusual of the unidentified objects are small clay balls, 7–12 mm in diameter. Five of these balls were found in the same excavation provenience outside the north wall of the church (unit 303N/316E), and the other two were from the aboriginal area. The balls are of hardened (but possibly unfired) sandy clay. Almost unbelievably, one of the smallest balls, recovered in the auger survey from the area of aboriginal structure, appears to have been incised with sets of parallel lines. One possible function of the balls was as part of a turtle-shell rattle, the presence of which is suggested by Goggin's recovery of drilled carapace fragments in the spring and our similar (but extremely fragile and fragmentary) find in Feature 43, a trash-filled pit along the north wall of the aboriginal structure. Pebbles, gravel, corn and bean seeds, and small "beads" are said to have been used by southeastern Indians to fill terrapin and gourd rattles in the historic period (Pierce 1825:134, Speck 1911:163, Swanton 1946:627). Unfortunately, no clay balls were found in features or in direct association with other artifacts that might help determine their use.

Small fragments of brass are another type of unidentified artifact found in limited quantity in the church, convento, and aboriginal areas. In the church and convento, fragments were found in general-level excavations around the presumed structural limits. In the aboriginal area, several cut irregular pieces were found in trash-filled pits.

Taken together, the Fig Springs artifacts speak of the broad range of activities that once occurred at the site and tell us something of its inhabitants. Unfortunately there are gaps in the material record. Artifacts comparable to the small wooden paddle and the plaited switch cane basketry or matting fragment found by Goggin in the springs were not (and are not likely to be) found in the terrestrial portion of the site. Of particular interest however, especially to an archaeologist in the early stages of excavation at a mission site, is the distribution of artifacts in the three major excavation areas. If one is beginning to dig a mission, which artifacts would be most useful in identifying specific buildings or site areas?

Clearly, the largest and richest source of artifacts is the aboriginal village, particularly those portions closest to the central mission complex because these are the areas of greatest and most diverse activity at the site. Here, virtually every class of artifact found across the site will be found, often in quantities and types not to be recovered elsewhere, especially aboriginal pottery and Spanish majolica. Even wrought-iron hardware is present, although its architectural use still remains in question. Most of the adornment artifacts also came from the aboriginal excavations, as did the religious medallion and possible rosary ornament. The aboriginal excavations also yielded the best preserved and most numerous plant and animal remains.

In terms of simple artifact counts, most of the identifiable nonceramic items in the church and convento areas were wrought-iron nails and spikes relating to wooden building construction. Aboriginal pottery and Spanish pottery also occurred in these areas but in lower quantities than in the aboriginal structure. It is notable that the church contained two varieties of very broad stamping (Jefferson Check Stamped, *var. Fort White*, Lamar Check Stamped, *var. Fort White*) which, with the exception of one sherd in the aboriginal structure, did not appear anywhere else on the site. Special use of the church and convento areas is suggested by the recovery of all but one (18 of 19) straight pins from these areas. The singular find of an iron chest lock in the presumed convento area suggests that the occupant of this structure, presumably the priest, had this standard piece of colonial furniture, whereas the residents of the aboriginal structure did not, or at least did not leave it behind. Conversely, the recovery of an iron hoe outside the aboriginal structure suggests that the inhabitants of this dwelling had full (and perhaps exclusive) access to an introduced agricultural technology.

Finally, in contrast to Christian interments unearthed at the Santa Catalina de Guale and Amelia Island missions (Saunders 1988), burials in the Fig Springs cemetery seem to lack both personal possessions and burial offerings. This generalization, based on evidence gathered in the 1988–89 excavations, applies to individuals buried close to the church and to those buried at some distance from it. Whether this lack of burial goods represents a departure from the prehistoric custom cannot be evaluated, since reliable excavation results from burial mounds in the vicinity of Fig Springs have not been reported.

7

Interpreting and Understanding Fig Springs Archaeology

✛   DESPITE THE MANY PAINSTAKING months spent in excavation at Fig Springs, it is surprisingly difficult to offer profound or absolute conclusions about the meaning of the findings. Certainly, the patterns of artifact distributions themselves defy easy generalization. With the exceptions of shell artifacts and religious objects, both of which are represented by only a few items each, and the singular recovery of the iron hoe outside the presumed aboriginal structure, the same kinds of artifacts are found in all areas of the mission complex. On the basis of simple artifact distributions, it is difficult if not futile to draw sharp lines between the different site areas such as the aboriginal structure and the church-cemetery-convento association. This itself perhaps leads to the meaningful conclusion that boundaries between priest and Indian such as might have existed were not reinforced through the means of personal possessions. This is not to say that all Indians were equal in terms of social status or position—indeed it cannot be determined until additional aboriginal households in the village are identified and excavated—but it might be said that priests at the frontier missions did not or were not set apart from the mission community they served by items they possessed and the Indians did not. The special position of the priest in the community undoubtedly derived from his unique association with the church and its functions and, as will be seen, is perhaps best archaeologically expressed through the unique architecture and construction of the church.

And although artifact patterns are in most cases too subtle to be understood through simple presence/absence relationships, artifacts are not found with equal frequency in the excavated areas of the mission complex. Artifact-frequency distributions have importance not only in inferring different functions or uses for different site areas (or structures) but may prove, when compared to other mission sites, to have importance in understanding aspects of mission-period society, politics, values, and beliefs.

For instance, all but four of the straight pins found in the excavations came from the floor area of the church or around the posts and wall line marking the interior room. This may have functional explanation if they were in fact pins used for fastening shrouds around the dead, an activity likely to take place in the church, before interment. Other artifact frequencies may have functional explanations as well. Almost one-half of the total glass sherds were found in and around the aboriginal structure, with the remaining half divided, roughly equally between the church and convento. Over 50 percent of the total olive jar came as well from the aboriginal structure and associated midden. Together, this may reflect a greater emphasis on food storage in this structure than in the mission buildings proper and, by inference, a greater emphasis on food preparation here as well. The single heaviest occurrence of olive jar on the site—in Feature 10, the cooking/roasting pit outside the aboriginal structure—may signify that foods (and liquids) were both stored and prepared in this area.

Strictly functional explanations may be less satisfactory in understanding other patterns of artifact distribution. Although the recovery of the gold medallion and the gilded rosary ornament from the aboriginal structure can scarcely be construed to represent a pattern, it is of interest that no similar items were found in the church and convento. Loucks made the same observation at the Baptizing Springs mission, where a religious medallion, the only certain religious object found at the site, came from her aboriginal structure "C" (Loucks 1979:266).

Another case where functional explanations by themselves fall short is the distribution of wrought nails and spikes. Less than 20 percent of the total nails and spikes came from the aboriginal structure; thus it is unlikely that the major portion of this building consisted of nailed-board framing as did the church and convento. But at the same time this distribution makes it difficult to conclude that the Indians were excluded or prevented from obtaining iron hardware for some purpose. The nails and spikes in the aboriginal area could, of course, have been pilfered from the standing mission buildings or during their construction or repair. Indeed a colonial order of 1630 required that all hardware unused in mission construction be returned to St. Augustine because the "poor Indians do not have the wherewithal for purchasing them" (Hann 1988b), thus indicating both their scarcity and value, but they may have been given to the Indians by the priest as gifts or rewards. How could these differences be detected in the archaeological record? The possible intentional burial of the iron chisel, awl, and large nails in a pit outside the aboriginal structure gives indication that these items had value, but whether they were obtained through gift, trade, purchase, or theft remains unanswered.

On the other hand, about 95 percent of the glass beads obtained in the excavation came from aboriginal contexts, and although this may in part be explained by the recovery of tiny seed beads in the fine mesh screening and detailed excavation of the trash-filled pits adjacent to the aboriginal structure, 17 of the total 19 large Ichtucknee Blue beads, often seen by the naked eye during excavation, were found in the aboriginal structure or related midden. Of course, European glass beads are known to have been favorite items of gift and trade from the earliest days of contact, and it is fully expected that the Indians at Fig Springs would have them.

Other artifact patterns conform to our expectations, based on the results of previous mission archaeology, and therefore present no great problems of interpretation. Finding virtually all of the mission-period stone projectile points and the greatest concentrations of waste flakes and shatter debris in aboriginal contexts is a pattern in common with San Luis and Baptizing Springs and is not surprising since hunting and stone-tool manufacture were typical aboriginal activities, and firearms and iron tools were not yet common. Similarly, if shell artifacts, which seem to be rare at mission sites, are indeed aboriginal status items as Loucks proposes for Baptizing Springs (Loucks 1979:267), then the recovery at Fig Springs of all shell artifacts from aboriginal contexts (except the columella plummet from the west wall line of the interior room of the church) can be explained in this light.

Patterns of aboriginal pottery distribution are not as straightforward as one would like. Aboriginal pottery was much more abundant in the aboriginal structure and midden (accounting for about 85 percent of total aboriginal pottery from the mission area, not including the south end village excavations) than in the church-cemetery-convento complex, but except for this, it is difficult to say with certainty that specific pottery types occur exclusively in one area and not in another. The single sherd of Jefferson Complicated Stamped *var. Baptizing Springs* was found in the church, as were nine of the ten sherds of the new broad check-stamped type called Jefferson Check Stamped *var. Fort White* (the other being found in the aboriginal structure). However, the small sample size obviates sure statements about the possible special meaning or significance of these check-stamped ceramics. In a similar comparison of pottery recovered in presumed Spanish versus Indian structures at Baptizing Springs, Loucks too was forced to conclude that, although several styles of complicated stamped pottery were more prevalent in the Spanish areas, the only category of ceramics distinctly aboriginal—that is, the only category that did not demonstrably cross-cut both Spanish and Indian site areas—was that of the Alachua Tradition. However, research at Fig Springs has shown that Alachua cord-marked and cob-marked ceramics, particularly in association with the roughened Suwannee Series types, are more likely to be found in premission contexts, so their "Indianness" may be more a factor of time than of mission-period ethnicity.

As to the question of Spanish preference for check-stamped ceramics, because of the purported functional superiority of check-stamped vessels, as is seen in urban St. Augustine (Deagan 1985:19), no certain answer is yet possible. The same is true of the Spanish influence in general on the aboriginal manufacture of pottery. Direct conclusions based on the Fig Springs tabulations are maddeningly elusive and do not seem to suggest strongly that the St. Augustine case can be applied to the interior missions. Perhaps this is as it should be, given the fact that, in contrast to St. Augustine, no Spanish households were known to have been present at the Fig Springs mission or the other frontier missions except for those of the priests. (This does not apply to San Luis, where a garrison and actual Spanish settlement were located.) The same explanation may apply to the scarcity of colono-Indian pottery forms at Fig Springs—that is, pottery made by the Indians to resemble in form European pitchers, plates, saucers, and the like. In the absence of a resident Spanish population, there would be little incentive or purpose for the production of these ceramics. Looking at the relationship of plain versus decorated aboriginal pottery in the different site areas of the mission complex, we find that plain pottery accounts for about 50–55 percent of the total assemblage in the church, convento (which actually has almost equal amounts of pottery being plain and decorated), cemetery, and aboriginal midden, whereas over 65 percent of pottery found in the aboriginal structure was plain.

Although the patterns of artifact distribution suggest a relatively open community, or at least that strong social boundaries were not maintained between priest and Indian, the architecture of the Fig Springs mission presents a picture of contrast, in which the respective architectural traditions of the European and aboriginal cultures are given expression in this frontier setting. The clay floor of the church and the square-hewn tapered posts of the church and convento clearly set these buildings apart from the aboriginal structure, where the posts are rounded and not tapered and where the floor was sand. The vertical board construction of the church was not an element used in aboriginal construction, nor were interior rooms in the aboriginal structure as clearly defined as in the church.

The cob-filled and wood-filled pits, trash-filled pits, cooking/roasting pits, and the basin-shaped pits or hearths are features found only in the aboriginal structure. This compares favorably to the finding of similar features in structures C and D at Baptizing Springs (Loucks 1979:141) and their absence in the Spanish structures A and B. (Several pit features were excavated in these structures, but Loucks suggested they may have been associated with or adapted from an earlier aboriginal structure [Loucks 1979:282].) The dog burial along the north wall line of the aboriginal structure at Fig Springs appears at this time to be unique to the site and could reflect either aboriginal or European influences.

Of special interest are those points of architecture where the Spanish and Indian traditions come together. The measurement of 1.7 m (roughly two Spanish *varas*) appears as the distance between the clay post-support pads and the edge of the floor in the church, and in the aboriginal structure as the distance between the wall and the first row of smudge pits. This suggests that the presumed sleeping benches were 1.7 m in length. Curiously, Burial 8, the only burial cleaned in its entirety, represents the remains of a 35–45-year-old woman who was about 1.45 m tall. It seems likely, as one would assume, that the church and aboriginal structures were constructed by the same builders or by builders sharing the same plans.

It is almost certain that it was the Indians who actually built the mission structures in the interior missions, at least in the early years before there was much of a military presence. When the Indians of Timucua first requested a resident priest in 1597, they were told first to build his church and living quarters, and the priest would follow (Hann 1988a). It is interesting to see how the Indians took what they had seen in St. Augustine as representing Spanish architecture and what they under-stood religious architecture to be to create buildings that fused both traditions. The several deep excavation cuts through the church floor, the first in Florida mission archaeology actually to reveal a construction sequence of this kind, show almost layer by layer the conceptual overlapping and synthesis of Spanish and Indian religious architecture. It is particularly striking how closely the preparation of the building site for the church, as understood through excavation, resembles the steps involved in mound building.

The sequence begins with the stripping of humus from the area where the building was to be placed. It is possible that the humus was dumped out and spread across the ground to the north of the building site, where a dark humus layer was encountered during excavation. After the humus had been removed, loads of clean sand fill were applied to the building site and graded to form a series of three low terraces, rising in elevation in steps from west to east. It was on these surfaces that the prepared clay floor was placed. The building burned at least once before the final episode, and new floor was laid down over several burnt posts, which were not replaced. Finally, after the building had been burned and was no longer in use, the ruins were capped with another layer of clean sand, presumably by Indians who lived at the site after the church had been destroyed. The ultimate visual effect, intentionally or not, was that of a low sand mound, raised some 10–15 cm above the level of the surrounding ground surface.

The Mission Community

What was life really like at the Fig Springs mission? Many more seasons of excavation in many more areas of the mission village will be necessary before this question can have a satisfactory answer. But it will take more than further archaeological research to bring about a new and more complete understanding of mission life. Previous assumptions and preconceptions about mission-period society should be carefully examined, and those that do not characterize the Florida missions as dynamic, functioning communities should be abandoned. As with all human communities of past and present, questions can be asked: Why did it exist? and, What kept it together?

If these questions had been put to individuals living in seventeenth-century Florida, the answers would have been as varied as their own interests in the colony. From the point of view of the Spanish Crown and the colonial administrators, the priests were agents of pacification, part of a master plan to conquer not only the natural resources of the territory but also the hearts, minds, and muscles of its native inhabitants. The priests, although far from politically naive, seem to have been genuinely inspired to gather souls for Christ, and to judge from their rates of conversion in Timucua and Potano, they could justifiably boast (and were required to do so in justifying their requests for additional supplies and provisions) of tremendous success in their efforts. In 1606 it is written that there was one Christian Indian in all of Potano, but by 1635 priests were claiming many thousands of conversions in this and the Timucua Province (Geiger 1940:12,90). Evidently the priests did not underrate their own accomplishments, nor could they really afford to in their constant competition with the military for the limited finances and compensation provided by the colonial government. In the words of one of the century's more outspoken friars, Father Pareja, "We are the ones who bear the burden and the heats, and we are the ones subduing and conquering the land" (Oré 1936:107).

We can only guess at what the Indians thought of the priests in the early years of the mission period and what they perceived as their role in the social milieu of the Spanish colonial frontier. The few documents that do exist give no hint of unanimity of opinion on the part of the natives. The aged cacique of Santa Ana in Potano Province remembered the horrors wrought by the de Soto expedition and at first wanted nothing to do with the robed Spaniards (Oré 1936:110), whereas other Indians of the interior sought out the priests, were readily baptized, and requested a Franciscan presence in their home villages. Their motives in so doing are lost to history, but both history and archaeology attest to the early flow of European goods from the Spaniards to Indians professing an obedience to God and King.

That the Spanish missions were able to exist in the Florida hinterland for nearly a century is thus in part due to the willingness of the Indians themselves to participate in the system. The fact that the long-term consequences of mission life were overwhelmingly negative in terms of loss of life from disease or relentless British-Indian raiding from the north is not relevant when viewed against the short-term experience of one person's life. It is probable that at least some of the natives thought it desirable to live at the missions and perceived it to be in their best interest to do so. It is also possible that the Indian rebellions that arose in Guale, Potano, and Timucua were native reactions to failed and unmet expectations, to promises made, under the table or otherwise, that were not kept. Certainly the southeastern Indians of the later historic period were shrewd traders and businessmen, and there is some indication that this generality applies to the mission Indians as well. By 1656 beads and knives were being shipped on Spanish frigates from Havana to Apalachee to barter for hens raised by the Indians. Also by this time the trade in deerskins had started up, and to the priests' dismay, the Indians were brought into close contact with the Spanish military (Hann 1987). Priests, however, were themselves blamed by Governor Rebolledo for causing native rebellions by conducting their own trade enterprises at the missions.

In archaeological terms, this interaction between priest and Indian is thought to have resulted in both areas of the site that contain relatively large numbers of Spanish artifacts and areas where Spanish materials are scarce or nonexistent. Areas with high densities of Spanish goods correlate with high-status occupation, while low-density areas correlate to low social standing. At first look, this interpretation seems reasonable, especially given that Spanish artifacts do seem to be differentially distributed at the few mission sites (Fig Springs and San Luis among them) where broad-scale archaeological surveys have been conducted. At San Luis, Spanish pottery (majolica and olive jar combined) accounted for 8.3 percent of total pottery from the presumed church-convento area and 2.1 percent of total pottery from the village area (Shapiro 1987b:111). At Baptizing Springs, these figures are 11.4 percent for the two Spanish structures and 2.9 percent for the village area. Spanish pottery on the average is 13 percent of the total at Fig Springs for the church and convento area, and 1.5 percent of total pottery in the aboriginal areas. The average figures for the three sites are about 11 percent Spanish pottery for presumed church-convento complex and 2.9 percent for village areas. Table 21 is a summary of percentages of aboriginal pottery, majolica, and

Table 21. Percentages of Spanish and Aboriginal Pottery in Different Excavation Contexts at Fig Springs

	Convento (count/% total)	Church	Cemetery	Abo. struc.	Midden
Aboriginal pottery	278/91.1	346/81.2	59/98.4	3108/97.1	365/96.6
Olive jar	17/5.6	54/12.7	—	76/2.4	10/2.6
Majolica	10/3.3	26/6.1	1/1.6	17/.5	3/0.8
Total	305/100	426/100	60/100	3201/100	378/100

olive jar present in different Fig Springs contexts. It is interesting to note that the percentages of majolica in the convento and church (3.3 and 6.1 percent, respectively) fall within the low end of the 4.1–7.8 percent range of majolica present in sixteenth-century St. Augustine Spanish households (Deagan 1985:28), suggesting that priests at the frontier missions may have had about as much majolica in their possession as a city dweller.

In social terms, however, the idea of a single fixed concept of status shared by all members of the community—at Fig Springs, 100 or more Indians and probably not more than one priest—is at best simplistic. It fails in terms of artifacts to take into account aboriginal prestige items such as shell ornaments (Loucks 1979:267), which may still have had value despite the presence of trade items. Fig Springs was strictly an aboriginal community, as were many of the interior missions. The Spanish presence, at least on a daily basis, was minimal, consisting as it did of a single priest. Anthropologists know from studying contemporary communities that they are composed of competing but cooperative groups of minorities, having consensus on an acceptable range of behavioral variation rather than on single values. At the missions, Christians versus infidels is a type of societal polarization, with the infidels presumably espousing traditional native values and religion and showing less affinity for Spanish goods. Why should status be determined (or marked) solely by the possession of Spanish items? In whose terms is this status defined? Is it not possible that members of the community whose roles were defined through traditional religious or political means (and not through the degree of their interaction with the Spanish) also were "high status" in the eyes of their followers?

Clearly, excavations are needed in mission villages if we are to understand how the communities were put together. This will require a shift in focus away from the central-mission complex (often casually, but erroneously, referred to by archaeologists as the Spanish sector) to the archaeological sampling of households in the village. If done right, it will be no small task. At Fig Springs, an estimated 300 2-m-by-2-m test units will be required to identify all of the probable household locations in the 12-acre village.

Excavations are also needed in early historic period, premission villages in Potano and Timucua. Such excavations will provide a baseline for evaluating what changes, if any, in aboriginal lifeways occurred as the result of mission living. Pottery obtained in the south-end village excavations at Fig Springs, when compared to pottery from the mission complex, suggests a dramatic increase in plain wares with the mission period, from about 15 percent of total aboriginal pottery being plain in the premission fifteenth century to greater than 65 percent of the total being plain in the seventeenth-century aboriginal structure of the mission complex. What trend of social change does this reflect? Lest this be interpreted as a direct indication of simplification of society, it must be noted that, with the mission period, there is an increase in diversity of rim styles and vessel form. Impressed, pinched, ticked, and notched rims are present in Jefferson pottery but not in the Suwannee Series. Changes in diet and subsistence practices are also detectable in the archaeological record. At Fig Springs, fauna recovered from trash-filled pits and the roasting pit associated with the aboriginal structure indicate a subsistence emphasis on wild terrestrial animals (primarily deer; see Appendix E), while plant foods were from a mix of wild and domesticated sources. Introduced species of plants and animals are present (pig, wheat, peaches, and, curiously, watermelon) but are not common. Several charred peach pits were found on the sand floor of the church along the south wall line of the interior room and occasionally in general-level excavations in the aboriginal structure. Were the subsistence practices at Fig Springs significantly different from the prehistoric pattern, and if so, what other changes in aboriginal society would be expected?

Not the least of the mysteries of the mission period is the cultural identity of the mission-period Indians themselves. The uncertainty has arisen because the aboriginal pottery assemblages in the three best-studied mission provinces—Apalachee, Timucua, and St. Augustine—seem to reflect an almost complete replacement of indigenous types by complicated stamped pottery of apparent Georgia origin. Archaeologists have understandably interpreted the rather abrupt appearance of stamped pottery in the Florida mission provinces as evidence for the undocumented migration of peoples from areas of the Georgia piedmont and coastal plain, where unlike Florida, the well-developed stamping tradition persisted into late prehistoric times. Indeed, in the documents, there is some hint of a population explosion early in the mission period. In his 1597 foray into Timucua from the lower Georgia coast, Fray Baltasar López noted that the territory consisted of one principal town and five satellite villages, with an overall population of about 1,500 persons (Hann 1988c). By 1608, just 11 years later, when Martín Prieto went also to Timucua, it contained 20 villages. In comparison, the de Soto narrative of Rodrigo Rangel records eight villages total for the territory representing the combined Potano and Timucua provinces (Swanton 1939:56), although of course unrecorded satellites may also have existed.

In the archaeological record, this striking phenomenon is not as straightforward and understandable as one might think. At Fig Springs, if the present interpretation of the internal chronology is sound, the indigenous roughened complex decreases in frequency from about 31 percent of the total decorated assemblage in the premission period to less than 5 percent in mission contexts. Similar decreases are noted for cord-marked pottery (about 35 percent to less than 8 percent, which actually is shell tempered) and Lochloosa Punctated (about 25 percent to about 6 percent). However, the frequency of cob-marked pottery actually increases, from less than 6 percent in presumed fifteenth-century contexts to almost 18 percent in the mission period. Bull's-eye complicated stamping, entirely absent prehistorically, seems to appear in the first decades of the seventeenth century (accounting for almost 35 percent of the decorated assemblage), swelling to 71 percent of the decorated assemblage by the 1630s–1640s. Curiously, in Apalachee, and perhaps Timucua as well, complicated stamping declines sharply in frequency after midcentury, as plain pottery comes to dominate the overall assemblage (seemingly increasing from about 50–60 percent of the combined mission assemblages to over 80 percent, as at San Luis; Shapiro and McEwan 1990).

In the St. Augustine missions there is a similar burst of stamped pottery, but here this may have occurred in the latter half of the seventeenth century. At the San Juan del Puerto mission, about 65 percent of the pottery is of stamped motifs belonging to the San Marcos Series, with origins on the central Georgia coast (McMurray 1973). There are documented movements of Guale Indians down the coast to resettle in the vicinity of St. Augustine after 1675 (McMurray 1973:70). Certainly the 50-foot-diameter council house or "war house" with interior benches or "cabins" described by Jonathan Dickinson in 1695 at San Juan del Puerto (Andrews and Andrews 1945) bears no resemblance to any aboriginal structure noted by Le Moyne and depicted in the de Bry engravings for the same area 130 years earlier (Lorant 1946).

Whether such evidence can be used to argue successfully for migration and population replacement awaits further research. The carryover to the grog-tempered mission period Jefferson Series of roughened and cob-marked Suwannee surface treatments suggests some continuity of the prehistoric population, although to what degree and by what means these peoples assimilated or were assimilated by immigrant populations are not known. In the St. Augustine area, migrations from Guale would also have meant replacement of the indigenous Timucuan language. In the Timucua Province of North Florida, this might not have been the case, as Timucua speakers may have inhabited South Georgia as far north as the Altamaha River. Movement of these peoples into the Timucua missions would represent a shift of population from one part of their territory to another.

Who were the mission Indians—migrants, mixed populations of migrants and indigenous Florida Timucuans, or native peoples who across the provinces began to make and use stamped pottery with grog-tempered paste? Inasmuch as these possibilities have been evident since Hale Smith (1948), Gordon Willey (1949), and John Goggin (1953) first looked at the mission question and proposed replacement models of mission demography, one must wonder how and when this question will be resolved. This is certainly an area of Florida archaeology where the basic facts of culture history—who lived where, and when, and where they came from—have not been revealed. The archaeology of Fig Springs indicates that these answers will not be easy to get, nor will the story of the Florida mission period, when finally told, be a simple one. Despite the many unknowns, it is certain that archaeologists studying the mission period have the rare opportunity to witness the birth of a new and unique culture, the product of the frontier interaction between priest and Indian.

APPENDIXES ✣

A

Inventory of Fig Springs Artifacts in the Florida Museum of Natural History

✛   ARTIFACT CLASSIFICATION FOLLOWS
the Florida Museum of Natural History catalog cards. Fig Springs accession is A-1964, a total of 4,657 specimens. Proveniences of the artifacts are unknown; most are probably from the springs itself.

Artifact counts are provided in parentheses.

See Deagan 1987 for recent discussion of "Ichtucknee" majolica types.

Aboriginal Pottery
Jefferson ware (2,669)
St. Johns Check Stamped (191)
St. Johns Plain (131)
St. Johns Simple Stamped (2)
St. Johns Linear Check Stamped (4)
Dunns Creek Red (6)
Pasco Plain (95)
Miller Plain (76)
Leon Check Stamped (42)
San Marcos Stamped (16)
Alachua Cob Marked (59)
Lochloosa Punctated (15)
Prairie Cord Marked (3)
Fort Walton Incised (13)
Aucilla Incised (10)
Ocmulgee Fields Incised (1)
shell tempered incised (5)
clay tempered brushed (12)
Orange Plain (23)

Orange Incised (2)
unique striated sand-tempered (5)
reconstructed Seminole plain vessel
lug handle (1)
strap handle (3)
sherd discs (plain gritty, olive jar, clay)
sherd hone (gritty, complicated stamped)
miniature vessel

Majolica and Olive Jar
  Columbia Plain (59) (31 plate, 8 tazza, 3 bowl, 15 jar, 2 unclassified) (58
    white, 1 green)
  Ichtucknee Blue on Blue (43)
  Ichtucknee Blue on White (42)
  Fig Springs Polychrome (66)
  Tallahassee Blue on White (17)
  unclassified blue on white (17)
  unclassified blue and orange on white (2)
  unclassified manganese and green on white (3)
  unclassified white (22)
  unclassified yellow (1)
  Olive Jar (594)

Metal
  iron hoe fragment
  thimble (1)
  small iron link (?) (1)
  old iron snaps (2)
  nails (8)
  iron fragments (20)
  sheet brass or copper (5)
  lead shot (20)
  lead plummetlike object (1)
  brass finger ring (1)
  lead cross (1)

Glass
  "Ichtucknee Blue" glass beads (16)
  glass bottle fragments (49)

Bone
    socketed antler point (2)
    bone pin fragment (1)
    worked canine tooth, beveled (1)
    turtle-shell rattles (3) (two are perforated, one sawn and perforated) (Box turtle carapace and plastron)

Wood
    wooden paddle

Lithics
    hammerstones (7)
    retouched flakes (14)
    stemmed points (10)
    stemless points (1 large, 16 small)
    stemmed knife (1)
    blade and fragments (8)
    flake drill (1)
    arrowshaft straightener (1)
    UID (1)
    flat grinding slab (?) frag. (1)
    side scrapers (2)
    core scrapers (5)
    flint chips (105)

Shell
    perforated shells (2)
    Cassis lip (1)
    Busycon dipper (1)
    UID object made of Busycon (1)

Plant Remains
    Peach pits (listed as "very common")
    Hickory nut hulls (common, may be recent)
    Cane (*Arundinaria* sp.) matting fragments
    Maize (plain and charred, very fragile, not saved)
    Gourd (fair-sized fragments; cracked, broken, and shrunken on removal from water)
    Corncob fragment (1)

Modern (?) China
  white ware (2)
  "peasant(?) painted" flowers (Gaudy Dutch?) (2)
  transfer print, blue floral (4)
  salt-glazed stoneware, brown inside (3)

Miscellaneous
  lime mortar and oyster shell chunks (2)
  wattle (?) fragments (20)

B

Burial Data from the Fig Springs Excavations

Burial No. 1 (1986 FMNH test excavations)
Excavation unit: TP-1 (FMNH designation)
Opening elevation: 15.35 mmsl (estimated)
Closing elevation: 14.55 mmsl (estimated)
Centimeters below surface (top of cranium): 75 cm (est.)
Stratigraphic definition: Below original humus or mixed cultural stratum of
  yellow to brown sand containing UID majolica and other artifacts, a
  possible burial pit at 14.83 mmsl (est.) of brown sand fill intrusive in tan
  sand matrix. This burial possibly intrusive on Burial 3.
Type of burial: primary
Condition: poor
Orientation: head to the east, facing west
Burial pit: probable
Burial form: extended (?)
Gender: undetermined
Age: child (?)
Artifacts: none recovered
Pathology: none recorded

Burial No. 2 (1986 FMNH test excavations)
Excavation unit: TP-2 (FMNH designation), 303N/307E
Opening elevation: 15.30 mmsl (est.)
Closing elevation: 14.40 mmsl (est.)
Centimeters below surface (top of cranium): 85 cm
Stratigraphic definition: Below a 20 cm stratum of dark brown sand (original
  humus and mixed cultural stratum), an intrusion at 14.95 mmsl (est.) of red
  to brown and tan to gray mottled sand (pit fill) in matrix of tan to brown sand
  (presumed sterile).
Type of burial: primary
Condition: good

Orientation: head to the east, facing west
Burial pit: present
Burial form: extended, supine
Gender: undetermined
Age: undetermined
Artifacts: none recovered
Pathology: none recorded

Burial No. 3 (1986 FMNH test excavations)
Excavation unit: TP-1, TP-3 (FMNH designation)
Opening elevation: 15.35 mmsl (est.)
Closing elevation: 14.45 mmsl (est.)
Centimeters below surface (top of cranium): 75 cm
Stratigraphic definition: Burial pit possibly originates below or through original humus and mixed cultural stratum associated with church, in matrix of sterile tan sand. Pit outlines may have been partially obliterated by intrusive Burial 1.
Type of burial: primary
Condition: good
Orientation: head to the east, facing west
Burial pit: probable
Burial form: extended, supine
Gender: undetermined
Age: undetermined
Artifacts: none recovered
Pathology: none recorded

Burial No. 4
Excavation unit: ST-6 (1986 FMNH test excavations)
Opening elevation: 15.35 mmsl (est.)
Closing elevation: 14.51 mmsl (est.)
Centimeters below surface (top of cranium): 82 cm
Stratigraphic definition: Burial pit of mixed sand fills and lumps of raw clay possibly originating at 15.02 mmsl (est.). Excavation stopped when cranium of Burial 4 encountered at 84 cmbs; no further excavation or cleaning of skeleton.
Type of burial: undetermined
Condition: good (cranium only)
Orientation: undetermined, but head probably to the east
Burial pit: probable but not observed
Burial form: undetermined
Gender: undetermined

Age: undetermined
Artifacts: none recovered
Pathology: none recorded

Burial No. 5

Excavation unit: 316N/316E, a 2 m × 2 m unit excavated in the 1988 season
Opening elevation: 15.25 mmsl (est.)
Closing elevation: 14.90 mmsl
Centimeters below surface (top of cranium): 40 cm (est.)
Stratigraphic definition: Below modern humus and intrusive through original
   humus and mixed cultural stratum of gray, white, and brown mottled sand,
   mixed fills of tan and yellow mottled sand with inclusions of raw clay (burial
   pit fill) in matrix of white (sterile) sand.
Type of burial: primary
Condition: good (based on legs only; cranium to pelvis in adjacent excavation
   unit were not excavated).
Orientation: head to the east, facing west. Long axis of burial approximately
   1–3° south of due east.
Burial pit: present
Burial form: extended, supine
Gender: undetermined
Age: undetermined
Artifacts: none recovered
Pathology: none recorded

Burial No. 6

Excavation unit: 316N/316E, a 2 m × 2 m unit excavated in 1988 season.
Opening elevation: 14.69 mmsl
Closing elevation: 14.44 mmsl
Centimeters below surface (top of cranium): 67 cm
Stratigraphic definition: Below stratum of tan and brown mottled sand, a
   mixed fill of tan and red mottled sand with inclusions of raw clay (burial pit
   fill), in matrix of white (sterile) sand. Burial 6 evidently predates Burial 5,
   as tan and brown sand stratum capping Burial 6 is intruded on by Burial 5
   pit.
Type of burial: primary
Condition: good (most elements present)
Orientation: head to the east, facing west. Long axis of skeleton approximately
   5° south of due east.
Burial pit: present
Burial form: extended, supine, arms folded over chest, hands crossed at chin.
   Head is upright against side of burial pit.

Gender: undetermined
Age: adult
Artifacts: none recovered
Pathology: none recorded

Burial No. 7

Excavation unit: 329N/319E, a 2 m × 2 m unit excavated in 1988 season.
Opening elevation: 15.16 mmsl
Closing elevation: 14.86 mmsl
Centimeters below surface (top of cranium): 58 cm
Stratigraphic definition: In stratum of tan and white mottled sand, a mixed fill of gray, brown, and white mottled sand with inclusions of raw clay (burial pit fill) down to white (sterile) sand.
Type of burial: primary
Condition: fair (bones somewhat soft)
Orientation: head to the east, facing west. Orientation of the long axis is approximately 5° south of due east.
Burial pit: present but difficult to distinguish because of highly mottled (disturbed?) associated strata. Pit may originate just below modern humus (15–20 cmbs) and intrude through original humus and mixed cultural stratum which contains a number of artifacts and faunal remains including alligator bone.
Burial form: extended, supine, head upright against side of burial pit.
Gender: undetermined
Age: 12–18 years (estimated)
Artifacts: single blue glass seed bead (FS 834) found in waterscreened soil from neck region.
Pathology: none recorded

Burial No. 8

Excavation unit: 303N/307E, a 2 m × 3 m unit excavated in the 1989 season.
Opening elevation: 14.84 mmsl
Closing elevation: 14.47 mmsl
Centimeters below surface (top of cranium): 50 cm
Stratigraphic definition: Below modern humus and lense of displaced original humus, mixed fills of tan and white mottled sand and numerous inclusions of raw clay and concretions (burial pit fill), in matrix of tan and white (sterile) sand. Burial 8 is intrusive on Burial 2. Cranium of Burial 8 is directly on top of Burial 2 pelvis; legs of Burial 2 are visible below Burial 8, with the feet of Burial 2 seen below the knees of Burial 8. There is no soil between the two skeletons.
Type of burial: primary

Condition: excellent
Orientation: head to the east, facing west. Long axis of skeleton is oriented approximately 3° south of due east.
Burial pit: present; burial excavated within pit. Remnant of undisturbed wider burial pit for Burial 2 also evident to the north and south of Burial 8 pit.
Burial form: extended, supine. Cranium is upright against side of burial pit. Arms folded across chest, hands crossed at chin.
Gender: female, based on subpubic angle, brow ridge, jaw line, and sacral notch.
Age: 35–45 years
Artifacts: none recovered
Pathology: none recorded

Burial No. 9
Excavation unit: 310N/311E, a 1 m × 4 m trench excavated in the 1989 season
Opening elevation: 14.97 mmsl
Closing elevation: 14.77 mmsl (excavation stopped at top of cranium)
Centimeters below surface (top of cranium): 50 cm
Stratigraphic definition: Below stratum of tan and gray mottled sand (original humus and mixed cultural stratum) and through stratum of tan, gray, and white mottled sand (subhumus, old root zone), a mixed fill of tan, brown, and gray mottled sand with numerous raw clay inclusions and chunks of limestone (burial pit fill) in matrix of white (sterile) sand.
Type of burial: undetermined (excavation stopped at top of cranium)
Condition: undetermined
Orientation: head to the east, facing west
Burial pit: present
Burial form: undetermined
Gender: undetermined
Age: undetermined
Artifacts: none recovered
Pathology: none recorded

Burial No. 10
Excavation unit: 306N/310E, a 1 m × 4 m trench excavated in the 1989 season
Opening elevation: 14.88 mmsl
Closing elevation: 14.34 mmsl
Centimeters below surface (top of cranium): 70 cm
Stratigraphic definition: Below stratum of tan and gray mottled sand (original humus and mixed cultural stratum) and through stratum of tan, gray, and

white mottled sand (subhumus, or old root zone), a mixed fill of tan to orange sand with numerous raw clay inclusions (burial pit fill), in matrix of white (sterile) sand. Burial 10 is intrusive on Burial 11.

Type of burial: primary

Condition: good

Orientation: head to the east, facing west

Burial pit: present, intrusive on Burial 11 pit

Burial form: extended (?), supine

Gender: undetermined

Age: undetermined

Artifacts: none recovered

Pathology: an 8-cm diameter concavity noted on top of frontal bone near coronal suture, with thin fracture extending from concavity to area of right eye socket

Burial No. 11

Excavation unit: 306N/310E, a 1 m × 4 m trench excavated in the 1989 season

Opening elevation: 14.88 mmsl

Closing elevation: 14.42 mmsl

Centimeters below surface (top of cranium): 70 cm

Stratigraphic definition: Below stratum of brown to gray mottled sand (displaced original humus?) and through stratum of tan, gray, and white mottled sand (subhumus, or old root zone), a mixed fill of tan, brown, and gray mottled sand with numerous inclusions of raw clay and chunks of limestone (burial pit fill), in matrix of white (sterile) sand. Burial 11 is intruded on by Burial 10, and the right ilium of Burial 11 was dug through and displaced as the result of the original excavation of the Burial 10 pit.

Type of burial: primary

Condition: good

Orientation: head to the east, facing west. Long axis of Burial 11 is oriented approximately 3° south of due east.

Burial pit: present

Burial form: extended, supine. Arms folded across chest, hands clasped at chin.

Gender: male (?)

Age: adult (?)

Artifacts: none recovered

Pathology: none recorded

C

Glass Beads from the 1988–1989 Fig Springs Excavations

✛   Kidd and Kidd is a standard
classification system for archaeological bead collections. See Kidd and Kidd
1970.

Dates, where provided, are taken from Deagan 1987, Table 4.

Description: Ichtucknee Blue
    Kidd and Kidd: drawn IIa40
    Manufacture: simple
    Form: oval to spherical with flat ends
    Diaphaneity: opaque
    Length (range in mm): 5–8 mm
    Weight (range in g): .2–.7 g
    Count/percentage of total collection: 19/11.6 percent
    Proveniences: church (1), convento (1), aboriginal structure (12), midden (5)
    Dates: 1575–1720

Description: Cobalt Blue Seed
    Kidd and Kidd: drawn IIa, drawn Ia
    Manufacture: simple
    Form: ring, doughnut, oval, spherical
    Diaphaneity: translucent
    Length (range in mm): 1–3 mm
    Weight (range in g): .1–.2 g
    Count/percentage of total collection: 109/66.1 percent
    Proveniences: church (1), convento (1), cemetery (burial 7)(1), aboriginal
        structure (106)
    Dates: 1550–1800

Description: Aqua Seed
  Kidd and Kidd: drawn Ia, IIa
  Manufacture: simple
  Form: ring, doughnut, oval
  Diaphaneity: opaque
  Length (range in mm): 1–3 mm
  Weight (range in g): .1 g
  Count/percentage of total collection: 4/2.5 percent
  Proveniences: aboriginal structure (4)
  Dates: 1550–1800

Description: Brown Seed
  Kidd and Kidd: drawn Ia, IIa
  Manufacture: simple
  Form: oval, doughnut, ring
  Diaphaneity: translucent
  Length (range in mm): 1.5–3 mm
  Weight (range in g): .1–.2 g
  Count/percentage of total collection: 4/2.5 percent
  Proveniences: aboriginal structure (4)
  Dates: 1550–1800

Description: Clear Seed
  Kidd and Kidd: drawn Ia
  Manufacture: simple
  Form: oval, ring
  Diaphaneity: transparent
  Length (range in mm): 1.5 mm
  Weight (range in g): .2 g
  Count/percentage of total collection: 4/2.5 percent
  Proveniences: aboriginal structure (4, Feature 16 only)
  Dates: ?

Description: Amber Seed
  Kidd and Kidd: drawn Ia
  Manufacture: simple
  Form: ring
  Diaphaneity: translucent
  Length (range in mm): 1 mm
  Weight (range in g): .1 g
  Count/percentage of total collection: 2/1.3 percent

Proveniences: aboriginal structure (Features 32 and 33 only)
Dates: 1550–1800

Description: Purple Seed
    Kidd and Kidd: drawn IIa
    Manufacture: simple
    Form: doughnut
    Diaphaneity: opaque
    Length (range in mm): 1 mm
    Weight (range in g): .1 g
    Count/percentage of total collection: 1/.7 percent
    Provenience: aboriginal structure (Feature 42 only)
    Dates: ?

Description: Yellow Seed
    Kidd and Kidd: drawn Ia
    Manufacture: simple
    Form: tube (?)
    Diaphaneity: translucent
    Length (range in mm): 1 mm
    Weight (range in g): .1 g
    Count/percentage of total collection: 1/.7 percent
    Provenience: aboriginal structure (Feature 16 only)
    Dates: 1550–1800

Description: Green Wire-wound
    Kidd and Kidd: W1b
    Manufacture: simple
    Form: spherical
    Diaphaneity: translucent
    Length (range in mm): 4.5–5 mm
    Weight (range in g): .3–.5 g
    Count/percentage of total collection: 2/1.3 percent
    Proveniences: aboriginal structure (Feature 32), aboriginal village (Auger
      Test 130N/250E)
    Dates: 1630–1800

Description: Black Drawn, heat-altered
    Kidd and Kidd: drawn IIa
    Manufacture: simple
    Form: oval

Diaphaneity: opaque
Length (range in mm): 5 mm
Weight (range in g): .2 g
Count/percentage of total collection: 1/.7 percent
Provenience: aboriginal structure (Feature 30 only)
Dates: ?

Description: Blue Drawn
    Kidd and Kidd: drawn IIa
    Manufacture: simple
    Form: spherical, oval, barrel
    Diaphaneity: translucent
    Length (range in mm): 6–8 mm
    Weight (range in g): .3–.4 g
    Count/percentage of total collection: 3/1.9 percent
    Proveniences: aboriginal structure (Feature 16, Feature 65, and occupation stratum)
    Dates: ?

Description: Aqua Drawn
    Kidd and Kidd: drawn IIa
    Manufacture: simple
    Form: oval, one specimen distorted into "peanut" shape
    Diaphaneity: opaque
    Length (range in mm): 3–12 mm
    Weight (range in g): .1–.4 g
    Count/percentage of total collections: 2/1.3 percent
    Proveniences: aboriginal structure (Feature 32 and occupation stratum)
    Dates: ?

Description: Green Drawn
    Kidd and Kidd: drawn IIa
    Manufacture: simple
    Form: oval
    Diaphaneity: translucent
    Length (range in mm): 7 mm
    Weight (range in g): .3 g
    Count/percentage of total collection: 1/.7 percent
    Provenience: aboriginal structure (occupation stratum)
    Dates: ?

Description: Clear Drawn
Kidd and Kidd: drawn IIa
Manufacture: simple
Form: spherical
Diaphaneity: transparent
Length (range in mm): 3 mm
Weight (range in g): .1 g
Count/percentage of total collection: 1/.7 percent
Provenience: aboriginal structure (Feature 60)
Dates: ?

Description: Brown Drawn
Kidd and Kidd: drawn IIa
Manufacture: simple
Form: spherical-doughnut
Diaphaneity: translucent
Length (range in mm): 5 mm
Weight (range in g): .4 g
Count/percentage of total collection: 1/.7 percent
Provenience: aboriginal structure (Feature 16)
Dates: ?

Description: Aqua Tube
Kidd and Kidd: drawn Ia
Manufacture: simple
Form: tube
Diaphaneity: opaque
Length (range in mm): 3 mm
Weight (range in g): .2 g
Count/percentage of total collection: 1/.7 percent
Provenience: convento
Dates: 1550–1800

Description: Amber Tube (possibly burnt)
Kidd and Kidd: drawn IIa
Manufacture: simple
Form: spherical, flat ends
Diaphaneity: translucent
Length (range in mm): 5 mm
Weight (range in g): .4 g

Count/percentage of total collection: 1/.7 percent
Proveniences: aboriginal structure (Feature 32)
Dates: ?

Description: Green Oval, heat-altered
 Kidd and Kidd: drawn IIa (?)
 Manufacture: simple
 Form: oval
 Diaphaneity: translucent
 Length (range in mm): 9 mm
 Weight (range in g): .5 g
 Count/percentage of total collection: 1/.7 percent
 Provenience: aboriginal structure (Feature 43)
 Dates: ? (similar to bead in FMNH-type collection from mound in Seminole
 County)

Description: Gilded Fluted
 Kidd and Kidd: ?
 Manufacture: simple
 Form: spherical, flat ends
 Diaphaneity: transparent, gilded
 Length (range in mm): 5 mm
 Weight (range in g): .3 g
 Count/percentage of total collection: 1/.7 percent
 Provenience: aboriginal structure (occupation stratum)
 Dates: 1550–1750

Description: Gilded Amber
 Kidd and Kidd: IIb
 Manufacture: simple
 Form: spherical
 Diaphaneity: transparent, gilded
 Length (range in mm): 6 mm
 Weight (range in g): .5 g
 Count/percentage of total collection: 1/.7 percent
 Provenience: cemetery (stratum above Burial 8)
 Dates: ?

Description: Burnt Glass Bead
 Kidd and Kidd: drawn ?
 Manufacture: ?
 Form: spherical

Diaphaneity: opaque
Length (range in mm): 7 mm
Weight (range in g): .7 g
Count/percentage of total collection: 1/.7 percent
Provenience: aboriginal structure (Feature 10, cooking or roasting pit)
Dates: if originally clear, possibly 1525–1600

Description: Heat altered, 5-layered blue, red, white, blue, and
dark blue chevron
    Kidd and Kidd: IVn
    Manufacture: compound
    Form: heat-altered fusing of two(?) beads
    Diaphaneity: opaque
    Length (range in mm): 12 mm
    Weight (range in g): 4.9 g
    Count/percentage of total assemblage: 1/.7 percent
    Provenience: auger test 420N/300E, presumed village context but no
      associated artifacts found.
    Dates: 1550–1650

Description: Blue Faceted
    Kidd and Kidd: WIIc or Ic
    Manufacture: simple
    Form: oval
    Diaphaneity: translucent
    Length (range in mm): 9 mm
    Weight: (range in g): .6 g
    Count/percentage of total assemblage: 1/.7 percent
    Provenience: convento
    Dates: 1500–1800 (if drawn), 1700–1800 (if wire-wound)

Description: Wire-wound (?) Cobalt Seed
    Kidd and Kidd: ?
    Manufacture: ?
    Form: doughnut
    Diaphaneity: transparent
    Length (range in mm): 2 mm
    Weight (range in g): .2 g
    Count/percentage of total assemblage: 1/.7 percent
    Provenience: aboriginal structure (occupation stratum, associated artifacts
      include an Ichtucknee Blue bead)
    Dates: ?

D

Revised Aboriginal Ceramic Typology for the Timucua Mission Province

John E. Worth

+   THIS REVISION OF THE EXISTING aboriginal ceramic typology for the Timucua Province of North Florida during the first half of the seventeenth century was initiated as a part of the long-term excavations at the Fig Springs site (8Co1), under the direction of Brent Weisman. On the basis of aboriginal ceramics recovered at Fig Springs, as well as comparative collections from other sites in the region that date to this period, the existing ceramic typology is unable to provide an effective analytical framework (see the discussion in Milanich et al. 1984).

A major factor in the revision of the existing typology was the recognition that most of the aboriginal ceramics recovered from Fig Springs were tempered with crushed sherds, or grog. This prompted a reevaluation of the utility of forcing both grit- and grog-tempered forms of the same surface treatment into a single type. The primary ceramic type in which grog dominates is a complicated stamped ware, which has gone under several names since its recognition in the 1940s. Hale Smith (1948) was the first to describe the complex of aboriginal ceramic types present on mission-period sites in Northwest Florida, and he characterized this assemblage as the Leon-Jefferson period. As the name implies, this description was based on collections from the Fort Walton area, specifically from the Scott Miller site (8Je2), a Spanish mission in the Apalachee Province in the vicinity of present-day Tallahassee. Willey (1949:488–495) subsequently adopted Smith's Leon-Jefferson period, and in this seminal description he affirms its basis in Northwest Florida collections.

Early work on the mission period in the North and North-Central Florida regions was marked by the recovery between 1949 and 1952 of a large collection of aboriginal and Spanish artifacts from the springs at Fig Springs by John Goggin and his students. This project resulted in the identification of aboriginal ceramics, which remained unclassified in 1953, when Goggin (1953:10) simply noted the predominance of "plain sherd-tempered ware, and complicated stamped sherd-tempered ware," which he noted had "not been adequately classified or tabulated." With regard to these ceramics, Goggin suggested that they "may be related to Jefferson ware, but are distinct."

Clearly, Goggin recognized the unusual character of this pottery. When these collections were finally subjected to intensive analysis almost twenty years later, Deagan classified the majority of this pottery as belonging to the Jefferson Series (Deagan 1972:28), while noting that "the Jefferson ceramics from Fig Springs differ from those of northwest Florida Leon-Jefferson sites, where clay tempering seems to be present only occasionally" (Deagan 1972:32) The classification of Fig Springs complicated stamped pottery as Jefferson ware followed earlier precedent for North-Central Florida, for Symes and Stephens (1965) had come to the same conclusion regarding the aboriginal ceramics at the contemporaneous Fox Pond site (8A272). Milanich (1971; 1972) reaffirmed this identification for both Fox Pond and the Richardson site within the Potano province, and Loucks (1979) also classified ceramics from the Baptizing Spring site in the Timucua Province within the Jefferson typology.

In sum, while the original identification of the Leon-Jefferson period and its complicated stamped ceramics was limited to the Northwest Florida region of the seventeenth-century Apalachee Province, and although Goggin apparently recognized that the North Florida equivalent of this assemblage was distinctive, researchers during the 1960s and 1970s expanded the Leon-Jefferson typology to both the North and North-Central Florida regions. This step has, in effect, linked the mission-period complicated stamped wares of the two regions under a single name. In addition, whereas the original published descriptions of Jefferson paste were never revised to incorporate the heavy grog temper in the North and North-Central Florida region, such a revision was implicit within the expansion of the Jefferson typology to include regions beyond Northwest Florida.

In his recent typology for the Fort Walton area, John Scarry (1985:222) recognized the overwhelming similarity of the Northwest Florida Jefferson Complicated Stamped pottery and the type Lamar Complicated Stamped. As a result, he subsumed the old Jefferson ware within the Lamar type name. This move was obviously a logical step for the Fort Walton area, but it effectively mandated a review of the situation in North and North-Central Florida. Although the complicated stamped ceramics in Northwest Florida were similar enough to established Lamar types to suggest the Lamar name, the great majority of such pottery in North and North-Central Florida is in fact tempered with large amounts of grog and thus sufficiently distinct from the Lamar series to exclude it from this category. Indeed the very fact that some grit-tempered Lamar ceramics were recognized within the predominantly grog-tempered collections at Fig Springs demonstrates that the latter cannot be classified as Lamar.

Intensive analysis of the Fig Springs collections revealed, in addition, that a number of different surface treatments were represented on grog-tempered vessels, including not only complicated stamping but also check stamping, incising, and most of the local prehistoric surface treatments of the Alachua tradition to the south. In fact, most types and varieties of sand- and grit-tempered pottery at Fig Springs possess a grog-tempered counterpart, although the ratio of grog to grit temper is by no means identical for each type. The existing typology is clearly unable to address the question of grog tempering without resorting to the use of modes, which would violate most if not all of the original type descriptions for the grit-tempered types involved.

The major advance of this revised typology is the creation of a category for these grog-tempered ceramics. There is ample precedent for such a move, and two major examples appear within the State of Florida. Both the St. Johns and Pasco series were defined and set apart on the basis of paste or, more specifically, temper. Goggin (1948:5–9) described these types on the basis of their easily sortable pastes (chalky sponge spicules and leached-out limestone chunks), and these types remain today, although their geographic and temporal distribution is vast indeed. While grog-tempered sherds are somewhat less rapidly sorted, the occurrence of this new series in North and North-Central Florida is apparently quite restricted, appearing only during the mission period and even then with limited distribution within the Spanish mission system.

For the new typology, all grog-tempered ceramic types will be classified within a single series—the Jefferson Series. The use of the original name is based on the fact that a large portion of the ceramics (that is, those from North and North-Central Florida), which have for years been classified under Smith's original Jefferson series, are in fact grog tempered, and thus will remain under the same name. The effective result of Scarry's (1985) typological revisions, combined with those proposed in this article, is to subdivide the original Jefferson Series (as broadly applied in the 1960s and 1970s) into two series, one grit tempered and thus classified as Lamar, and one grog tempered and thus still classified as Jefferson.

Although Smith's original description of Jefferson paste (1948:317) will no longer fully apply to the proposed definition of the Jefferson Series as grog tempered, this original definition actually has been obsolete since the Jefferson name was applied to grog-tempered ceramics in the 1960s and 1970s. Within the revised typology, the Jefferson name will apply to much of the same pottery as before (as well as to several minority surface treatments on the same paste). In fact, for the North and North-Central Florida region, the Jefferson Series will still connote the mission-period aboriginal assemblage, whereas this is no longer the case in Northwest Florida.

Some scholars may argue that such a major revision in the existing ceramic typology, based on grog temper, is unwarranted, but it seems clear that the significance, if any, of grog temper in the mission period cannot be determined if the existing typological framework is inadequate for such analysis. This revised typology will permit detailed examination of this problem. Further typological revisions presented here primarily constitute refinement and expansion of the existing typology, based on new data, although in one case, a new series with three new types is defined for a previously unrecognized shell-tempered ware present at Fig Springs and other regional sites. In addition, a new ceramic series is defined for the late prehistoric period in North Florida, including one new ceramic type and several types also within the Alachua tradition of North-Central Florida (Milanich 1971). In general, the goal of the present revision of the aboriginal ceramic typology for this region of Florida is to provide a simplified and logical analytical framework that better represents the data in hand and may easily be expanded with future research.

The provisional typology is presented below, followed by a discussion of its potential significance to mission-period research.

Provisional Typology

Suwannee Valley Series

The Suwannee Valley Series represents the regional late prehistoric ceramic assemblage for North Florida. Although this assemblage possesses a number of typological similarities to the Alachua tradition of North-Central Florida (Milanich 1971), the ceramics recovered in the southern portion of the Fig Springs site, both in the auger survey (Weisman 1988a) and test excavations in 1989, appears sufficiently distinct to be classified as a separate regional ceramic series. Previously, the unusual post-Weeden Island ceramics of North Florida were characterized as Weeden Island II (Milanich et al. 1984). Recent survey work in North Florida (Johnson 1987; Johnson and Nelson 1990) has resulted in the initial clarification of the late prehistoric ceramic assemblage in this region. On the basis of a number of seriations across North Florida, Johnson and Nelson (1990) identify the Indian Pond complex as distinct from the Alachua tradition to the south.

Many ceramic types and varieties described here are present in both regions, but the percentages of specific types within each complex vary considerably. With the present addition of one major new type and the refinement of the existing typology for the Alachua tradition to reflect regional characteristics, a new typological framework may be defined for North Florida: the Suwannee Valley Series. This step will effectively serve both to recognize the typological similarity between the ceramics of each region and to facilitate comparisons and contrasts regarding the differences that are apparent. As a result, the late prehistoric ceramic assemblages of North-Central and North Florida will be classified within the Alachua Series and the Suwannee Valley Series respectively. Although ceramics of the Alachua and Suwannee Valley Series are more similar to one another than to any contemporaneous ceramic assemblages in adjacent regions, they will remain typologically separate for the present time. If other regional variants are recognized in the future, the Suwannee Valley Series may be subdivided or expanded as data warrant.

The Suwannee Valley Series will be defined primarily on the basis of ceramic collections excavated from the apparently single-component occupation at the south end of the Fig Springs village. Collections from the Richardson site (Milanich 1972) and other early seventeenth-century occupations in the North-Central Florida region were also examined for comparative purposes.

The Suwannee Valley Series as a whole is characterized by a limited range of simple vessel forms generally decorated over the entire vessel surface with one or more of a variety of surface treatments apparently designed to roughen the exterior of each vessel. Vessels were impressed or scraped with items commonly available within any village, including corncobs, cord or twine, bundles of straw or sticks, fabric, and perhaps comblike tools. The clay was tempered with

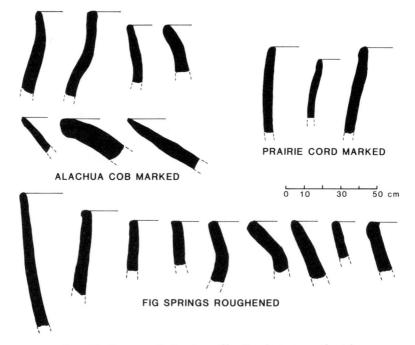

FIG. 75. *Suwannee Series rim profiles. Vessel interiors to the right.*

moderate to large amounts of sand or grit, and formed into either simple bowls or jars ranging from conoidal forms with slightly incurvate rims to jars with straight or slightly flaring rims (fig. 75). Vessel-wall thickness typically ranges from 6 to 9 mm, averaging roughly 7 mm. Vessel lips are simple, either flattened or rounded, and no appendages are known. Vessels were occasionally drilled just below the rim, presumably to provide for suspension of the vessel.

Although the Suwannee Valley Series, as defined here, presents an overall coherence in terms of paste, vessel form, and decoration, individual type descriptions are presented below in order to illuminate the distinctions that are apparent.

Alachua Cob Marked

Alachua Cob Marked has surface decoration consisting of corncob impressions, typically applied over the entire vessel surface, though occasionally only around the neck. Cob markings are often partially erased or modified by smoothing. The type conforms to Milanich's (1971:32) description of Alachua Cob Marked.

Var. Alachua is a variety conforming in all respects to Alachua Cob Marked (Milanich 1971:32; and see Scarry 1985:210) and is characterized by cob impressions over the entire surface of the vessel. The conoidal jar form is known for this variety, as is a wide, shallow bowl form with a drilled hole below the rim.

Prairie Cord Marked

Prairie Cord Marked possesses surface decoration consisting of cord impressions over the entire surface of the vessel and includes the type Prairie Cord Marked described by Milanich (1971:33). Cord impressions are typically more or less vertical with respect to the lip, but cross-stamping occurs frequently, often almost obliterating the linear cord patterns. Cords are generally comparatively thick, ranging from 1 to 2 mm (typically closer to 2 mm), and are almost always tightly spaced, although some cords are separated by as much as 5 mm. Vessel forms for this type are remarkably consistent at Fig Springs—only the conoidal jar with slightly incurvate rim is known. Cord marking appears all the way up to the lip of the vessel, which ranges from rounded to flattened.

Var. Prairie is currently the only recognized variety of Prairie Cord Marked present during the early seventeenth century. It conforms to Milanich's (1971:33) Prairie Cord Marked. Although his Prairie Punctated-over-Cord Marked is considered a separate variety of Prairie Cord Marked, it has not been recognized this late in either region. There is evidence for roughening or brushing over some cord impressions, but until further examples come to light no variety will be defined for this treatment.

Lochloosa Punctated

Lochloosa Punctated is marked by surface treatment consisting of apparently random punctations applied over the entire surface of the vessel and thus incorporates the original type Lochloosa Punctated (Milanich 1971:33–34). Punctations are typically heavy and may be randomly spaced or tightly packed (see varieties below). Rims are rare at Fig Springs, and thus known vessel forms include only the simple bowl.

Var. Lochloosa conforms to the type Lochloosa Punctated (Milanich 1971:33–34) and is characterized by random punctations or clusters of punctations with some blank space in between. There is often evidence of dragging or brushing in and around the punctations and spaces between them (see fig. 61).

Var. Grassy Flats, a new variety, is characterized by densely packed heavy punctations with no space between and no evidence of dragging or brushing. The entire surface appears stippled due to the mauling by bunches of straw or sticks (see fig. 60).

Prairie Fabric Impressed

Prairie Fabric Impressed has impressions of woven fabric over the entire vessel surface and conforms to the type Prairie Fabric Impressed defined by Milanich (1971:35–36). It is difficult to distinguish from Prairie Cord Marked, especially when overstamped, but the presence of woven patterns of cord marks it. No varieties have been defined for this type.

Fig Springs Roughened

A new type, Fig Springs Roughened constitutes a major portion of the Suwannee Valley Series in North Florida and as such represents the major departure of the Suwannee Valley Series from the Alachua tradition ceramic assemblage to the south. It is characterized by an apparently brushed or scraped decoration of parallel grooves, frequently crossed. In overall appearance, the decoration of this type is coherent, yet closer examination reveals at least two varieties of this brushing, one of which is visually similar to simple stamped wares. After extensive consideration, this form of decoration was classified as roughened in order to preserve the similarity in visual effect without addressing the precise manufacturing technique. There is historical precedent for the use of the term "roughened" for such decoration, as in the case of the type Walnut Roughened (Jennings and Fairbanks 1939). It is my opinion that neither variety was created in a manner consistent with the term "simple stamped," but the name Fig Springs Roughened should avoid confusion in this area. Vessel forms include a simple bowl form and an apparently conoidal jar form, sometimes with a slightly flaring rim. Two examples of drilling below the rim are known.

Although most sherds may be classified as one or the other of the two varieties described below, some sherds are indistinct and must be classified as Fig Springs Roughened, variety unspecified.

Var. Ichetucknee is marked by wide (ca. 2 mm), evenly spaced parallel grooves, which are generally clear and bold, and often have striations within the grooves (usually two smaller grooves on either side). The visual effect of this variety gives an initial impression of a simple stamped decoration (see fig. 60), but it is more likely that this decoration is the result of a toothed tool, or perhaps a comb with wide spines, being dragged across the clay surface and partially smoothed over in some cases.

Var. Santa Fe is marked by narrow grooves, which are applied in a more random fashion, generally less parallel, less evenly spaced (typically between 2 and 4 mm), and ranging from very light brushing (usually) to heavier incisions, occasionally quite deep (though still applied in a similarly random manner). This variety is far more similar to classic brushed wares and, as such, may have been made by bundles of pinestraw, or even a fine-toothed-comblike tool in some cases (see fig. 60). One example has been recovered of a jar of this variety with a row of pinches on the vessel surface below the lip.

Alachua Plain

The type Alachua Plain conforms to the same type described by Milanich (1971:31–32) and is marked by undecorated sherds with the same paste and vessel forms described above for the Suwannee Valley Series.

Lamar Series

The Lamar ceramic series corresponds to those types originally described for the Lamar culture in middle Georgia (Jennings and Fairbanks 1939). These original types were characterized by a number of distinctive features, yet the temper of Lamar pottery types was uniformly described as moderate to abundant amounts of medium to coarse grit. While Hale Smith (1948) noted that his complicated stamped Jefferson ware, defined for mission-period sites in Northwest Florida, possessed a "strong correlation with the Late Lamar stamped ware of Georgia" (Smith 1948:317), but it was not until Scarry's (1985) work that this relationship led to the characterization of mission-period complicated stamped ceramics in the Fort Walton area as Lamar Complicated Stamped (Scarry 1985:222). Ceramics corresponding to the Lamar Complicated Stamped and Plain paste-and-style descriptions are uncommon in North-Central Florida mission contexts, but they do comprise a small percentage of recovered collections.

In addition to these types, other associated ceramic types have here been subsumed within the Lamar Series on the basis of similarities (both in paste and style) to corresponding types in classic Lamar assemblages from Georgia. Specific details for each type are provided below.

Lamar Complicated Stamped

The type Lamar Complicated Stamped conforms to the original type of the same name, described by Jennings and Fairbanks (1939). Although no concrete evidence for vessel form has yet been recognized for this type, it seems likely that some form of the flaring rim jar is represented. Only a single variety has been recognized for this type because the collection is small.

Var. Early has concentric circles, or "bull's-eye" design, conforming to the same type and variety described by Scarry (1985:222).

Lamar Check Stamped

Lamar Check Stamped was created in recognition of the similarity in paste and vessel-wall thickness of these check-stamped varieties with other Lamar types. In addition, the presence of check stamping in the context of several Late Lamar assemblages in western Georgia suggests the inclusion of these check-stamped varieties within the Lamar series.

Var. Leon corresponds to the type Leon Check Stamped, *var. Leon* described by Scarry (1985:225). Checks are generally in a diamond configuration, of ca. 1 cm or slightly less, and are frequently marked by raised dots in the center, giving the surface a sort of "pineapple" appearance (see fig. 62). Stamping ranges from bold and clear to light and indistinct. There is no clear evidence for the vessel form of this variety.

Var. Fort White, a new variety, is quite distinctive. It is characterized by extremely broad checks, generally ranging between 1.5 and 2.1 cm in width (see fig. 62). Stamping is uniformly light, and checks are almost perfectly square, with narrow lands (ca. 2 mm). No vessel forms are known for this variety.

Lamar Incised

Lamar Incised includes the original Lamar Bold Incised described by Jennings and Fairbanks (1939). Following Knight (1985:189–90), both bold and fine forms of incised decoration will be subsumed under the single type name Lamar Incised, with varieties serving to distinguish between wide- and narrow-incised decoration. Although stylistic analysis of the designs created by such incision is impossible using the small collections available, such evaluation seems best suited for the sub-*variety* level (and thus beyond the scope of the present typology), particularly due to the level of variation in freehand designs created individually for each vessel.

Lamar Incised vessels appear to be restricted to the carinated bowl form. Paste is typically finer than other Lamar types, and surfaces are generally smoothed if not burnished. Incised decoration is generally curvilinear in form, and apparently conforms in general to that described for Scarry's (1985:221,227) corresponding types.

Var. Columbia is marked by bold incision (2 mm +) and conforms to the type Lamar Bold Incised, described by Scarry (1985:221).

Var. Ocmulgee Fields is marked by narrow incision, and corresponds to the same type and variety described by Knight (1985:190) and to the type Ocmulgee Fields described by Scarry (1985:227).

Lamar Plain

The type Lamar Plain, although it undoubtedly constitutes a major portion of any Lamar assemblage, is somewhat problematic in terms of distinguishing body sherds of this type from those of Alachua Plain. The presence of folded and pinched or punctated rims in the Lamar style serves to characterize rim sherds, but only the paste may be utilized with other sherds. In general, Lamar Plain sherds possess coarser grit temper than the sand temper of Alachua Plain. In addition, Lamar sherds tend to be smoother-surfaced and thicker, and the Lamar vessel forms such as the flaring-rim jar and carinated bowl apparently have no correlate within the Suwannee Valley Series. Although these types may be problematic, their excavated context may provide a solution, for Lamar sherds seem to occur only in association with mission-period Jefferson assemblages, and there only in small quantities.

Jefferson Series

The new Jefferson Series includes all grog-tempered aboriginal ceramics, regardless of surface treatment. Grog is present in moderate to large quantities within the clay paste. Particles range from fine to coarse (>2mm) in size, and typically appear in shades of tan, cream, or orange in contrast to the darker surrounding matrix. Occasional mineral inclusions, such as quartz particles, do appear within grog-tempered sherds but are almost always rounded and probably naturally present within the clay source. Although several Jefferson types possess surface treatments that correspond to local prehistoric wares, there is apparently no regional prehistoric correlate for the heavy grog temper of Jefferson paste.

For effective sorting of these types from their grit-tempered counterparts, sherds, particularly sherd edges, must be well cleaned. Initial examination should be under a bright direct light (sunlight seems particularly effective). Whereas grit-tempered sherds tend to sparkle because of the abundant angular mineral fragments within the clay, grog-tempered sherds only rarely possess any reflective particles. Instead, light-colored patches appear within the darker clay, and although their texture is generally identical to the surrounding clay, there is frequent evidence of flat surfaces on grog particles, almost certainly portions of the surfaces of crushed sherds. When initial examination proves insufficient, sherds should be lightly dampened, which proves effective in bringing out the color contrasts.

Jefferson Series vessels as a group are generally thicker-walled than Suwannee Valley types, typically ranging from 7 to 10 mm in thickness, and often around 8 or 9 mm. Vessel forms are diverse, and include carinated and hemispherical bowls as well as flaring-rim and straight-neck jars. Rims are generally simple, but flaring-rim jars are often folded and pinched in the Lamar fashion (fig. 76). As a rule, Jefferson vessels exhibit more and sharper breaks in

JEFFERSON SERIES

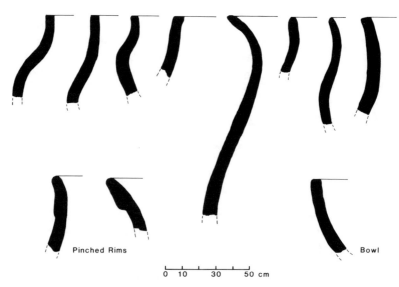

Pinched Rims

Bowl

0   10   30   50 cm

FIG. 76. *Jefferson rim profiles. Vessel interiors to the right.*

profile, typically around the neck and shoulder, than do vessels of the earlier Suwannee Valley Series. In addition, sherds tend to be smoother on the exterior surfaces and possess sharper edges on the fractures than Suwannee Valley sherds, perhaps because of the paste composition or firing temperature.

Jefferson Complicated Stamped

The new type Jefferson Complicated Stamped corresponds in most respects to the original type Lamar Complicated Stamped (Jennings and Fairbanks 1939), of course excluding temper. Vessels are boldly stamped with a variety of designs, described below, and stamping extends all the way up to the lip of the vessel (or to the base of the rim fold). Two forms of jars are represented for this type—the flaring-rim jar and the straight-neck jar (see fig. 76). Flaring-rim jars typically possess simple rims, although folded and pinched rims are occasionally present. The straight-neck jar is always marked by a simple rim.

Var. Early has concentric circles, or bull's-eye design (see fig. 64), conforming to the same variety described by Scarry (1985:222–23). It is extremely common in this region.

Var. Jefferson has nested parallelograms, conforming to the same variety described by Scarry (1985:222–23). It is very uncommon in this region.

Var. Curlee has a herringbone design, heavily overstamped and poorly defined, conforming to the same variety described by Scarry (1985:222–23). It is very uncommon in this region.

Var. Fig Springs has an unusual design consisting of rectilinear borders around large, raised dots, apparently in sets of threes (see fig. 64). This design was first described by Deagan (1972:28–29). It is uncommon but present at several contemporaneous sites.

Var. Baptizing Spring has a design consisting of nested crosses, generally rectilinear in execution but occasionally rounded (see fig. 64). This design was first described by Loucks (1979). Further work may permit the rounded form to be classified as a separate variety. This variety is comparatively common, second only to *var. Early*.

Var. Suwannee has a design consisting of interlocking waves of four parallel lines around a central, raised oval (see fig. 64). Loucks (1979:202) characterized this design as "interlocking circles." It is uncommon but present at several sites.

Jefferson Check Stamped

The new type Jefferson Check Stamped corresponds to the grit-tempered Lamar Check Stamped and as such occupies a similar position within the Jefferson Series.

Var. Leon is a variety that conforms to the type Lamar Check Stamped, *var. Leon*, in terms of surface treatment. The only vessel form recognized for this variety is the flaring-rim jar with a folded and pinched rim.

Var. Fort White is a variety that conforms to the description of the surface treatment of Lamar Check Stamped, *var. Fort White* (see fig. 64).

Jefferson Incised

The new type Jefferson Incised corresponds to the grit-tempered Lamar Incised and is subdivided on the same basis.

Var. Columbia conforms to the surface treatment of the same variety of Lamar Incised (see fig. 64).

Var. Ocmulgee Fields conforms to the surface treatment described for the same variety of Lamar Incised.

Jefferson Cob Marked

The new type Jefferson Cob Marked is characterized by essentially the same surface treatment as the type Alachua Cob Marked. The only evident distinction, save the paste, is the appearance of a flaring-rim jar form in addition to the wide, shallow bowl.

Var. Alachua conforms in all above respects to the same variety of Alachua Cob Marked.

Jefferson Punctated

The type Jefferson Punctated corresponds to the same type within the Suwannee Valley Series in terms of surface treatment, yet only one of the two varieties of Lochloosa Punctated is known for the Jefferson Series.

Var. Lochloosa is the only variety of this type recovered and apparently conforms in all respects save paste to Lochloosa Punctated, *var. Lochloosa*.

Jefferson Roughened

The surface treatment of Jefferson Roughened corresponds to the type Fig Springs Roughened. Although both varieties of Jefferson Roughened appear to fall within the range of variation in surface treatment for the same varieties of Fig Springs Roughened, there are minor differences noted below. In addition, the only vessel form currently recognized for this type is the flaring-rim jar. This type is not common at Fig Springs.

Var. Ichetucknee conforms to the same variety of Fig Springs Roughened; however the brushing is lighter in general on the few Jefferson sherds.

Var. Santa Fe corresponds to the same variety of Fig Springs Roughened, but its application is both lighter and more sparse than most examples of the sand-tempered type.

Jefferson Plain

The new type Jefferson Plain includes all grog-tempered sherds with a plain surface. Paste is identical to other types of the Jefferson Series. Vessel forms include hemispherical bowls and both straight-neck and flaring-rim jars. Folded and pinched rims are more common on Jefferson Plain flaring-rim jars than on those of Jefferson Complicated Stamped. There is some evidence for strap and lug handles on Jefferson plain vessels, and at least one small dipper with a thick handle is represented.

Goggin Series

The new Goggin ceramic series consists of three types of pottery, which are distinguished from all other North and North-Central Florida ceramics by their heavy shell temper. The Goggin Series appears to be exclusive to the historic period in this region in that it is only known from mission-period sites. Although shell-tempered ceramics in Florida are almost uniformly assumed, on the basis of proximity, to be of the Pensacola Series (see Deagan 1972:33), this appears to be miscalculated. Intensive examination of shell-tempered sherds recovered at Fig Springs demonstrates that they are apparently unrelated to the Pensacola Series or other related ceramics in southern Alabama in terms of vessel form, rim treatment, and surface decoration.

Analysis of a ceramic collection, consisting of sherds both from John Goggin's collections from Fig Springs and from recently excavated contexts within the seventeenth-century aboriginal structure and associated midden, has determined the parameters of this type. This shell-tempered pottery is most similar to the Dallas and related wares of eastern Tennessee, northwestern Georgia, and northeastern Alabama. The presence of notched appliqué strips and folded and pinched rims on flaring-rim jar forms, as well as parallel diagonal-line incising on the necks of some vessels, combined with the presence of a fine cord-marked shell-tempered ware, makes this ceramic series a striking anomaly in the North Florida region. This pottery is probably ultimately derived from a Dallas or

Dallas-related source, but it is sufficiently distinct from named types to preclude the use of Dallas-type names in describing it (David Hally and Marvin Smith, personal communication 1989).

As a result, these ceramics are here defined as a distinct series, on the bases both of their apparent dissimilarity with named ceramic types and of their remoteness from their ultimate northern point of origin. In memory of John Goggin, the pioneering Florida archaeologist who first collected ceramics of this series, and in order to detach the name of this series from any geographic implications, these shell-tempered ceramics at Fig Springs will be defined as the Goggin Series, consisting of the types described in detail below.

The Goggin Series is marked by a fine-textured paste, with moderate to large amounts of crushed-shell tempering. This shell is typically leached out on the surface, although this is not always the case with sherds recovered from the springs. In general, Goggin vessels are thin-walled compared to both the Suwannee Valley Series and the thicker Jefferson Series. Sherds of both Goggin Incised and Goggin Plain range between 4 and 5 mm in thickness, and Goggin Cord Marked is uniformly thin, typically between 4 and 4.5 mm. Sherds of all three types exhibit a similarity in paste and overall appearance that permits their inclusion within a single series, although any original cultural or historical relationship among the three has yet to be positively demonstrated.

Goggin Incised

The new type Goggin Incised is characterized by incised decoration on the necks of shell-tempered jars. Vessel forms are apparently limited to jars with restricted necks, flaring rims, and well-defined shoulders. Although the overall shape of these jars is presently unknown, they most likely resemble the flaring-rim jar or Mississippian jar forms. Incised decoration is restricted to the necks of these jars (see fig. 66) and is marked by parallel lines oriented diagonally with the lip of the vessel (in all but one case from lower left to upper right). These lines are grouped (generally in pairs), with lines 4–16 mm apart (usually around 10 mm or so). Incisions range between 1 and 2 mm in width and are often deep and always burred on the edges, indicating that the clay was still wet when incisions were carried out (unlike the Pensacola Incised decoration). All examples of Goggin Incised that include both the neck and shoulder of the jar display a row of large ovoid punctations along the break in profile at the shoulder. These punctations are 4–5 mm in size, and are spaced roughly 6–8 mm apart. No rims are known for this type, but they may resemble those of Goggin Plain.

Goggin Plain

The new type Goggin Plain is similar in vessel form (and possibly rim style as well) to Goggin Incised. Only jar forms are known, and these may be

GOGGIN PLAIN

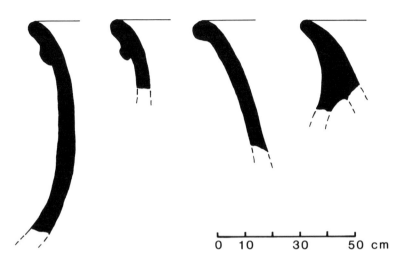

FIG. 77. *Goggin rim profiles. Vessel interiors to the right.*

characterized as flaring-rim jars or Mississippian jars with various forms of rim modification (fig. 77). Some rims possess a notched or pinched appliqué fillet strip of clay below the lip of the vessel. One such strip joins with a wide strap handle, which originates just below the lip of the jar. Other rims have a narrow, pinched or notched fold of clay at the lip of the flaring rim of the jar. In addition, some vessels appear to have a notched appliqué fillet strip of clay at the shoulder of the jar, probably in the same position as the row of punctations on Goggin Incised vessels (see fig. 66).

Goggin Cord Marked

The new type Goggin Cord Marked is perhaps the most internally coherent and distinctive type of pottery present at Fig Springs. Although its name implies a similarity to Prairie Cord Marked, the types are dissimilar both in paste and style (see fig. 65). Goggin Cord Marked is characterized by fine cord impressions over the surface of extremely thin-walled vessels. Cord thickness ranges from 0.5 mm to 1 mm, with occasional examples just under 1.5 mm, and is neatly arranged in parallel rows roughly 2 mm apart. Overstamping is common, producing a crossed effect. No rims are present to give a clue as to vessel form, but it seems clear that these vessels were not particularly small despite the thin 4–4.5 mm vessel walls. Although the paste is similar to the other Goggin Series types,

Goggin Cord Marked shows no evidence of similarity in vessel form. Such analysis must await larger sherds and collections.

Fort Walton Series

The Fort Walton Series consists of grit-tempered wares conforming to the types originally described for the Fort Walton culture (Willey 1949). The single type recognized for this region occurs only occasionally.

Fort Walton Incised

The type Fort Walton Incised is recognized by its incised and punctated surface treatment (see fig. 66). No varieties have been recognized for this region, probably because the type is rare.

St. Johns Series

All ceramics tempered with sponge spicules, regardless of surface treatment (see fig. 67), fall into the St. Johns Series, as described by Goggin (1948:5–8) for North and North-Central Florida. Ceramics of this series, while distinctive in character, remain a consistent minority in this region.

St. Johns Check Stamped

The type St. Johns Check Stamped is marked by fine check impressions, generally lightly applied on the St. Johns paste.

St. Johns Plain

The type St. Johns Plain possesses a smooth and unmarked surface and is marked by the unmistakable St. Johns chalky paste.

Discussion

The typology presented has been developed primarily on the basis of intensive analysis of the aboriginal ceramics recovered from the Fig Springs site. Existing collections from contemporaneous sites in North and North-Central Florida were additionally examined in order to expand the applicability of the typological system created at Fig Springs. Because of the undisturbed nature of this site, however, and the detailed excavations carried out in the 1988–1989 field seasons, the aboriginal ceramic collection from Fig Springs is considered uniquely suitable to be the basis for this typological revision.

Indeed, the utility of the new typology has been demonstrated in practice at Fig Springs, for it has already permitted a number of insights regarding the details of the mission period, which would have been largely impossible using the existing typology. Not only has the revised typology proved an aid in the sorting of ceramics at Fig Springs, but it has also provided a far more complete view of the fundamental differences between the late prehistoric ceramic assemblage of North and North-Central Florida and that of the mission-period provinces of Timucua and Potano. The seventeenth century witnessed a revolution in surface decoration, rim modification, vessel forms, and, particularly, ceramic technology. To the late prehistoric Suwannee Valley Series ceramic inventory was added the Lamar Series, the Jefferson Series, and the Goggin Series. The revised typology clearly indicates the merging of ceramic traditions, with Suwannee Valley surface treatments appearing on vessels with a different clay paste and vessel form. Many of these observations would have been impossible using the earlier typology.

As noted, the primary goal of this revised typology is to create a logical analytical framework, which will permit the maximum amount of information possible to be derived from aboriginal ceramic collections. Integral to this typology is the potential for expansion and refinement promised by future research. I hope that the typology proposed here will prove effective for archaeological research into the dynamics of the initial years of the Spanish mission effort in the Timucua and Potano provinces.

E

Archaeobotanical and Faunal Remains

Lee Newsom and Irvy R. Quitmyer

✛ THE 1988–1989 EXCAVATIONS AT the Fig Springs site have yielded quantities of material suitable for paleoethnobiological analysis. This investigation represents the first systematic collection of ethnobiological remains at this site. This study incorporates analyses of botanical and faunal remains from a large aboriginal structure associated with the excavated mission complex. The analysis of these materials was conducted at the Zooarchaeology Laboratory of Florida Museum of Natural History under the direction of Elizabeth S. Wing. All specimens have been deposited for permanent curation at the Zooarchaeology Lab.

Between 1949 and 1952, John Goggin and his students extracted large quantities of plant remains, degraded wood, animal remains, and other waterlogged material from Fig Springs, from the underwater portion of the site that appeared to have functioned as a refuse dump for material of Spanish-Indian origin (Deagan 1972). Because these collections of plant and animal remains were not collected with stratigraphic controls, their value is limited. This study reconciles this problem and forms a basis for further interpretive work.

Previous efforts to make systematic recoveries of faunal refuse from upland sites in Florida have been thwarted by poor bone preservation, resulting from burial in the excessively drained acidic soils predominant in this region. It is for this reason that little is known about the zooarchaeological aspect of subsistence behavior of the interior mission populations early in the seventeenth century.

Nineteen samples were analyzed for plant remains. Six of the nineteen also underwent faunal analysis. Four additional samples were processed for faunal remains only. All of the samples were extracted from features or special contexts located and defined within the confines of the aboriginal structure. This analysis did not extend to samples of general depositional context (floor/living surfaces) from the structure or to other areas of the site, which are deferred for future work.

Since the data here are derived from a limited number of contexts within a single large structure, the information they provide about foodways and environment at the mission is incomplete and does not necessarily reflect the full range of adaptation and exploitation of the environment. Insights gained from this analysis, however, add to the growing corpus of ethnobiological data and can be compared to similar studies under way at the San Luis mission, Santa Catalina de Guale, and seventeenth-century components in Spanish St. Augustine.

Data Base

Botanical Samples

The plant data are derived from two functionally specific contexts: maize cob and wood concentrations believed to have functioned as smudge pits (see, for example, C. M. Scarry 1988) and samples for subsistence and environmental data taken from hearths and midden fill. By virtue of this functional distinction, the two sample types are uneven, although complementary in terms of their information potential. Smudge pits are highly specialized depositional contexts and thus cannot be used to estimate the relative contribution of maize to other plants in the diet. Hearth and midden samples are less specialized, and a broader spectrum of remains tends to occur. These samples have the potential of providing greater insights into plant use—including fuelwood selection, diet, and crop production. Cobs from smudge pits can also be incorporated into analyses of food production strategies but must be regarded with more caution because of the selective nature of deposition (see C. M. Scarry 1988 for a complete discussion). Table 22 is a list of the samples examined for plant data.

Maize (Zea mays) Features

Seven samples of maize remains are included in this analysis. Four samples are concentrations of cobs and wood that may have functioned as smudge pits. The pits with maize cobs are nearly identical in size, roughly circular at the base, with restricted necks (see fig. 42). These four cob pits (Features 8, 11, 12, 13; Field Samples 880, 886, 888, 889) were discovered close to a dog burial located within the walls of the aboriginal structure.

A concentration of carbonized wood and cobs that defined the bottom of Feature 45 (FS 1110) is analyzed here with the four pits containing cobs because of its general similarity of contents. Two additional collections of cob remains added to the maize analytical data: a single cob from Feature 50 and two cobs from Feature 48.

One other sample with cob remains—FS 1092 "cob concentration in a larger Feature 38"—was not incorporated here because only one cob was recovered, and its condition is too poor for accurate measurement of the diagnostic features.

Table 22. Samples for Botanical Analysis from 1988–1989 excavations at Fig Springs (8Co1)

FS	FEA	Sample type	Volume (ltr)	Weight (g)
880	8	cob pit	1	
886	11	cob pit	4	
888	12	cob pit	3	
889	13	cob pit	1	
1110	45	cob pit	2	
	48	isolated cobs	—	
	50	isolated cob	—	
1057	10	posthole fill	3	150
1058	10	upper strat. hearth	27	2100
1059	10	ash assoc. with 1058	10	524
1060	10	?earlier hearth	31	1702
1066	10	trash pit/hearth	35	2973
1068	10	orig. hearth/fill	19	1363
885	10	½ feat., bulk samp.	45	—
1029	32	sherd assoc. matrix	1	—
1034	32	trash filled pit	—	150
1039	32	sherd assoc. matrix	1	—
974	22	wood sample		178
	57	carboniz. twigs	—	trace

Trash pit/hearth deposits

The contents of two large features with strata variously representative of hearths or midden fill were analyzed. Feature 32 is a midden-filled pit (see fig. 42), from which four samples were extracted for ethnobiological analysis. The fill was excavated in two sections, comprising northern and southern halves. The southern half of the deposit (FS 1034) was chosen for botanical analysis. In addition, two samples of soil/feature matrix in direct contact with large ceramic sherds were collected separately for potential analysis of jar contents. The latter samples are designated Field Samples 1029 and 1039, respectively.

Feature 10 is a large stratified pit. Distinct layers and concentrations of remains were defined in the field that are believed to represent separate episodes of midden deposition, perhaps also in-situ fire pits/hearths, and natural soil accumulation (see figs. 53, 54). Originally, half of the feature was excavated as a single bulk sample (FS 885). The exposed profile after extraction of the bulk sample facilitated the definition of stratigraphic layering in the remaining half-feature, which was then excavated by individual layers and concentrations of remains.

Only the coarsest size fraction (see methods below) from bulk sample 885 was analyzed for plant remains, and because this sample is comprised of mixed proveniences, the identifications are not treated quantitatively. All but one of the samples from the stratigraphically excavated portion of the feature were analyzed. These samples were processed and analyzed in their entirety (see methods, below). Field Sample 1067 from Feature 10 was not analyzed for plant remains because the sample is more or less a replication of another sample (two arbitrarily defined levels from the same provenience; see below).

The Feature 10 samples are defined as follows (beginning with the uppermost stratum):

FS 1057—posthole fill
FS 1058—upper stratum of hearth fill
FS 1059—ash associated with hearth 1058
FS 1060—possible earlier hearth
FS 1066—upper 10 cm of trash pit/hearth
FS 1067—lower 11 cm of FS 1066 (not analyzed for plant remains)
FS 1068—original hearth/fill deposit.

Faunal remains from all but samples 1057 and 1060 were analyzed.

Miscellaneous plant samples

Field Sample 974 is a collection of large-sized carbonized wood fragments from Feature 22, a charred post in the presumed church structure. An attempt was made to see if the post showed evidence of having been hewn.

The final sample is a collection of small carbonized twigs from Feature 57 that were recognized and notable in the field for their curious concentration.

Faunal Samples

Animal bone from Features 10, 16, and 32 (10 samples) was analyzed. Features 10 and 32 are described above in the section on the botanical data. Both the southern and northern halves of Feature 32 (FS 1034 and 1038) underwent zooarchaeological analysis. Five of the stratigraphic samples from Feature 10 were analyzed as was a portion of the bulk-sampled half of the feature (see methods below).

Feature 16 is a refuse-filled pit similar in size and content to Feature 32. One sample (FS 1113) of the pit fill from Feature 16 was incorporated in this study.

Methods

Archaeobotany

All botanical samples (table 22) were processed in the Zooarchaeology Laboratory of the Florida Museum of Natural History, except for FS 1034 which was water-screened in the field through $1/16$-inch mesh screen.

The volumes of the Feature 10 stratigraphic samples and the bulk sample (FS 885) from Feature 10 (45 liters) were recorded, then sieved through nested screens sizes 4 mm, 2 mm, 1 mm, and .42 mm with water. Following air drying, the material from the four size fractions was weighed so that larger samples could be subsampled for analysis according to fraction size and weight (below).

Field Sample 1034 from Feature 32, which was screened in the field, was weighed and then passed dry through geologic sieves noted above. The volumes of the two samples collected as possible vessel contents from this feature were measured, then passed dry through the geologic sieve series. Individual size fractions were not weighed but were examined in their entirety.

Following sieving, remains recovered in the 4 mm-sized mesh were completely sorted and identified. The next largest size component (2 mm) was either processed in its entirety or, if a large sample, was divided in half by weight and one half examined. A 10 percent subsample by weight of the finer components resulting from the sieving process was selected for analysis. The 2 mm and finer fractions were scanned for whole seeds and other identifiable plant remains under $20 \times$ magnification, but were not otherwise sorted.

Field Sample 974 (wood sample) and the twig sample from Feature 57 were weighed and then examined without further processing.

The features with maize were first examined for whole and fragmentary cobs. If present, cobs were carefully removed for individual analysis and measurement. The residue was then passed through the geologic sieves listed above and the resulting fractions weighed, then scanned for seeds and additional maize remains.

Plant identifications were made using standard archaeobotanical techniques. Nut and seed remains were identified on the basis of morphological features with the aid of pictorial guides and by reference to comparative specimens housed at the Florida Museum. Charcoal was prepared for identification by fracturing each specimen along three planes. Wood species identification proceeded on the basis of three-dimensional anatomy according to diagnostic features and keys to anatomical structure (Record and Hess 1943; Urling and Smith 1953; Panshin and de Zeeuw 1980). Thirty fragments of charcoal per sample were employed as the minimum number identified. Suitable specimens for identification were randomly drawn from the 4 mm- and 2 mm-size fractions.

Morphometric analysis of corn remains included both qualitative and quantitative measurements of cobs, cupules, and kernels, following C. M. Scarry (1988).

Zooarchaeology

Fauna from Features 16 and 32 were processed in the field with $1/16$-inch water-screening. Three methods were used to subsample the fauna contained in Feature 10: (1) Approximately 50 percent of Feature 10 was excavated in natural stratigraphic levels, as described above, and water-screened in the laboratory through successive gauges of $1/14$-, $1/16$-, $1/32$-, and $1/64$-inch screens (the same screen sizes used in the botanical analyses); (2) A 25 percent sample of the bulk-sampled (nonstratigraphic) portion of the feature was water-screened with the same successive gauges of screen; and (3) 25 percent of the feature was water-screened through $1/16$-inch gauge screen in the field. Faunal remains from all three of these constituents was examined.

All of the fauna were identified to the lowest possible taxon by direct comparison with a series of reference specimens, which are a part of the collections of the Zooarchaeology Laboratory of the Florida Museum of Natural History (table 23).

Table 23. Scientific and Common Names of Fauna Identified from Fig Springs Mission

Taxon Scientific Name	Common Name	F-10	F-16	F-32
VERTEBRATA	Vertebrates	X	X	X
Mammalia	Mammals	X	X	X
Medium mammalia	e.g., opossum	X		
Large mammalia	e.g., white-tailed deer	X	X	X
Didelphis virginiana	Opossum	X		
Canidae cf. *Urocyon cinereoargenteus*	Gray fox	X		
cf. *Mephitis mephitis*	Skunk	X		
Artiodactyla	Even-toed ungulates	X		
Sus scrofa	Domestic pig			X
Odocoileus virginianus	White-tailed deer	X	X	X
Aves	Birds	X		
Meleagris gallopavo	Wild turkey		X	
Testudines	Turtles	X	X	X
Kinosternidae	Musk and mud turtles	X		
Gopherus polyphemus	Gopher tortoise	X	X	
Osteichthyes	Fishes	X	X	X
Lepisosteus spp.	Garfish		X	
Amia calva	Bowfin	X		
Ictalurus spp.	Freshwater catfish		X	X
Centrarchidae	Sunfishes	X	X	X
Lepomis spp.	Sunfishes		X	
Micropterus salmoides	Largemouth bass		X	
MOLLUSCA	Bivalves and gastropods		X	X
Bivalvia	Bivalves	X	X	

Standard zooarchaeological methods were used to quantify the remains (Reitz 1979, Wing and Brown 1979; Lee et al. 1984; Bense 1985; Reitz and Quitmyer 1988). Minimum numbers of individuals (MNI) were estimated by the use of paired elements and size. If, for example, an assemblage contains three left and five right pectoral spines of freshwater catfish (*Ictalurus* spp.), five minimum number of individuals are represented.

When animals of varying body mass are present in a faunal assemblage, the use of MNI may not always be a good indicator of the relative importance of the various taxa. Clearly the meat of eight sunfishes (Centrarchidae) are not greater than that provided by four white-tailed deer. Skeletal mass allometry used in conjunction with MNI can help to clarify the importance of different taxa in the diet (table 24).

The principle of allometry holds that there is a predictable log-log relationship between the weight or dimensional measurement of supporting tissue (bone) and biomass (Peters 1983; Schmidt-Nielsen 1984; Reitz et al. 1987). When skeletal mass allometry is used, it is assumed that only the meat adhering to the fragment of bone is represented. It is for this reason that skeletal mass allometry provides a proportional estimate of biomass. One inaccuracy that can be introduced is when the weight of the bone is either increased by mineralization or decreased by fire (von den Driesch 1976:3; Wing and Brown 1979:129). Biomass was calculated for only those species where MNI could be determined (Reitz and Quitmyer 1988).

When measurements could be obtained from the skeletal elements, dimensional allometry was used to estimate the biomass of those species (Wing and Brown 1979:127–29; Peters 1983; Quitmyer 1985; Reitz et al. 1987). These data are provided as a means of determining catch or hunt technology and to serve as a background for future research (table 25).

Table 24. Allometric Values Used in Study

Species	N	A	Slope (b)	r^2	Notes
Skeletal Mass Allometry Constants					
Mammalia	97	1.12	0.90	0.94	a
Aves	307	1.04	0.91	0.97	a
Testudines	26	0.51	0.67	0.55	a
Osteichthyes	393	0.90	0.81	0.80	a
Siluriformes	36	1.15	0.95	0.87	a

*Key to abbreviations: Formula is $Y = aX^b$; where Y is the biomass or meat weight; X is the weight of the remains; a is the Y-intercept; b is the slope; n is the number of observations; and r^2 is the correlation coefficient (Reitz and Cordier 1983; Reitz et al. 1987; Wing and Brown 1979).
a. Enter bone weight in kg to determine minimum estimate of body weight (biomass) in kg.

Table 25. Anatomic Measurements and Estimated Biomass of Specimens Identified in Features 10, 16, and 32, Fig Springs Mission (8Co1)

Taxon	Measurement (mm)	Estimated biomass (g)
Feature 10—F.S. 885		
Urocyon cinereoargenteus	10.73[a]	3178.63
Amia calva	4.57[b]	325.72
Centrarchidae	4.45[b]	308.46
	6.65[b]	701.97
Feature 10—F.S. 1058		
Centrarchidae	5.88[b]	545.65
Feature 10—F.S. 1067		
Centrarchidae	6.88[b]	752.56
	6.27[b]	622.31
Feature 16—F.S. 1113		
Lepisosteus spp.	3.89[c]	266.79
	4.08[c]	301.58
	4.35[c]	355.56
	6.23[c]	895.02
Ictalurus spp.	3.41[b]	178.87
Centrarchidae	2.34[b]	82.75
	2.74[b]	92.44
	2.74[b]	92.44
	2.83[b]	122.13
	2.85[b]	123.90
	4.27[b]	283.46
	4.33[b]	291.67
	4.74[b]	351.01
	5.10[b]	407.75
	5.68[b]	508.34
	6.07[b]	582.35
	6.21[b]	610.18
	6.26[b]	620.28
	6.50[b]	669.94

(continued)

a. Width of femur head (acetabulum) in terrestrial mammals to biomass
  $\log Y = 2.5569 (\log x) + 0.8671$; $r^2 = 0.72$; N = 50
    x = greatest diameter (mm) of the femur head (acetabulum)
    y = estimated biomass (g) (Wing and Brown 1979:128)
b. Teleost vertebrae width to biomass
  $\log Y = 2.047 (\log x) + 1.162$; $r^2 = 0.72$; N = 50
    x = anterior width (mm) of the centrum of the atlas vertebrae of bony fish
    y = estimated biomass (g) (Wing and Brown 1979:128)
c. Average width of thoracic vertebrae in *Lepisosteus* spp.
  $\log Y = 2.57 (\log x) + 0.91$; $r^2 = 0.96$; N = 9
    x = anterior width (mm) of the centrum of the thoracic vertebrae
    y = estimated biomass (g) less supportive tissue and viscera (Quitmyer 1985:40)
d. Direct comparison of distal tibia of the archaeological specimen with modern comparative materials in the collections of the Florida Museum of Natural History.

Table 25. *Continued*

Taxon	Measurement (mm)	Estimated biomass (g)
Micropterus salmoides	16.31[b]	4404.47
	16.99[b]	4788.57
	18.78[b]	5878.34
	18.80[b]	5891.16
	19.49[b]	6342.27
	19.69[b]	6476.21
Feature 32—F.S. 1034		
Osteichthyes	2.77[b]	77.65
Centrarchidae	4.10[b]	260.83
Feature 32—F.S. 1038		
Odocoileus virginianus	31.11[d]	44038.00
Centrarchidae	3.03[b]	140.45
	3.23[b]	160.08
	3.16[b]	153.06

Faunal identifications from Features 10, 16, and 32 were combined as a single analytical unit. In addition to giving an increased sample size, the combined faunal list from the three features can be used to account for several kinds of human behavior. Tables 26, 27, and 28 are faunal lists from the individual features. Table 29 is a list of combined faunal remains from all features analyzed.

Results

Archaeobotanical analysis

Botanical analysis resulted in the identification of at least 23 species, including both wild and domesticated taxa. I discuss the maize features first, followed by an account of the samples from the two refuse pit–hearth contexts and miscellaneous plant samples.

Maize Features

The four cob-filled pits and the cob and wood concentration from the bottom of Feature 45 are nearly identical in content. Maize cob fragments and loose cupules are abundant, as is wood charcoal. In contrast, maize kernels, seeds, and other evidence of plants are absent from these contexts.

In three of the cob-filled pits only a single species of wood occurs with the

Table 26. Faunal Remains Identified from Feature 10, Fig Springs
Mission Site (8Co1)

Species	Count #	Count %	MNI #	MNI %	Weight g	Weight %
VERTEBRATA	828	53.70	—	—	134.72	19.91
Mammalia	26	1.69	—	—	4.75	0.70
Medium mammalia	1	0.06	—	—	0.38	0.06
Large mammalia	150	9.73	—	—	130.38	19.27
Medium-large mammalia	176	11.41	—	—	161.49	23.86
Didelphis virginiana	2	0.13	1	10.00	0.63	0.09
Canidae cf. *Urocyon cinereoargenteus*	2	0.13	1	10.00	1.35	0.20
cf. *Mephitis mephitis*	1	0.06	1	10.00	0.12	0.02
Artiodactyla	2	0.13	—	—	2.20	0.33
Odocoileus virginianus	76	4.93	1	10.00	115.53	17.07
Aves	1	0.06	1	10.00	0.26	0.04
Testudines	175	11.35	—	—	63.24	9.35
Kinosternidae	1	0.06	1	10.00	0.11	0.02
Gopherus polyphemus	88	5.71	1	10.00	60.29	8.91
Osteichthyes	6	0.39	—	—	0.31	0.05
Amia calva	2	0.13	1	10.00	0.25	0.04
Centrarchidae	3	0.19	1	10.00	0.53	0.08
Bivalvia	2	0.13	1	10.00	0.16	0.02
Total taxon	1542	100	10	100	676.70	100

maize remains. This may be evidence for rather ephemeral, discrete episodes of use, perhaps even single-event burnings. Pine of the hard or dentate section, a group that includes all of the native hard or yellow pines, is the only wood type in Features 8 and 11. Similarly, black cherry was the only species identified in Feature 13. The curvature of the growth rings of the pine specimens indicates collection of large-sized, older branch and/or stem wood, as opposed to twigs and young, small-diametered branch wood. The cherry specimens were not large enough in size for this type of examination.

Feature 12, the fourth cob concentration, differed from the other cob-filled pits in the presence of three wood species rather than one. Feature 12 was otherwise identical to the other three cob pits. Live oak, hickory of the true group (includes pignut and other common native species except water hickory), and pine of the

Table 27. Faunal Remains Identified from Feature 16 (F.S.1113),
Fig Springs Mission[a]

Species	Count #	Count %	MNI #	MNI %	Weight g	Weight %
VERTEBRATA	46	9.20	—	—	3.08	0.75
Mammalia	44	8.80	—	—	5.29	1.29
Large mammalia	36	7.20	—	—	39.83	9.75
Odocoileus virginianus	31	6.20	2	15.38	320.57	78.44
Meleagris gallopavo	1	0.20	1	—	0.31	0.08
Testudines	2	0.40	—	—	0.58	0.14
Gopherus polyphemus	8	1.60	1	7.69	3.30	0.81
Osteichthyes	209	41.80	—	—	9.67	2.37
Lepisosteus spp.	59	11.80	1	7.69	6.23	1.52
Ictalurus spp.	21	4.20	2	15.38	3.20	0.78
Centrarchidae	28	5.60	5	38.46	3.20	0.78
Lepomis spp.	6	1.20	b	—	0.32	0.08
Micropterus salmoides	9	1.80	1	7.69	13.10	3.21
Total sample	500	100	13	100	408.68	100

a. Water-screened in the field with $1/16$-inch screen.
b. Due to the difficulty in distinguishing the various species of Centrarchidae (with the exception of *M. salmoides*) MNI was determined at the family level. One *Lepomis* spp. was identified in Feature 16.

Table 28. Faunal Remains Identified from Feature 32 (F.S. 1034 + 1038), Fig
Springs Mission

Species	Count #	Count %	MNI #	MNI %	Weight g	Weight %
VERTEBRATA	70	64.22	—	—	2.80	3.47
Mammalia	4	3.67	—	—	0.46	0.57
Large mammalia	13	11.93	—	—	22.78	28.26
Sus scrofa	1	0.92	1	16.67	13.33	16.54
Odocoileus virginiana	7	6.42	1	16.67	40.59	50.35
Testudines	1	0.92	1	16.67	0.04	0.05
Osteichthyes	2	1.83	—	—	0.01	0.01
Centrarchidae	4	3.67	1	16.67	0.12	0.15
Ictalurus spp.	1	0.92	1	16.67	0.03	0.04
MOLLUSCA	6	5.50	1	16.67	0.45	0.56
Total sample	109	100	6	100	80.61	100

Note: Water-screened in the field through $1/16$-inch screen.

Table 29. Faunal Remains Identified from Features 10, 16, and 32, Fig Springs Mission (8Co1)

Species	Count #	Count %	MNI #	MNI %	Weight g	Weight %	Skeletal mass[a] estimate of biomass g	Skeletal mass[a] estimate of biomass %
VERTEBRATA	946	43.78	—	—	140.60	12.06	—	—
Mammalia	74	3.42	—	—	10.50	0.90	—	—
Medium mammalia	1	0.05	—	—	0.38	0.03	—	—
Large mammalia	207	9.58	—	—	192.99	16.55	—	—
Medium-large mammalia	176	8.14	—	—	161.49	13.85	—	—
Didelphis virginiana	2	0.09	1	3.45	0.63	0.05	17.35	0.20
Canidae cf. *Urocyon cinereoargenteus*	2	0.09	1	3.45	1.35	0.12	34.46	0.40
cf. *Mephitis mephitis*	1	0.05	1	3.45	0.12	0.01	3.90	0.04
Artiodactyla	2	0.09	—	—	2.20	0.19	—	—
Sus scrofa	1	0.05	1	3.45	13.33	1.14	270.61	3.12
Odocoileus virginianus	114	5.28	4	13.79	476.69	40.88	6767.25	77.99
Aves	1	0.05	1	3.45	0.26	0.02	6.00	0.07
Meleagris gallopavo	1	0.05	1	3.45	0.31	0.03	7.03	0.08
Testudines	178	8.24	1	3.45	63.82	5.47	512.06	5.90
Kinosternidae	1	0.05	1	3.45	0.11	0.01	7.21	0.08
Gopherus polyphemus	96	4.44	2	6.90	63.59	5.45	510.82	5.89
Osteichthyes	217	10.04	—	—	9.99	0.86	—	—
Lepisosteus spp.	59	2.73	1	3.45	6.23	0.53	129.88	1.50
Amia calva	2	0.09	1	3.45	0.25	0.02	9.60	0.11
Ictalurus spp.	22	1.02	3	10.34	3.23	0.28	76.29	0.88
Centrarchidae	35	1.62	7	24.14	3.85	0.33	87.95	1.01
Lepomis spp.	6	0.28	b	b	0.32	0.03	b	b
Micropterus salmoides	9	0.42	1	3.45	13.10	1.12	237.13	2.73
MOLLUSCA	6	0.28	1	3.45	0.45	0.04	c	c
Bivalvia	2	0.09	1	3.45	0.16	0.01	c	c
Total taxon	2161	100	29	100	1165.95	100	8677.54	100

a. Biomass was determined only for those species represented by MNI.
b. Due to the difficulty in distinguishing the various species of Centrarchidae (with the exception of *M. salmoides*) MNI was determined at the family level. There was one *Lepomis* spp. identified.
c. Biomass not calculated for Mollusca because they may be fossils.

Table 30. Row Number Distribution of Maize Cobs from Fig Springs (8Co1) (cob midsections only)

Row number	6	8	10	12
Number	1	22	8	3
Percent	3	65	23	9

Average row number = 8.76 (n = 34)
Absolute cob count including tips = 53

dentate section were identified. Pine, however, is far more abundant (92 percent) than the other two woods (7 percent and 1 percent, respectively), and thus, Feature 12 differs little from Features 8 and 11, in which pine was the only wood identified. Likewise, the pine growth rings are indicative of mature growth.

The Feature 45 carbon concentration (FS 1110) mirrors the cob-filled pits in composition. Like Features 8 and 11, all of the wood in Feature 45 is hard-pine group.

Table 30 is a summary of the maize remains from the four pits and Features 45, 48, and 50. Analytical data for the individual contexts is reported in table 31.

Table 31a. *Zea mays* Measurements, Fig Springs (8Co1): Summary for Feature 8 (FS 880) Cob Pit

Measurable cobs = 6 midsections
Cob tips/butts = 1

Percent row number	6	0
	8	83
	10	17
	12	0

Average row number = 8.3

8-row
Average cob diameter	14.37 mm
Average cupule width	10.94 mm
Median cupule width	9.37 mm
Average cupule length,	3.70 mm
cupule width/length	2.95

10-row
Average cob diameter	16.55 mm (n = 2)
Average cupule width	8.26 mm (n = 3)
Median cupule width	8.20 mm
Average cupule length,	3.17 mm (n = 2)
cupule width/length	2.60

Table 31b. *Zea mays* Measurements, Fig Springs (8Co1): Summary for Feature 11 (FS 886) Cob Pit

Measurable cobs = 10 midsections
Cob tips/butts = 3

Percent row number	6	0
	8	40
	10	30
	12	30

Average row number = 9.8

8-row
Average cob diameter	15.80 mm
Average cupule width	9.76 mm
Median cupule width	10.10 mm
Average cupule length,	3.44 mm
cupule width/length	2.84

10-row
Average cob diameter	18.11 mm
Average cupule width	9.05 mm
Median cupule width	9.61 mm
Average cupule length,	3.35 mm
cupule width/length	2.70

12-row
Average cob diameter	16.70 mm
Average cupule width	8.12 mm
Median cupule width	8.25 mm
Average cupule length,	3.52 mm
cupule width/length	2.30

Grouping the cobs as a single population, row number is predominantly 8-row (65 percent), with 10-row cobs being the second most frequent (23 percent). Rare is 12-row (9 percent) and 6-row (3 percent) maize. Average row number for the combined sample is 8.76. Strength of row pairing (moderate to strong), cob morphology, and cupule size are within the limit of native eastern complex maize commonly known as Eastern Eight Row (C. M. Scarry 1988). Evidence for hybridization with imported varieties of maize from tropical America is not present in these sample measurements, though the possible biases of small sample size should be kept in mind. Kernel size and morphology (Feature 10, see below) is consistent with Eastern Eight Row maize: the single intact kernel is crescent-shaped and smooth-surfaced (nondent).

The plant identifications from the maize features, as well as the rest of the samples analyzed here, are listed by provenience in table 32.

Table 31c. *Zea mays* Measurements, Fig Springs (8Co1): Summary for Feature 12 (FS 888) Cob Pit

---

Measurable cobs = 12 midsections
Cob tips/butts = 4

Percent row number	6	9
	8	73
	10	18
	12	0

Average row number = 8.18

8-row
  Average cob diameter   15.10 mm
  Average cupule width   9.60 mm
  Median cupule width   9.50 mm
  Average cupule length,   3.78 mm
    cupule width/length   2.54
10-row
  Average cob diameter   15.44 mm
  Average cupule width   7.90 mm
  Median cupule width   8.20 mm
  Average cupule length,   3.10 mm
    cupule width/length   2.55
6-row
  Average cob diameter   14.05 mm (n = 2)
  Average cupule width   9.50 mm (n = 3)
  Median cupule width   9.50 mm
  Average cupule length,   3.34 mm (n = 5)
    cupule width/length   2.84

Trash pit–hearth deposits

Three samples from Feature 32, a midden-filled pit, were analyzed for plant remains. The two samples taken as possible vessel contents (FS 1029 and 1039) provided little information. No seeds or bone are present, and only a few fragments of wood charcoal and a single acorn-hull fragment were recovered. Pine charcoal is present in both samples. Charcoal of the red oak group is identified in FS 1039 and a hardwood (oak or hickory) in FS 1029.

The third sample from Feature 32 (FS 1034) was of the fill proper. Remains of food plants are noteworthy. Nut food remains are present, though not particularly abundant. Eighteen fragments of hickory nut shell were recovered, as was a single fragment of acorn hull. Three domesticated plants are represented. These are a small quantity of maize cupules of native origin, six peach pit fragments of Old World origin, and, most importantly, a single wheat grain, also coming from the Old World.

Table 31d. *Zea mays* Measurements, Fig Springs (8Co1): Summary for Feature 13 (FS 889) Cob Pit

Measurable cobs = 5 midsections		
Cob tips/butts = 0		
Percent row number	6	0
	8	60
	10	40
	12	0
Average row number = 8.8		
8-row		
Average cob diameter		13.90 mm
Average cupule width		7.86 mm
Median cupule width		8.20 mm
Average cupule length,		3.14 mm
cupule width/length		2.50
10-row		
Average cob diameter		17.01 mm
(Average) cupule width		8.20 mm (one measured)
Average cupule length,		3.10 mm (n = 2)
cupule width/length		2.64

Actual remains of early imported wheat are rare in New World archaeological sites (see Ruhl 1990 for a summary). This specimen measures 5 mm in length, 3.4 mm at its largest width, and 3.0 mm in thickness. The germ is medium sized, 1 mm long, and enough of the embryo is present that the shape of the germ is obscured (measurements and confirmation of the identification were made by Donna Ruhl, Florida Museum of Natural History).

Charcoal identifications from FS 1034 are consistent with those from the cob-filled pits. Pine of the dentate section comprised 93 percent of the sample identified, and black cherry 7 percent. Charcoal identifications by sample are summarized in table 33.

Feature 10 (the cooking/roasting pit)

The six samples from Feature 10—the large stratified pit—are very like the sample from Feature 32, just described, even though the latter was not sieved through as fine a screen. The Feature 10 samples add to the list of wild and domesticated plants. The samples are presented here in descending order as they occurred stratigraphically in the feature.

Field Sample 1057 (Feature 10 posthole fill) contained evidence of several plant foods, including both native and introduced species. Hickory nut and acorn

Table 31e. *Zea mays* Measurements, Fig Springs (8Col): Summary for Feature 45 (FS 1110) ?HEARTH

Measurable cobs = 2 midsections
Cob tips/butts = 3

Percent row number	6	0
	8	50
	10	50
	12	0

Average row number = 9

8-row
Average cob diameter	16.80 mm
Average cupule width	11.11 mm
Median cupule width	11.33 mm
Average cupule length,	3.25 mm
cupule width/length	3.41

10-row
Average cob diameter	(fragmented)
Average cupule width	9.85 mm
Median cupule width	9.85 mm
Average cupule length,	3.89 mm
cupule width/length	2.53

remains are present, but, as in Feature 32 described above, both plants are represented by few specimens (nine fragments total). Four small fragments of maize cob were recovered, as was one fragment of peach pit. Another European food plant may be present in FS 1057 in the form of a tentatively identified fragment of hazel nut. Following C. M. Scarry (1989), this specimen, if it is indeed hazel nut, is presumed to be from the European species rather than the native tree, which has a natural range well north of the site. Finally, a single saw palmetto seed was identified and was probably used as a native plant food.

Charcoal identifications from FS 1057 are predominately of pine (90 percent). One fragment of oak and two of black cherry were also identified.

Four seeds of watermelon, another Old World cultivar, were found in FS 1058, the next deepest sample from Feature 10. Other domesticated species include maize (one cob fragment and 20 cupules and fragments), peach-pit fragments (six), and a tentatively identified hilum (seed coat scar) from domestic bean. Another interesting inclusion in this sample is sand spur (one fruit), an Old World weed that was unintentionally introduced early into North America. Seeds of two wild fruits were recovered—saw palmetto (two seeds) and maypop (one seed). Finally, three fragments of hickory-nut shell were recovered.

Table 32. Distribution of Plant Remains by Provenience

	Features															
Taxon	45	8	11	12	13	32			10	-	-	-	-	-	-	
						1029	1039	1034	1057	1058	1059	1060	1066	1068	885	974
Indigenous food																
Corn	X	X	X	X	X				X	X	X	X	X	X	X	
Common bean										X			X			
Acorn						X		X	X				X	X	X	
Hickory nut								X	X	X	X	X	X	X	X	
Palmetto									X	X	X	X	X	X	X	
Maypop										X						
Persimmon													X			
Old World food																
Peach pit								X	X		X	X	X	X	X	
Wheat grain								X								
Watermelon										X			X			
Cf. hazelnut									X							
Non-food plants																
Sandspur										X		X				
Monocot stem										X		X	X	X	X	
Palm petiole										X						
Fuelwoods																
Wood charcoal	X	X	X	X	X	X	X	X	X	X	X	X	X	X	X	X
Pine	X	X	X	X		X	X	X	X	X	X	X	X	X	X	X
Cherry							X		X	X			X	X		
Oak		X						X	X	X			X	X	X	
Hickory		X											X			

Wood charcoal from this level (FS 1058) includes two species, pine (97 percent) and live oak (3 percent). Also present in the nonfood remains is carbonized monocot stem, probably native switch cane but possibly cornstalk, an unidentified woody herb (one fragment) of small diameter, and fragments of palm leaf petiole.

Field Sample 1059 is an ashy deposit directly underlying, and probably resulting from, the hearth designated FS 1058. This sample is very much like 1058 in plant species composition. Fragments of peach pit (nine), maize cob (one) and cupules (seven) are present, as is a small amount of hickory-nut shell

Table 33. Relative Frequencies of Fuelwood Taxa from Seven Features at Fig Springs (8Co1)

Provenience		Pine	Cherry	Red oak	Live oak	Hickory
Feature 10						
1057		90	7	1		
1058		97			3	
1059		97	3			
1060		90	3	3		3
1066		97			3	
1068		100				
885		97			3	
Feature 32	1034	93	7			
Feature 08	880	100				
Feature 11	886	100				
Feature 12	888	70			10	20
Feature 13	889		100			
Feature 45	1110	100				

(12 fragments) and a single saw palmetto seed. Also, as in FS 1058, a palm petiole fragment and one fragment of the same small dicot stem were reccvered. Again, pine charcoal is dominant—pine comprised 97 percent of the identified wood and black cherry 3 percent (table 32).

Field Sample 1060 of Feature 10 is described as "mixed deposits, possible earlier hearth." This sample is rich in botanical remains. Domesticated taxa are represented by peach-pit fragments (13), maize cupules and fragments (33), and a single maize kernel. This is the only sample in the analysis in which a kernel was recovered (although a tentatively identified kernel is present in FS 1066). The maize kernel is crescent shaped and without a dent, typical characteristics of indigenous Eastern Eight Row maize. It measures 8.85 mm in width, 6.45 mm height, and 5.75 mm thickness.

Like Sample 1059, a single sand spur was recovered from FS 1060. Two saw palmetto seed fragments were identified, as was a small quantity of hickory-nut shell (29 fragments, all less than 2 mm in size). Three wedge-shaped seeds of the same type remain unidentified from this sample; they should, with additional time and comparative material, be identifiable.

Charcoal identifications from FS 1060 are slightly more diverse than the other samples from Feature 10. Four species are present: hard group pine (90 percent), black cherry (3 percent), red group oak (3 percent), and pecan group hickory (3 percent). Other nonsubsistence remains include four fragments of vine, probably grape vine, monocot stem, cane or cornstalk, a male cone from a pine, and two small dicotyledonous twigs with a star-shaped pith (not the same woody herb as is present in FS 1058 and FS 1059).

Field Sample 1066 of Feature 10 is a sample representative of the upper 10 cm of a midden stratum. Four cultivated species are present, including domestic bean. Beans are rarely recovered in archaeological contexts because they are usually consumed whole. (Also, pods and vines degrade readily and are easily consumed by fire.) This specimen appears to be a form of *Phaseolus vulgaris,* or common bean. Measurements are 8.1 mm in length and 4.225 mm width.

Other species of domesticated plants found in the FS 1066 midden deposit are maize (one cob fragment, 46 cupules), peach (28 pit fragments), and two watermelon seeds. Evidence of persimmon (one seed), an important wild fruit, is exclusive to this sample. Seven intact and two fragmentary saw palmetto seeds were identified. Also identified are a single fragment of what may be a cabbage palm seed, an unidentified seed of the grass family, and an identifiable seed that is morphologically similar to morning glory. Consistent with the rest of the samples, nut remains are scarce in FS 1066 (22 small fragments of hickory shell, 8 of acorn).

Also in keeping the other samples, pine charcoal is ubiquitous (200 + fragments) in FS 1066. The subsample of 30 identified specimens consisted of 97 percent pine (hard group) and 3 percent live oak (one identification). Other nonsubsistence remains include three fragments of monocot stem, cane, or maize as above, five fragments of possible grapevine, a single male pine cone, three small unidentified dicot twigs, and two small unidentified (?) monocotyledonous stems.

Field Sample 1068 is the stratigraphically deepest sample from Feature 10 and is believed to represent the original hearth or deposition of fill. The content of this sample is consistent with those in superior position described above. Maize (38 cupules and one possible kernel) and peach (six pit fragments) represent the domesticated taxa and saw palmetto (one seed), hickory (21 small fragments) and acorn (7 small fragments) are present as wild plant subsistence remains. One poorly preserved seed remains unidentified.

Pine (30 + fragments) is the only wood identified from FS 1068. Other nonsubsistence remains include one fragment of probable grapevine, and two fragments of monocot stem, possibly cane or maize as in the other samples.

Not surprisingly, archaeobotanical identifications from the bulk sample from Feature 10 (FS 885) followed those of the stratigraphic samples just described. Maize and peach were identified, as were saw palmetto seeds and one petiole fragment. Fragments of acorn and hickory-nut shell are present, and two unidentified seed fragments were also noted. The charcoal is overwhelmingly pine, with one specimen of live oak observed. Switch cane, possible grapevine, and stem fragments from an unidentified member of the grass family (possibly cane) were also recovered.

Miscellaneous botanical samples

Field Sample 974 is a wood sample from a charred post in the church (Feature 22). The sample is composed of numerous large-sized fragments of pine charcoal that came from a single large (10 cm × 10 cm) post. Tool marks were not discernible.

The last sample is a collection of small-diameter (1.0–1.5 mm) twigs from Feature 57, a wood smudge near the north wall of the large aboriginal structure. These appear to be dicotyledonous and have a solid, star-shaped pith. These small stems are probably too immature for accurate identification. It is possible that the unidentified plant is an annual herb.

Zooarchaeological Results

The Fig Springs faunal assemblage contains 2,161 fragments of bone and mollusc shell for a total weight of 1,165.95 grams. This represents 14 animal species and at least 29 individual animals (see table 29). Less than 1 percent of the bone in Features 16 and 32 showed signs of being altered by fire. Feature 10, on the other hand, probably in part served as a hearth. Supporting evidence for this is that over 99 percent of the fauna are burned.

By the measure of MNI, domestic animals (a single pig, *Sus scrofa*) account for 3.7 percent of the total faunal assemblage (fig. 78). Wild terrestrial animals contribute 37 percent of the individuals, dominated by white-tailed deer *Odocoileus virginiana* at 13.8 percent. Opossum *Didelphis virginiana* (3.45 percent), skunk *Mephitis mephitis* (3.45 percent), gray fox *Urocyon cinereoargenteus* (3.45 percent), and gopher tortoise *Gopherus polyphemus* (6.9 percent) are the remaining species of wild terrestrial animals represented in the three features. A mud turtle *Kinosternon* spp. (3.45 percent) is the only aquatic reptile identified in the faunal assemblage. Freshwater fishes account for 48.18 percent (MNI) of the aquatic faunal. Garfish *Lepisosteus* spp. (3.45 percent), bowfin *Amia calva* (3.45 percent), freshwater catfish *Ictalurus* spp. (10.34 percent), and sunfishes Centrarchidae (27.59 percent) are the fish species identified in the assemblage. Sunfish *Lepomis* spp. and largemouth bass *Micropterus salmoides* are the two centrarchids that were identified.

The estimated proportional biomass of the categories of fauna show that wild terrestrial animals (90.42 percent) contribute the largest portion of the meat represented in the three features (fig. 79). The major contributor to this classification is the white-tailed deer (77.99 percent). Domestic swine, on the other hand, provide only 3.12 percent of the estimated meat in the faunal assemblage. Freshwater fishes account for 6.32 percent of the biomass, while aquatic reptile (0.05 percent) and wild bird (0.15 percent) represent only a trace of the estimated biomass.

Measurements of the skeletal elements from Features 10, 16, and 32 are

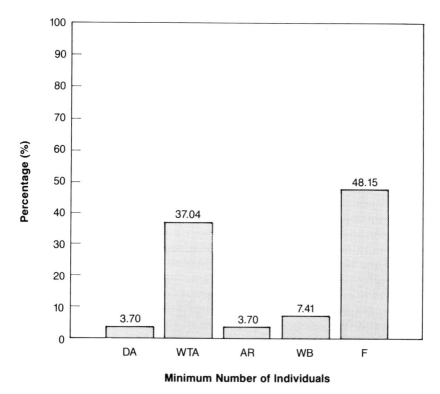

FIG. 78. *Minimum number of individuals (MNI) summary of proveniences analyzed for zooarchaeological remains.*

presented in table 25. Direct comparison of the archaeological white-tailed deer bone with reference specimens with known weights show that the white-tailed deer weighed approximately 44,038 grams. The measured lateral width of the thoracic vertebra of freshwater catfish indicate an estimated body weight of 178.87 grams. Sunfish thoracic vertebrae were the most numerous elements available for measurement. The estimated body mass of the sunfish in the three features is between 82.75 grams and 752.56 grams, while the body mass of the largemouth bass ranges between 4,404.47 and 6,476.21 grams.

Summary and Discussion of Ethnobiological Data

This study was directed toward discerning the extent and nature of plant and animal preservation at Fig Springs and the potential for a paleoethnobiological study of the mission and accompanying Indian village. Both prospects look favorable. No

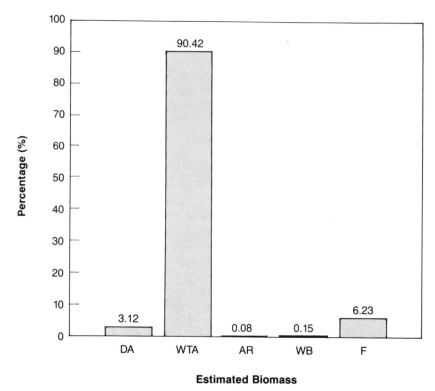

FIG. 79. *Biomass summary of proveniences analyzed for zooarchaeological remains.*

systematic collections of biological remains from Fig Springs exist previous to this work. There is, however, a growing data base of contact- and mission-period plant remains with which to compare (C. M. Scarry 1986, 1988, 1989; Ruhl 1990; Russo et al. 1989). Unfortunately, however, well-preserved faunal assemblages from inland contact and mission-period sites are dramatically lacking.

Summary of Plant Remains

Plant remains from 11 closed contexts (19 samples total) at Fig Springs were examined in this study. All of the samples were excavated from the area of a large seventeenth-century aboriginal structure, archaeologically associated with the church, convento, and cemetery of the mission complex.

Eleven plants were identified among the subsistence remains from Fig Springs, including three (perhaps four) Old World domesticates, two New World domesticates, and five native wild taxa with edible fruit. These plants are listed in table 34. Goggin's earlier collections supplement this list with gourd rind

Table 34. Plant Taxa Identified from Fig Springs (8Co1)

Old World cultivated species	
Citrillus vulgaris	watermelon
Corylus avellana[a]	hazelnut
Prunus persica	peach
Triticum sp.	wheat
Indigenous cultivated species	
Phaseolus vulgaris	common bean
Zea mays	maize
Wild nuts	
Carya sp.	hickory nut
Quercus sp.	acorn
Wild fruit	
Diospyros virginiana	persimmon
Passiflora incarnata	maypop
Sabal palmetto	cabbage palm
Serenoa repens	saw palmetto
Commensals	
Cenchrus pauciflorus	sandspur
Poaceae	grass family
Fuelwoods	
Carya sp., pecan group	pecan; water hickory
Carya sp., true group	e.g. pignut hickory
Pinus sp., section diploxylon	Southern hard pine
Prunus serotina	black cherry
Quercus sp., red group	red oak section
Quercus virginiana	live oak
Miscellaneous	
Dicotyledonae	herbaceous stem
Monocotyledonae	cane/cornstalk
Palmae	palm frond
Pinus sp.	male strobilus
Vitaceae	grape vine

a. Tentative identification.

(presumably bottle gourd, but the taxonomic identification is not given [Deagan 1972]). Other plants recovered by Goggin are maize cobs, hickory nuts, and hundreds of peach pits (see Appendix A).

On the whole, the various strata of Feature 10 are fairly consistent in terms of species represented. Old World taxa occur throughout. The Feature 32 sample is similar to Feature 10 in containing both native and introduced species.

This assemblage of introduced and native, domesticated and wild taxa is consistent with plant recovery from other mission sites—including San Luis (Le4), San Juan de Aspalaga (Je1), and Nuestra Señora de la Purissima Concepción de Ayubale (Je2) (C. M. Scarry 1986, 1988)—as well as sixteenth-

and seventeenth-century St. Augustine (C. M. Scarry 1984, 1989; Reitz and Scarry 1985). Wheat and watermelon, both Old World taxa, tend to be scarce in mission and contact period sites, while peach pits are abundant. This undoubtedly reflects the durability of peach pits relative to other less resistant seeds. The same problem exists when comparing the abundance of hickory nut to other seed/fruit remains.

Old World taxa not present in the Fig Springs samples examined thus far, but present at other mission and contact period sites, include melon (*Cucumis melo*), common pea (*Pisum sativum*), fig (*Ficus carica*), olive (*Olea europa*), and the European wine grape (*Vitis vinifera*). Fig trees reportedly grew wild in the area of the site around 1820 and are presumed to have come from the Spanish occupation some time previous (Deagan 1972). To the extent this is true, we might expect evidence of this plant in the archaeobotanical record at some point.

Also absent from the present sample is evidence of exotic New World cultigens such as butternut squash (*Cucurbita moschata*) and chili pepper (*Capsicum annuum*). These native plants and others were adopted by the Spanish early in the colonial period (see discussion in Reitz and Scarry 1985). The maize from Fig Springs likewise shows no evidence of hybridization with introduced cultivars from tropical America, nor are such cultivars evidenced here as distinct forms. At later mission sites, there is good evidence for the introduction of nonlocal maize cultivars (C. M. Scarry 1988).

In general, the plant assemblage from Fig Springs is consistent with assemblages from prehistoric sites in Florida, particularly in regard to the wild species like maypop and persimmon. Reliance on maize and beans is more a pattern of groups in the Fort Walton–Apalachee area than peninsular Florida, but their presence at Fig Springs is not surprising. Fuelwood use indicating a strong emphasis on pine is also consistent with the prehistoric pattern. This analysis seems to indicate a continuity with the basic aboriginal pattern of reliance on wild plants, with at least limited emphasis on cultivated species and perhaps also the first indication of a shift toward greater emphasis on cultivated species and introduced taxa. Certainly the presence of wheat is a reflection of the Spanish insistence in having this plant in their diet and not necessarily a reflection of the Indians' acceptance of this plant. How long the missionaries were able to maintain or ensure a supply of wheat is uncertain since wheat was unsuccessful in Florida (Reitz and Scarry 1985).

Summary of Faunal Remains

There are three primary aspects of faunal sampling that have to be emphasized in the analysis of animal remains. The first is the choice of the appropriate screen size for the optimum recovery of the fauna. Over the past 40 years southeastern archaeologists have chosen either ½-inch or ¼-inch screen for the recovery of artifacts from prehistoric sites. With the relatively recent emergence of faunal analysis in archaeological inquiry, it has become evident that while ¼-inch screen may be adequate for the recovery of artifacts, a finer gauge of screen (¹/₁₆-inch) is necessary for the recovery of animal remains (Wing and Quitmyer 1983).

The use of ¹/₁₆-inch screen in the excavation of faunal remains assures the equal recovery of large animal (e.g., white-tailed deer) remains and those of smaller species (e.g., sunfishes). Without exception in prehistoric southeastern coastal sites where ¹/₁₆-inch screen has been used for the recovery of animal remains, small fishes have been the major constituent of the faunal assemblage (Lee et al. 1984; Bense 1985; Reitz and Quitmyer 1988), and terrestrial fauna are of minor consequence (e.g., Reitz and Quitmyer 1988). This pattern is indicative of the use of shallow water habitats and mass capture of juvenile fishes with the aid of fine mesh nets (Reitz and Quitmyer 1988). Evidence contrary to this pattern could mark changes in technology, resource selection or exploitation of different habitats. Fine screen (¹/₁₆-inch) faunal recovery from historic period sites should therefore be continued so as to facilitate the comparison of fauna from prehistoric and historic sites.

The importance of ¹/₁₆-inch screen recovery of fauna is apparent in the Fig Springs faunal assemblage. Even though skeletal elements of large terrestrial animals are most prevalent in the samples, osteological remains of small fishes would not have been recovered if fine screen (¹/₁₆-inch) had not been used. For example, fish vertebrae with lateral dimensions of less than 6.35 mm (¼-inch) potentially would have passed through ¼-inch screen (table 25). This would have been 75 percent of the 36 fish vertebrae measured. The lack of fishes from Goggin's inventory of faunal remains from Fig Springs further attests to the importance of ¹/₁₆-inch screen for the recovery of faunal remains (Deagan 1972:39–40). All of the species represented were large animal forms such as deer, alligator (*Alligator mississipiensis*), gopher tortoise, salt/fresh water molluscs (Deagan 1972:39–40)

Second, there is the question of sample size adequacy. A measure of how appropriate the sample size is is the relationship of MNI to the number of species identified in the faunal sample (Wing and Brown 1979:19). The goal is to reach a point where few, if any, new species are added to the assemblage with the identification of greater numbers of individuals. For example, in the circum-Caribbean coastal plain, an adequate sample is estimated to be 200 MNI and 29 vertebrate species (Wing and Brown 1979:19). The relationship of MNI to species count has to be made for each locality because of the natural diversity of faunal resources and the use of those resources by human beings. At this time sample-size adequacy cannot be determined for Fig Springs because too few samples have been analyzed from this locality. This will require further sampling from a variety of proveniences at Fig Springs.

The third consideration is sampling location in the archaeological site. Faunal materials need to be obtained from a variety of places in the archaeological site. One feature, or sample from a midden, probably does not account for the variability in human behavior present in the site. Fauna from a hearth may only represent food acquisition and food distribution behavior of a select nature, while the midden outside a house might represent a greater variety of acquisitions, food storage, preparation, and or distribution of resources to the community.

The faunal analysis of the Fig Springs assemblage is based on the contents of three features from an aboriginal structure associated with the convento and mission church. A more diverse array of samples of larger sample size are goals for future research. The present faunal assemblage, however, provides a basis against which future samples can be compared.

A general theme of faunal use seems to be present in the Fig Springs faunal assemblage (tables 25 and 28). By the measure of MNI and biomass it is apparent that terrestrial animals that can be hunted and gathered in the forests and open brushy areas represent an important part of the diet (Carr and Goin 1959; Burt and Grossenheider 1964; Bull and Farrand 1977). White-tailed deer and gopher tortoise are among the more important of terrestrial animals identified. If allowed to roam freely European domestic pig could have also been hunted in these habitats. These hunting enterprises are further supported by the large number of projectile points found in Feature 10.

Aquatic fauna identified from Fig Springs represents a less important aspect of the diet, but it accounts for some dietary diversity. This pattern contrasts with coastal sites, as noted above. Sunfishes and freshwater catfishes are the two most important of the species found in the assemblage. Hook and line technology and spearing of fish may have been practiced in the waters of the Ichetucknee River or nearby Santa Fe River. The presence of bottom-dwelling fishes (e.g., catfish and bowfin) and the smaller sunfishes indicate the possible use of mass capture devices such as traps or nets. At the present time artifacts associated with hook and line fishing (e.g., hooks and or weights) or netting (e.g., net weights) are not among the artifacts identified at Fig Springs, with the possible exception of a "lead curl" net weight found in the church excavations (see fig. 30d).

Conclusions

The ethnobiological materials analyzed for this study document an initial phase of aboriginal contact with colonial Europeans. Heavy use of native resources and low-intensity use of Old World plants and animals is indicated. Further, the maize sample gives no indication of the presence of cultivars from tropical America such as has been documented for later mission contexts in other areas. A greater number of samples will have to be analyzed before this observation can be confirmed.

The ethnobiological materials also provide insight into the diversity of aboriginal subsistence behavior. Although terrestrial plants and animals from forested and open brushy areas dominate the assemblage, a variety of aquatic resources (e.g., fish and aquatic turtle) were identified. This diversity shows a well-developed hunting, fishing, and gathering economy integrated with the horticultural system.

This study represents a preliminary inquiry that needs to be tested with a larger number of samples from a variety of proveniences in the site. Refuse-pit remains from the convento, if found, could be contrasted with contemporaneous aboriginal households, and such households could be compared with each other. It would also be instructive to compare ethnobiological data from components of the site associated with the mission period with samples from the earlier precontact period. One cannot understand the changes in life-style that occurred as the result of contact with Europeans without first grounding the data in an understanding of the precontact aboriginal pattern.

REFERENCES CITED

Andrews, E. W., and C. M. Andrews, eds.
    1945   *Jonathan Dickinson's Journal; or God's Protecting Providence*. New Haven: Yale University Press.

Baker, Henry A.
    1968   Archaeological Investigations at Panama Vieja. M.A. thesis, University of Florida.

Bartram, John
    1942   Diary of a Journey Through the Carolinas, Georgia, and Florida From July 1, 1765 to April 10, 1766. Edited by Francis Harper. *Transactions of the American Philosophical Society* 33 (1).

Bartram, William
    1955   *The Travels of William Bartram*. Edited by Mark Van Doren. New York: Dover Press.

Bense, Judith A., ed.
    1985   *Hawkshaw: Prehistory in an Urban Neighborhood in Pensacola, Florida*. University of West Florida Office of Cultural and Archaeological Research Report of Investigation no. 7, Pensacola.

Boyd, Mark F.
    1939   Spanish Mission Sites in Florida. *Florida Historical Quarterly* 17:254–80.
    1949   Diego Peña's expedition to Apalachee and Apalachicola in 1716. *Florida Historical Quarterly* 28:1–27.

Bull, John, and John Farrand, Jr.
    1977   *The Audubon Society Field Guide to North American Birds: Eastern Region*. New York: Alfred A. Knopf.

Bullen, Ripley P.
    1975   *A Guide to the Identification of Florida Projectile Points*. Gainesville: Kendall Books.

Burt, William Henry, and Richard P. Grossenheider.
    1964   *A Field Guide to Mammals*. Boston: Houghton Mifflin Company.

Bushnell, Amy
    1988   Translation of Three Documents from the Edict on Afuyca, Archivo de Indias Santo Domingo 58-1-25/82. March 22, 1685. Manuscript on file, Florida Bureau of Archaeological Research, Tallahassee.

Carr, Archie, and Coleman J. Goin
1959   *A Guide to the Reptiles, Amphibians and Fresh-Water Fishes of Florida.*
        Gainesville: University of Florida Press.

Clausen, Carl J.
1970   The Fort Pierce Collection. *Bureau of Historic Sites and Properties
        Bulletin* 1:1–24. Florida Department of State, Tallahassee.

Deagan, Kathleen
1972   Fig Springs: The Mid-Seventeenth Century in North-Central
        Florida. *Historical Archaeology* 6:23–46.
1978   Cultures in Transition: Fusion and Assimilation among the Eastern
        Timucua. In *Tacachale: Essays on the Indians of Florida and Southeast-
        ern Georgia during the Historic Period,* edited by Jerald T. Milanich
        and Samuel Proctor, 89–119. Gainesville: University Presses of
        Florida.
1985   The Archaeology of Sixteenth-Century St. Augustine. *Florida
        Anthropologist* 38:6–33.
1987   *Artifacts of the Spanish Colonies of Florida and the Caribbean,
        1500–1800.* Volume 1: *Ceramics, Glassware, and Beads.* Washington,
        D.C.: Smithsonian Institution Press.

Gannon, Michael V.
1965   *The Cross in the Sand.* Gainesville: University of Florida Press.

Geiger, Maynard
1936   *The Early Franciscans in Florida.* Paterson, N.J.: St. Anthony Guild
        Press.
1940   *Biographical Dictionary of the Franciscans in Spanish Florida and Cuba.*
        Paterson, N.J.: St. Anthony Guild Press.

Goggin, John M.
1948   *Some Pottery Types from Central Florida.* Gainesville Anthropological
        Association, Bulletin 1.
1949   Field Book for Florida, 1949. Box 9 in the Goggin collection, P.K.
        Yonge Library of Florida History, Gainesville.
1953   An Introductory Outline of Timucua Archaeology. *Southeastern
        Archaeological Conference Newsletter* 3 (3):4–17.
1960a   *The Spanish Olive Jar: An Introductory Study.* New Haven: Yale
        University Press.
1960b   Underwater Archaeology: Its Nature and Limitations. *American
        Antiquity* 25:348–54.
1968   *Spanish Majolica in the New World.* Yale University Publications in
        Anthropology, no. 72. New Haven: Yale University Press.

Hally, David J.
  1988   Archaeology and Settlement Plan of the King Site. In *The King Site: Continuity and Contact in Sixteenth Century Georgia*, ed. by Robert Blakely, 3–16. Athens: University of Georgia Press.
Hann, John H.
  1987   Translation of AGI Santo Domingo 235, Letter of the Religious of Santa Elena, Sept. 10, 1657. Woodbury Lowery Collection, Florida State University, Tallahassee. Translation in possession of John Hann, Tallahassee.
  1988a   Translation of AGI Santo Domingo 231, testimony of Francisco Machado, June–July 1597. Woodbury Lowery Collection, Florida State University. Translation in possession of John Hann, Tallahassee.
  1988b   Translation of AGI Santo Domingo 235, DeJesus Petition. P. K. Yonge Library of Florida History, Microfilm 28K, Reel 36. University of Florida, Gainesville. Translation in the possession of John Hann, Tallahassee.
  1988c   Translation of AGI 235, letter form Baltasar López to Fray Blas de Montes, Sept. 15, 1602. Woodbury Lowery Collection, Florida State University.
  1989   Translation of AGI Santo Domingo 865, Fray Bullones 1728 Report on the Spanish Missions, Oct. 5, 1728. Stetson Collection, P. K. Yonge Library of Florida History, University of Florida, Gainesville. Translation in the possession of John Hann, Tallahassee.
Hume, Ivor Noël
  1972   *A Guide to the Artifacts of Colonial America*. New York: Alfred A. Knopf.
Jennings, Jesse D., and Charles H. Fairbanks
  1939   Ceramic Type Descriptions. *Southeastern Archaeological Conference Newsletter* 3(3):4–17.
Johnson, Kenneth W.
  1987   *The Search for Aquacaleyquen and Cali: Archaeological Survey of Portions of Alachua, Bradford, Citrus, Clay, Columbia, Marion, Sumter, and Union Counties, Florida.* Miscellaneous Project Report 33, Department of Anthropology, Florida Museum of Natural History, Gainesville.
  1990   The Discovery of a Seventeenth-Century Spanish Mission in Ichetucknee State Park, 1986. *Florida Journal of Anthropology* 15:39–46.
Johnson, Kenneth W., and Bruce C. Nelson
  1990   The Utina: Seriations and Chronology. *Florida Anthropologist* 43:48–62.

Jones, B. Calvin, and Gary Shapiro
1987   Nine Mission Sites in Apalachee. Paper presented at the Society for Historical Archaeology annual meeting, Savannah, Ga.
Jones, Grant D., Robert R. Kautz, and Elizabeth Graham
1986   Tipu: A Maya Town on the Spanish Colonial Frontier. *Archaeology* 39(1): 40–47.
Kidd, Kenneth, and Martha Kidd
1970   A Classification System for Glass Beads for the Use of Field Archaeologists. *Canadian Historical Sites Occasional Papers in Archaeology and History* 1:45–89.
Knight, Vernon J., Jr.
1985   *Tukabatchee: Archaeological Investigations at an Historic Creek Town, Elmore County, Alabama, 1984.* Report of Investigations 45. University of Alabama, Office of Archaeological Research.
Kubler, George
1948   *Mexican Architecture of the Sixteenth Century.* Vol. 2. New Haven: Yale University Press.
Lee, Chung H., I.R. Quitmyer, C.T. Espenshade, and R.E. Johnson
1984   *Estuarine Adaptations during the Late Prehistoric Period: Archaeology of Two Shell Midden Sites on the St. Johns River.* University of West Florida Office of Cultural and Archaeological Research, Report of Investigations no. 5, Pensacola.
Lorant, Stefan
1946   *The New World.* New York: Duell, Sloan, & Pearce.
Loucks, Lana Jill
1979   Political and Economic Interactions Between Spaniards and Indians: Archeological and Ethnohistorical Perspectives of the Mission System in Florida. Ph.D. dissertation, University of Florida.
Lyon, Eugene
1988   Towards a Typology of Spanish Colonial Nails. In *Spanish Artifacts from Santa Catalina,* ed. Stanley South, Russell K. Skowronek, and Richard E. Johnson, 325–409. University of South Carolina, South Carolina Institute of Archaeology and Anthropology Anthropological Studies 7. Columbia.
McMurray, Judith A.
1973   The Definition of the Ceramic Complex at San Juan del Puerto. M.A. thesis, University of Florida.
Manucy, Albert
1985   The Physical Setting of Sixteenth-Century St. Augustine. *Florida Anthropologist* 38:34–53.
Marrinan, Rochelle
1985   The Archaeology of the Spanish Missions in Florida. In *Indians, Colonists, and Slaves: Essays in Memory of Charles H. Fairbanks,* ed.

Kenneth W. Johnson, Jonathan M. Leader, and Robert C. Wilson, 241–52. Florida Journal of Anthropology Special Publication 4, Gainesville.

Milanich, Jerald T.
1971   *The Alachua Tradition of North-Central Florida.* Contributions of the Florida State Museum, Anthropology and History, no. 17, Gainesville.
1972   Excavations at the Richardson Site, Alachua County, Florida: An Early Seventeenth-Century Potano Indian Village (with Notes on Potano Culture Change). *Bureau of Historic Sites and Properties Bulletin* 2, 35–61. Florida Department of State, Tallahassee.
1978   The Western Timucua: Patterns of Acculturation and Change. In *Tacachale: Essays on the Indians of Florida and Southeastern Georgia during the Historic Period,* edited by Jerald T. Milanich and Samuel Proctor, 59–88. Gainesville: University Presses of Florida.

Milanich, Jerald T., and Charles H. Fairbanks
1980   *Florida Archaeology.* New York: Academic Press.

Milanich, Jerald T., and Susan Milbrath, eds.
1989   *First Encounters: Spanish Exploration in the Caribbean and the United States, 1492–1570.* Gainesville: University of Florida Press.

Milanich, Jerald T., and William Sturtevant
1972   *Francisco Pareja's 1613 Confessionario: A Documentary Source for Timucuan Ethnography.* Tallahassee: Florida Department of State.

Milanich, Jerald T., with Carlos A. Martinez, Karl T. Steinen, and Ronald Wallace
1976   Georgia Origins of the Alachua Tradition. *Bureau of Historic Sites and Properties Bulletin* 5, 47–56. Florida Department of State, Tallahassee.

Milanich, Jerald T., Ann S. Cordell, Vernon J. Knight, Jr., Timothy Kohler, and Brenda J. Sigler-Lavelle
1984   *McKeithen Weeden Island: The Culture of Northern Florida, A.D. 200–900.* Orlando, Fla.: Academic Press.

Morrell, L. Ross, and B. Calvin Jones
1970   San Juan de Aspalaga: A Preliminary Architectural Study. *Bureau of Historic Sites and Properties Bulletin* 1:25–43. Tallahassee: Florida Department of State.

Mueller, Patricia
1972   *Jewels of Spain.* New York: Hispanic Society of America.

Oré, Luís Gerónimo de
1936   The Martyrs of Florida (1513–1616). Ed. and trans. Maynard J. Geiger. *Franciscan Studies* 18, New York: J. F. Wagner.

Panshin, A. J., and C. de Zeeuw
1980   *Textbook of Wood Technology.* 4th ed. New York: McGraw-Hill.

Peters, Robert H.
  1983   *The Ecological Implications of Body Size.* Cambridge: Cambridge University Press.
Pierce, James
  1825   Notices of the Agriculture, Scenery, Geology, and Animal, Vegetable, and Mineral Productions of the Floridas, and of the Indian Tribes, Made During a Recent Tour in These Countries. *American Journal of Science*, series 1, 9:119–36.
Purcell, Joseph
  1778   *A Map of the Road from Pensacola in W. Florida to St. Augustine in East Florida from a Survey Made by Order of the Late Hon. Col. John Stuart.* Copy available in the P.K. Yonge Library of Florida History, Gainesville.
Quitmyer, Irvy R.
  1985   Zooarchaeological Methods for the Analysis of Shell Middens at Kings Bay. In *Aboriginal Subsistence and Settlement Archaeology of the Kings Bay Locality*, vol. 2, ed. William Hampton Adams, 33–39. University of Florida Department of Anthropology Reports of Investigations 2, Gainesville.
Radisch, William H.
  1988   Classification and Interpretation of Metal Stars from Santa Elena. In *Spanish Artifacts from Santa Elena*, ed. Stanley South, Russell K. Skowronek, and Richard E. Johnson, 145–151. University of South Carolina, South Carolina Institute of Archaeology and Anthropology, Anthropological Studies 7, Columbia.
Record, S. J., and R. W. Hess
  1943   *Timbers of the New World.* New Haven: Yale University Press.
Reitz, Elizabeth J.
  1979   Spanish and British Subsistence Strategies at St. Augustine, Florida, and Frederica, Georgia, Between 1565 and 1783. Ph.D. dissertation, University of Florida.
Reitz, Elizabeth J., and Dan Cordier
  1983   Use of Allometry in Zooarchaeological Analysis. In *Animals and Archaeology: Shell Middens, Fishes, and Birds*, ed. C. Grigson and J. Clutton-Brock, 237–52. BAR International Series 183, London.
Reitz, Elizabeth J., and Irvy R. Quitmyer
  1988   Faunal Remains from Two Coastal Georgia Swift Creek Sites. *Southeastern Archaeology* 7:95–108.
Reitz, Elizabeth J., I. R. Quitmyer, H. S. Hale, S. J. Scudder, and E. S. Wing
  1987   Application of Allometry to Zooarchaeology. *American Antiquity* 52:304–7.
Reitz, Elizabeth J., and C. Margaret Scarry
  1985   *Reconstructing Historic Subsistence with an Example from Sixteenth-*

Century Spanish Florida. Society for Historical Archaeology, Special Publication Series 3.

Ruhl, Donna L.
1987   First Impressions in and on Daub: A Paleoethnobotanical and Ceramic Technological Analysis of Some Burned Clay from Three Mission Sites in *La Florida.* Paper presented at the 44th Annual Meeting of the Southeastern Archaeological Conference, Charleston, S.C.

1988   Old Customs and Traditions in New Terrain: Adaptations, Accommodations, and Preferences as Seen in the Sixteenth and Seventeenth Century Paleoethnobotanical Data from *La Florida.* Paper presented at the 45th Annual Meeting of the Southeastern Archaeological Conference, New Orleans.

1990   Spanish Mission Paleoethnobotany and Culture Change: A Survey of the Archaeobotanical Data and Some Speculations on Aboriginal and Spanish Agrarian Interactions in *La Florida.* In *Columbian Consequences,* vol. 2, ed. D. H. Thomas, pp. 555–80. Washington, D.C.: Smithsonian Institution Press.

Russo, M., J. R. Ballo, R. J. Austin, L. Newsom, S. Scudder, and V. Rowland
1989   *Phase II Archaeological Excavations at the Riverbend Site (8Vo2567), Volusia County, Florida.* Report submitted to the State of Florida by Piper Archaeological Research, Inc.

Saunders, Rebecca
1988   *Excavations at 8Na41: Two Mission Period Sites on Amelia Island, Florida.* Miscellaneous Project Report Series no. 35, Department of Anthropology, Florida State Museum, Gainesville.

Scarry, C. Margaret
1984   Analysis of the Plant Remains from the 1983 Excavations at the Ximénez-Fatio Site, St. Augustine. In Final Report on the 1982–1983 Excavations at the Ximénez-Fatio House, by C. R. Ewen. Manuscript on file, Department of Anthropology, Florida Museum of Natural History, Gainesville.

1986   A Preliminary Examination of Plant Remains From Test Excavations at San Luis. Manuscript on file, Florida Bureau of Archaeological Research, Tallahassee.

1988   Plant Remains from the San Luis Council House. Manuscript on file, Florida Bureau of Archaeological Research, Tallahassee.

1989   Plant Remains from the Fountain of Youth Park Site (8SJ31). Manuscript on file, Department of Anthropology, Florida Museum of Natural History, Gainesville.

Scarry, John F.
1985   A Proposed Revision of the Fort Walton Ceramic Typology: A Type-Variety System. *Florida Anthropologist* 38:199–233.

Schmidt-Nielsen, Knut
  1984   *Scaling: Why Animal Size Is So Important.* Cambridge: Cambridge University Press.
Shapiro, Gary
  1987a   Inside the Apalachee Council House at San Luis. Paper presented at the 44th Annual Meeting of the Southeastern Archaeological Conference, Charleston, S.C.
  1987b   *Archaeology at San Luis: Broad-Scale Testing, 1984–1985.* Florida Bureau of Archaeological Research, Florida Archaeology 3.
Shapiro, Gary, and Bonnie McEwan
  1990   Excavations in the San Luis Council House. Manuscript in preparation for publication as *Florida Archaeology* 6. Tallahassee: Florida Bureau of Archaeological Research.
Smith, Hale G.
  1948   Two Historical Archaeological Periods in Florida. *American Antiquity* 4:313–19.
  1956   *The European and the Indian, European-Indian Contacts in Georgia and Florida.* Florida Anthropological Society Publications no. 4, Gainesville.
South, Stanley, Russell K. Skowronek, and Richard E. Johnson
  1988   *Spanish Artifacts from Santa Elena.* University of South Carolina, South Carolina Institute of Archaeology and Anthropology, Anthropological Studies 7.
Speck, Frank G.
  1911   Ceremonial Songs of the Creek and Yuchi Indians. *University of Pennsylvania Museum, Anthropological Publications* 1:157–245.
Swanton, John R.
  1939   *Final Report of the United States De Soto Commission.* Washington, D.C.: U.S. Government Printing Office.
  1946   *The Indians of the Southeastern United States.* Bureau of American Ethnology Bulletin 137. Smithsonian Institution, Washington, D.C.
Symes, M. I., and M. E. Stephens
  1965   A 272: The Fox Pond Site. *Florida Anthropologist* 18:65–76.
Thomas, David Hurst
  1987   *The Archaeology of Mission Santa Catalina De Guale: 1. Search and Discovery.* Anthropological Papers of the American Museum of Natural History, vol. 63, part 2, New York.
United States Department of Agriculture (USDA)
  1984   *Soil Survey for Columbia County, Florida.*
Urling, G. P., and R. B. Smith
  1953   An Anatomical Study of Twenty Lesser Known Woods from Florida. *Quarterly Journal of the Florida Academy of Sciences* 16:163–80.

Vernon, Richard H.
1984   Northeast Florida Prehistory: A Synthesis and Research Design. M.A. thesis, Florida State University.

Vernon, Richard H., and Bonnie McEwan
1990   *Town Plan and Town Life of Seventeenth-Century San Luis.* Florida Archaeology Reports 18. Tallahassee: Florida Bureau of Archaeological Research.

von den Driesch, A.
1976   *A Guide to the Measurement of Animal Bones from Archaeological Sites.* Peabody Museum Bulletin no. 1, Harvard University.

Weisman, Brent R.
1988a   Archaeological Investigations at the Fig Springs Mission (8Co1). Draft report submitted to the Florida Department of Natural Resources, Division of Recreation and Parks, Tallahassee.

1988b   *1988 Excavations at Fig Springs (8Co1), Season 2, July–December 1988.* Florida Archaeology Reports 4. Florida Bureau of Archaeological Research, Tallahassee.

1989   *Like Beads on a String: A Culture History of the Seminole Indians in North Peninsular Florida.* Tuscaloosa: University of Alabama Press.

Willey, Gordon
1949   *Archeology of the Florida Gulf Coast.* Smithsonian Miscellaneous Collections, vol. 113. Washington, D.C.

Willis, Raymond F.
1984   Empire and Architecture at Sixteenth-Century Puerto Real, Hispaniola. Ph.D. dissertation, University of Florida.

Wing, Elizabeth S., and Antoinette B. Brown
1979   *Paleonutrition: Method and Theory in Prehistoric Foodways.* New York: Academic Press.

Wing, Elizabeth S., and Irvy R. Quitmyer
1983   Recovery of Animal Remains from Archaeological Contexts. Paper presented at the meeting of the Society for American Archaeology, Pittsburgh.

Worth, John E.
1989   The Goggin Series: Extralocal Shell-tempered Ceramics in the Timucua Mission Province. Paper presented at the 46th Annual Meeting of the Southeastern Archaeological Conference, Tampa.

INDEX

Page numbers given in italics indicate that the reference is to a figure or table on that page.

Ripley P. Bullen Series
Jerald T. Milanich, General Editor

Tacachale: Essays on the Indians of Florida and Southeastern Georgia during the Historic Period, edited by Jerald T. Milanich and Samuel Proctor (1978).

Aboriginal Subsistence Technology on the Southeastern Coastal Plain during the Late Prehistoric Period, by Lewis H. Larson (1980).

Cemochechobee: Archaeology of a Mississippian Ceremonial Center of the Chattahoochee River, by Frank T. Schnell, Vernon J. Knight, Jr., and Gail S. Schnell (1981).

Fort Center: An Archaeological Site in the Lake Okeechobee Basin, by William H. Sears, with contributions by Elsie O'R. Sears and Karl T. Steinen (1982).

Perspectives on Gulf Coast Prehistory, edited by Dave D. Davis (1984).

Archaeology of Aboriginal Culture Change in the Interior Southeast: Depopulation during the Early Historic Period, by Marvin T. Smith (1987).

Apalachee: The Land between the Rivers, by John H. Hann (1988).

Key Marco's Buried Treasure: Archaeology and Adventure in the Nineteenth Century, by Marion Spjut Gilliland (1989).

First Encounters: Spanish Explorations in the Caribbean and the United States, 1492–1570, edited by Jerald T. Milanich and Susan Milbrath (1989).

Missions to the Calusa, edited and translated by John H. Hann, with introduction by William H. Marquardt (1991).

Excavations on the Franciscan Frontier: Archaeology at the Fig Springs Mission, by Brent Richards Weisman, with contributions by John E. Worth, Lee Newsom, and Irvy R. Quitmyer (1992).

Library of Congress Cataloging-in-Publication Data

Weisman, Brent Richards, 1952–
    Excavations on the Franciscan frontier: archaeology at the Fig
Springs Mission / Brent R. Weisman.
        p.   cm. — (Ripley P. Bullen series) (Columbus quincentenary
    series)
    Includes bibliographical references (p.   ) and index.
    ISBN 0–8130–1119–1 (alk. paper)
    1. Fig Springs Mission.   2. Spanish mission buildings—Florida.
I. Title.   II. Series.   III. Series: Columbus quincentenary series.
F319.F54W45   1992   91–32487
975.9—dc20   CIP